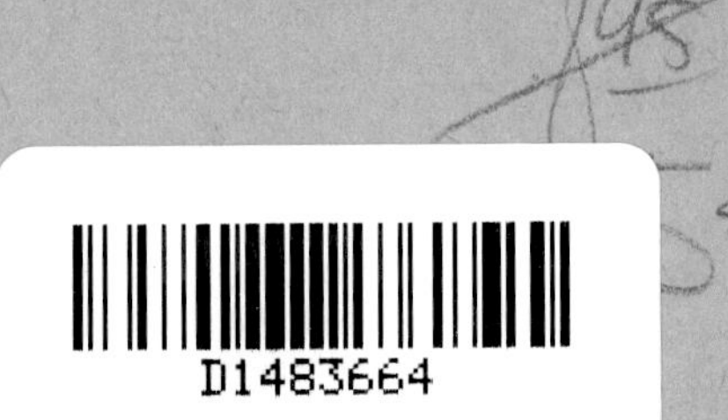

THE SEARCH FOR SAM GOLDWYN

By Carol Easton

THE SEARCH FOR SAM GOLDWYN
STRAIGHT AHEAD: THE STORY OF STAN KENTON

The Search for *SAM GOLDWYN*

A Biography

by Carol Easton

WILLIAM MORROW AND COMPANY, INC.
NEW YORK 1976

Special thanks to the reference librarians at the Redondo Beach Public Library, who went far beyond the call of duty to help me research this book.

Printed in the United States of America.

1 2 3 4 5 80 79 78 77 76

Library of Congress Cataloging in Publication Data

Easton, Carol.
The search for Sam Goldwyn.

Bibliography: p.
Includes index.
1. Goldwyn, Samuel, 1882-1974. I. Title.
PN1998.A3G64 1976 791.43'0232'0924 [B] 75-28167
ISBN 0-688-03007-6

BOOK DESIGN: HELEN ROBERTS

to Jeannie, Kelly and Andy,
who had to live through this with me;

to Riley, who chose to;

and to r.v.l.

Contents

THE SEARCH FOR SAM GOLDWYN

Establishing Shot

My father was a Hollywood agent who died thinking he was a failure because he never made a lot of money. Sam Goldwyn was a Hollywood producer who left an estate of $19,000,000 and died thinking he was a success.

They had a lot in common, my father and Mr. Goldwyn. Money was their motive and their measure. My father made friends instead of money; but he wouldn't play the game. Goldwyn invented the game; he made up the rules as he went along, and had all the friends money could buy.

Indeed, Goldwyn had everything money could buy; status, fame, power, prestige, servants; every luxury, including the most expensive one of all—insulation from reality.

In the country of the blind, Sam Goldwyn had class.

I grew up literally in the shadow of Sam Goldwyn, in a stucco duplex a block away from his studio. On warm summer evenings and a few daring days, I climbed the fence behind the back lot, hid from the patrolling guards, and played on the sets. It became a familiar magic. Once I persuaded a neighborhood boy, younger and smaller but vulnerable to a dare, to come along. In a castle surrounded by a moat, built for *The Princess* (Virginia Mayo) *and the Pirate* (Bob Hope), he revealed to me the astonishing difference between little boys and little girls—an incident long forgotten . . . until the search for Sam Goldwyn triggered a relentless, around-the-clock assault on my memory.

I was moviesick as some children are lovesick; a lonely only child, I ached to be a movie star. At nine, I wrote and mailed a letter to Sam Goldwyn. "All I'm asking for is a chance," I pleaded. Mr. Goldwyn did not reply.

In my tenth year, my father, thinking to cure me of my obsession (never dreaming how consuming it was), persuaded a casting director friend to hire me as an extra for *The North Star*, a Goldwyn epic about the heroism of Russian peasants during World War II. A Russian village was constructed on the back lot—thatched huts for the peasants, corrals for an assortment of farm animals including cows which we, city kids dressed in peasant's costumes, furtively attempted to milk.

I was ecstatic. Instead of being disenchanted, as my father had hoped, by the dreary repetitiveness of the movie-making process, I became even more firmly hooked. Nothing was beyond my ability to romanticize: the lessons with the studio tutor; the commissary lunches; the prop food I bit into, expecting ambrosia and tasting wax; the hush that descended upon the company when the great Mr. Goldwyn made his brief daily visits to the set; the other extras, moviewise children with precociously cynical eyes; and the stars!—larger-than-life Walter Huston, awesome Ann Harding, glamorous Ann Baxter, Jane (Josephine the Plumber) Withers and Goldwyn's newest discovery, Farley Granger, whom I worshipped from afar until one reckless afternoon when I wordlessly thrust a coke into his hands, panicked and ran like hell. I knew it was only a matter of time before I, too, would be discovered. One day the eyes of the director, Lewis Milestone, would focus upon me; he would instantly recognize my untapped talent and beckon me to stardom. But although the experience only exacerbated my moviesickness, *The North Star* was my swan song in pictures.

Thirty years later, I thought I would go home again.

1. From Ghetto to Gloversville

In 1947, a handful of Hollywood's royalty attended a dinner party given by Mr. and Mrs. Samuel Goldwyn in their sixteen-room home in Beverly Hills, just down the road from Pickfair and adjacent to the William Randolph Hearst estate. The five-acre Goldwyn spread contained all the obligatory Hollywood status symbols: swimming pool, tennis courts, manicured gardens and, as an added touch of opulence (an anniversary gift from Mrs. Goldwyn to her husband), croquet courts.

The menu, planned by Mrs. Goldwyn, was elegant; the wines, selected by Mrs. Goldwyn, superb. Every detail was first class, just like a Goldwyn movie. The party broke up around eleven. Getting into her car, one of the guests realized she'd left her gloves in the house; her husband, a director, went back to retrieve them. Passing the dining room doorway, the director got a rare glimpse of the real Sam Goldwyn: alone in the room, he was carefully pouring the wine left in the glasses back into a wine bottle.

Goldwyn had left the Warsaw ghetto at the age of eleven; but the ghetto never left Goldwyn.

Samuel Goldwyn was born in 1918 by order of the Superior Court of the State of New York; but the original, genuine article was born to Abraham and Hannah Goldfisch on or about August 27, 1882, in the infamous Warsaw ghetto.

Facts about his family background are sketchy and contradictory; in his memoirs, Goldwyn said only, "My early boyhood was spent in Europe." One consistent fact is that he left home at the age of eleven; but under what circumstances? Goldwyn told Adolph Zukor, who knew him from 1915 until the end of his career, that he had run away to London following the death of his parents; and in 1943, a journalist reported in *The New York Times* that "There was a distant look in his eyes as he told of being left an orphan." But a few years earlier, his biographer, Alva Johnson, wrote that when Goldwyn was eighteen and already a successful salesman, he "took two months off and went to Europe, meeting his mother at Karlsbad." Goldwyn, who loved Johnston's book, never disputed anything in it.

There was no premium on truth in the Warsaw ghetto of the 1890's. There was only constant, grinding poverty, and the terror of pogroms. Much has been made of Goldwyn's lack of formal education—but at the age of eleven, he matriculated from the toughest survival school in the world. The boy was father to the man.

The education he received in the ghetto uniquely equipped him for Hollywood, a world of which he reportedly said, "It's dog eat dog—and nobody's going to eat me." As the overvalued firstborn son of Orthodox Jews, his birth conferred on his mother her only status in life. The first lesson she taught him was that he was a prince, not subject to the rules that governed ordinary mortals. He was expected only to pray, visit the temple with his father, and generally allow himself to be pampered. What Sam wanted, if it was humanly possible, *whatever the means,* Sam—presumably—got. This was the lesson drummed into him by word and deed.

To survive among the embattled minority that overpopulated the ghetto required sharp wits, obsessive drive, monstrous arrogance and a suspiciousness conducive to paranoia. Nobody was to be trusted. Wheeling and dealing was a way of life. Morality was elastic; bribery, for example, was neither right nor wrong but merely necessary when corrupt officials threatened one's means of livelihood or the destruction of one's house in a "spontaneous" raid. "Money for the devil" it was called; no Jew wanted to be without it. Boys grew up under the approaching threat of conscription. And given the lack of privacy in the unbelievably cramped quarters of the ghetto, is it not reasonable to assume, and to understand, how a child might come to long for . . . space? Space. Sixteen rooms. Five acres. Space.

When the eleven-year-old Sam Goldfisch ran away/was sent to an aunt in Birmingham, England, he left behind two brothers—one seven, the other an infant—and his parents, living or dead. According to legend, under his arm he carried a loaf of bread; and under his skin, surely a load of guilt.

Birmingham was not his destination—merely a stopping-off place en route to America. He worked as a "dogsbody" (slang for flunky), first pushing a coal cart, then for a blacksmith, finally for a safe manufacturing firm, and after two years had accumulated enough money for steerage passage across the Atlantic. It is likely that the boy did little during those years but work long hours, eat whatever was available, and sleep. It is conceivable that in Birmingham he saw, for the first time, floors of wood rather than dirt, tablecloths, white bread and other such luxuries. It is certain that he thought obsessively of the promised land, America.

He arrived in New York harbor penniless, possibly with forged papers (not an uncommon practice), programmed for success—Sam Goldfish now, without the *c* (courtesy of an immigration official who took a phonetic guess at the name of the boy who spoke fluent Yiddish, some Polish, but almost no English). A government agency promptly placed him in Gloversville—a company town named for its product—near Albany. In Gloversville, his ambition was unleashed.

Poles were emigrating by the millions at the turn of the century, and Gloversville contained a substantial colony of them, at various stages of Americanization. Goldfish had no relatives there, but he was quickly absorbed into the community. The owner of the glove factory—Samuel Lehr, who had himself emigrated from Warsaw—enjoyed considerable status in Gloversville society.

Goldfish's first job was sweeping floors at the factory for three dollars a week. He was industrious, a veritable sorcerer's apprentice, and quickly graduated to operating a glovemaking machine. There is no reason to doubt his later claim that he got up at six A.M. to tramp through zero weather to work standing up at the machine all day long.

He learned to cut skins, for which he was paid by the piece. He made, quite possibly cultivated, the friendship of the boy who shared his workbench. Abe, two years Sam's junior, undoubtedly admired the older boy for his adventures and independence. Abe was Samuel Lehr's son.

Goldfish never outgrew the values he acquired in Gloversville. There he began his lifelong pursuit of the trappings, the ornaments, the ostentatious badges of success. In the overblown, ghostwritten prose of his memoirs, written ten years after he left Gloversville, one of the rare passages with the ring of truth refers to his envy of the drummers he saw through the window of the town's leading hotel: "those splendid adventurers with their hats and their massive cigars both at an angle!"

By the time he was sixteen, he had completed a year of night school and acquired enough rudimentary English to get by. His horizons had widened, and he found the factory confining. He persuaded Samuel Lehr to let him go on the road as a salesman and, armed with his sample case—his ticket to immortality—the prince set out to claim his kingdom.

In the haberdashery and general stores of New England cities and towns, Goldfish came into his own. The resistance of cautious Yankee buyers only sharpened his wits and his determination. Bedeviled by cravings for the things he knew money could buy, he charmed, blustered, badgered, wheedled, wheeled and dealed his way through the Northeast, outtalking, outfoxing and outdistancing the competition. He would not acknowledge, let alone accept, rejection. He had an answer for every argument, a ploy for every occasion. He could not be insulted. He could not be deterred. He could not be withstood.

His years on the road refined his technique and gave him a reputation as the highest-paid glove salesman in the country. He earned up to $10,000 a year—more than enough to indulge his lifelong passion for expensive clothes. He traveled to Europe first class, steerage now and forever beneath him. He accepted an offer to manage the New York office of a rival glove company;

but he began to find the glove business confining; restless, he cast about for new worlds, preferably with no limits.

His new boss was a man named Joe Moses, who had a dazzlingly beautiful niece named Bessie Ginzberg. Bessie became the object of Goldfish's affections. The depth of his passion will never be known, but Goldfish was, above all, conventional, and convention dictated that a man in his late twenties should acquire a suitable wife. Sam was too crude and aggressive for Bessie's taste, however, and she turned him down in favor of a gentler young man, a vaudeville performer turned producer named Jesse Lasky.

The Laskys settled in New York, and Goldfish sometimes dropped in to visit. The household was dominated by Jesse's mother Sarah, a widow whose world revolved around her children, and Jesse's sister, Blanche. These two strong-minded women had already driven Bessie to the brink of divorce; Blanche even told Bessie what clothes to wear.

Jesse and Blanche were San Francisco-born, grandchildren of German immigrants. Jesse had joined a vaudeville troupe as a child, playing cornet; later Blanche learned to play the instrument and joined the act. With stage mother Sarah in the wings, they toured the country from the Barbary Coast to the Bowery. But Blanche never enjoyed performing as Jesse did, and repeatedly pointed out to her brother that the people who were making money in vaudeville were not on the stage, but in management. Eventually, she persuaded him to open an office and book acts, which he also produced. Blanche ran the office, supervised the sets and selected the costumes. She was industrious and efficient—qualities greatly admired by Sam Goldfish—and she was a remarkably handsome young woman. By the time she met Goldfish, whatever glamour show business had held for Blanche had worn exceedingly thin. She dreamed of marrying a solid, respectable businessman, and Sam entered right on cue. Handicapped by his abysmal awe and ignorance of women, he soon found himself at the mercy of someone as adept as himself at manipulation. In 1910, they were married.

Sam lived with his wife and in-laws (including Jesse's infant son) in a crowded apartment on Broadway. To his wife's dismay, he was intrigued by Jesse's show business world; the glove business looked increasingly tame by comparison. The gamble, the unpredictability, the high stakes to be won (he refused to consider the possible losses) excited him. He joined Lasky in backing a Broadway play called *Cheer Up*—a farce written by Mary Roberts Rinehart and produced by a friend of Jesse's named Cecil De Mille. *Cheer Up* cheered no one; it was a disastrous flop. But Goldfish was hooked.

Early in 1911, in a Times Square nickelodeon, Goldfish had viewed his first film—a Western called *Broncho Billy's Adventures*. He was transfixed—not by the film, but by the steady stream of coins that accumulated at the ticket window. He tried to persuade Jesse to go into the motion picture business, but Jesse, who had just lost $100,000 on another venture, was not in the mood for a gamble—especially with Sam, whom he disliked.

Motion pictures had been popular since 1903, but for what Lasky considered the wrong reasons: as intermissions between vaudeville shows. Crude two-reelers, seven to ten minutes long,* were called "chasers" because they cleared out the house. When Goldfish characteristically refused to take no for an answer, Jesse, *un*characteristically, became furious. "Now listen, Sam," he said, "and get this straight. I'm a showman. You don't have any idea what a showman is, so I'm going to tell you. A showman is a man who produces shows that attract people into the theater. God damn it, you're asking me to go into something that chases them out! Now you can go to hell!"

Goldfish paid no attention whatever. A couple of weeks later he told Lasky, "I've been around to the General Film Company. There's a trust. We can get into it or break it up!"

"I told you what I thought of it," said Lasky. "Now let me alone!"

Goldfish's prescience was sheer practicality, not artistic vision. Congress had lowered the tariff on imported gloves, and Sam feared this would result in the bottom dropping out of the domestic glove business. In 1912, Adolph Zukor, an immigrant whose past paralleled Goldfish's—substitute Hungary for Poland

* The average mind was not believed capable of concentrating on a film longer than twenty minutes; even if it could, such concentration was certain to cause blinding headaches, double vision, perhaps eventual blindness.

and furs for gloves—produced a four-reel, hour-long extravaganza starring Sarah Bernhardt as Queen Elizabeth, and booked it into legitimate theaters on its own merits. *Voilà*—respectability.

In the original notes for his autobiography—considerably more revealing than the published version—Lasky wrote, "At about this time, two shabbily dressed men visited my office. One of them said, 'It's an honor to meet you, sir. We are about to embark in the motion picture business and we need a trademark to attract the better public into the nickelodeons. We want to buy your name as a trademark and we are prepared to offer you $10,000.' I nearly dropped dead. I would like to have had that $10,000, but I couldn't bring myself to add my name to anything like that—I, the top vaudeville producer in America. I turned them down. It was a great temptation. I never heard of them again."

That same day, Lasky lunched with his friend Cecil De Mille at a theatrical club. Heavily in debt, fed up with Broadway and restless, De Mille confided his plan to join the revolution in Mexico. "If you want adventure," said Lasky impulsively, "I've got a better idea than that. Let's go into the picture business."

Lasky recalled that De Mille "looked at me with those strange eyes of his for a moment. 'Let's,' he said. We shook hands." On their way out of the club they ran into Dustin Farnum and Edwin Royale, the star and the writer of a hit play called *The Squaw Man*. On the spot, Lasky optioned the movie rights to the play. Then he telephoned Goldfish. "You win," he told him. "We're going into the picture business."

The average two-reeler cost $1,000. Lasky and Goldfish budgeted their epic at $20,000. They borrowed $5,000 from Bessie's uncle, Joe Moses, and invested $15,000 of their own. De Mille had no money to invest, but was to serve as "Director General" for a salary of $100 a week. But De Mille, although cocky and confident, had never directed a picture or even witnessed the making of one. Goldfish insisted, in the interest of protecting their investment, on hiring an experienced director. He approached a young man named David Griffith, who had already experimented with a "long" film. They met for lunch.

Goldfish was impressed. Griffith was not. "Show me a bank balance of $250,000," he said, "and then we'll talk." Goldfish settled for De Mille.

The Lasky Feature Play Company was formed. Lasky was president. Goldfish was vice-president and business manager. Blanche Lasky Goldfish was treasurer and Arthur Friend, a lawyer acquaintance, was secretary and legal consultant.

In the fall of 1913, Goldfish placed newspaper ads grandly announcing the company's intention to produce twelve five-reel pictures a year. The first production (and the only one to which they were actually committed) would be *The Squaw Man.*

2. The Squaw Man

The villain of the embryonic movie industry was the General Film Company, a monopoly commonly known as The Trust. It had been formed in 1909 by a group of producers who used their patents on cameras as a means of keeping potential competitors out of the action. The Trust exercised airtight control over the length, distribution and cost of its films; it also controlled the exchanges that bought the pictures which they in turn rented to theater owners for whatever the traffic would bear. The Trust even collected protection money—two dollars a week, called a "license fee"—from each of the 15,000 theaters that exhibited its product.

Strongarm tactics were not beyond The Trust. It was known to employ deputy marshals, detectives, even a goon squad headed by an All-American football star; on one occasion they carried out their mission with such enthusiasm that seven members of an independent cast wound up in the hospital. Maverick moviemakers began migrating westward in 1910 as a defensive measure. Their first Hollywood encampments, too primitive to be called studios, were enclosed by high fences and guarded by lookouts, at whose signal the offending bootleg equipment was stashed in fast cars and smuggled across the border into Mexico, one hundred miles away, until the threat subsided.

Safety was only one factor in the Lasky Company's choice of Hollywood for its location; the availability of cheap land, cheap labor and year-round sunlight—as well as the Western setting of *The Squaw Man*—lured De Mille West—but not to Hollywood. During discussions of a location more appropriate than Fort Lee, New Jersey, where most pictures were then produced, Lasky remembered that "Once when appearing on a vaudeville bill with Herman The Great, we played Flagstaff for a matinee and a night. The town was filled with cowboys, Indian blankets, silver things and so forth. Let's do this in a big way. Let's go to Flagstaff, Arizona!" But when De Mille detrained at Flagstaff, the view from the station platform seemed wrong. He ordered his party back on the train to the end of the line: Los Angeles.

The section of town called Hollywood was four years younger than Goldfish—born and christened in 1896 by one Mrs. Daeida Hartell Wilcox, who left the Midwest with a mission: to establish a sinfree community, God-fearing and teetotaling, under a sunny and cloudless sky. She and her husband bought and subdivided 120 acres of land surrounding what would become the intersection of Hollywood and Vine. The vegetation included holly and live oak; thus, Mrs. Wilcox's inspiration.

De Mille was accompanied by Oscar Apfel, a director with some motion picture experience; Alfred Gandolfi, a cameraman; Dustin Farnum (who turned down a stock interest in the company for the security of $5,000 cash); and Farnum's dresser. None of them had ever been west of the Rockies.

Instructed by Goldfish to make no long-term commitments, De Mille rented a barn in the then wilderness (now Sunset and Vine), converted the horses' stalls into dressing rooms, rounded up extras off the streets and proceeded—already an advertisement for himself in jodhpurs, leather puttees and broad-brimmed hat—to make his movie.

Lasky and Goldfish remained in New York. They rented offices opposite the Public Library on Fifth Avenue, and Goldfish, still hanging on to his glove job, went to work selling what was called "states rights"—exclusive distribution rights for one or more states. He sold New York for $7,000, Pennsylvania for $5,000, the New England states for $9,000. Every couple of days he would burst into Lasky's office, gleefully announce something like "What a break! Just sold the Middle West for $5,000!" and rush out again to call on a glove account. On the strength of his sales techniques and Lasky's reputation, he soon accumulated over $60,000 worth of contracts from theater owners and operators willing to buck the dreaded Trust.

The Squaw Man, begun on December 29, 1913, was the first feature-length movie made in Hollywood. In six weeks it was completed. Lasky went to California for the first gala showing, while Goldfish waited in New York for glowing reports of their hit. Instead, he heard only an ominous silence. With exhibitors breathing down his neck for prints of the film (for which they had paid in advance), Goldfish grew panicky. His telegrams to Lasky asking for confirmation of release dates for the film went unanswered. Meanwhile, back at the barn, Lasky and DeMille were in despair. Three attempts to screen their picture had produced only chaos—the equivalent of a television picture with its vertical hold gone berserk. The film seemed in order, so did the projector; yet the top and bottom of the picture would not hold. Facing bankruptcy and possible criminal charges—having spent moneys advanced for a product that now seemed worthless—the two men finally wired Goldfish that there was "something wrong," and returned to New York with their apparently calamitous film.

Salvation came from an unexpected quarter: The Trust. One of its members was the Lubin Film Laboratory in Philadelphia. Goldfish felt the situation called for desperate measures and suggested they throw themselves on the mercy of Sig Lubin, the greatest expert in his field. (Goldwyn later claimed full credit for enlisting Lubin's help. "I told him the story of my life," he told a reporter twenty-two years later. "I got so dramatic I began to cry." But DeMille claimed it was *he* who persuaded Lubin to save the day). Whatever his reasons, Lubin—possibly touched by their plight, surely not perceiving their clumsy attempt at moviemaking as any serious threat—assured them that the problem was a minor one, a matter of the sprocket holes on the film not being at the proper intervals. Lubin's technicians simply corrected the perforations, and the Lasky feature Play Company was back in business.

The Squaw Man opened in New York on February 15, 1914. Three weeks later it was playing to full houses in forty-four states, thanks largely to Goldfish's relentless promotion. When the picture opened at Tally's Broadway Theater in Los

Angeles, thousands of flyers, called "Tallygrams," were circulated, announcing:

THE SQUAW MAN
A Six-Act Motion Picture Production

It may appear at first blush that the producers of THE SQUAW MAN had an easy time because they were provided with a thrilling and gripping story. But there was nothing easy about it. The story is one which must be presented in the right way or it loses its grip and its thrills, and the infinitely larger number of settings than in the stage production makes the task all the harder. Viewing the film as a whole, one is strongly tempted to say that it is perfect. Of course no film can be quite that, but this one seems to be as near it as anyone is likely to get for some time. From the first scene to last, the settings, whether interiors or exteriors, are extraordinarily good. The interiors are not bizzare or spectacular, but represent what they are supposed to be so well that one hardly notices them. This is the highest form of stage-setting art. Exteriors are of unusual beauty and all of the western scenes were made in the very country where the story is laid. The photographic work is perfect and it includes many particularly fine effects such as the scenes in which Nat-U-Ritch is kneeling on the mountain top in the light of the setting sun. The snow views are also extremely beautiful. The burning of the schooner is a strong piece of realism. THE SQUAW MAN represents the triumph of the picture over stage productions.

We Call For And Deliver Dry Cleaning
Special: Suits Dry or Steam Cleaned $1.00

Eventually, *The Squaw Man* would gross a quarter of a million dollars.

Process Shot

Sam Goldwyn seemed a natural subject for a biographer, certainly a legitimate one. His career spanned the life cycle of Hollywood; its last lingering illness was in sync with his own. He was the most stubbornly independent producer in the business, financing his own pictures, beholden to no one, passing no bucks (except his own). He was a public figure who spent fortunes advertising himself along with his pictures; colorful "Goldwynisms" contributed to his legend. Most intriguing of all, nothing of any depth had ever been written about him. His long, active life seemed to promise untapped veins of rich material—the man, the metaphor, the movies. I set out with (in hindsight) embarrassing naïveté, eager to exhume Goldwyn's past and, in the process, some of my own. It never occurred to me to question why, in the recent proliferation of Hollywood biographies, Goldwyn had been overlooked.

The search for Sam Goldwyn led through an obstacle course of exaggerations, evasions, ambiguities, insults, humiliations, vacillations, contradictions, absurdities and outright lies. It entailed sifting through tons of propaganda to find microscopic fragments of facts and feelings, to be laboriously fitted together until the shadowy shape of a human being began to emerge. I examined old guild (labor union) directories, museum collections, court records, newspaper files, obituaries and my memory for tenuous leads, feeling at times like an archaelogist, at others like a skip tracer. Primary sources are dead, or senile, or otherwise unreliable. Memories and memoirs are at best selective, at worst distorted. Lasky, Zukor, Goldwyn and both De Milles, Cecil and William, all wrote their *Rashomon*-like versions of the Lasky Feature Play Company story. All five books are self-serving. William De Mille's is the most introspective; Goldwyn's the most superficial; Lasky's the most fair. The books reveal more than they intended of the mood, the time, the scrambling for position, the self-absorption of individuals and industry, the evolution of the inevitable split between the artists and the merchants. But on Goldwyn, there is no definitive source; only bits and pieces of the mosaic.

After Goldfish became Goldwyn in 1918, an army of publicists systematically covered his tracks. Mountains of press releases extolled his taste, his insistence on excellence, his independence, his wardrobe. His wardrobe! In a town obsessed with fashion, Goldfish, marching to the beat of those distant Gloversville drummers, was the best-dressed man. He bragged of refusing to carry a billfold, lest it spoil the elegant line of his suits. Onlookers were either too dazzled, too preoccupied with their own appearance or too fearful of losing their jobs to call attention to the emperor's nakedness.

Naked, Sam Goldfish/Goldwyn was infinitely more interesting than clothed, however fine the fabrics. Why, then, the intensive campaign to renounce reality for PR rhetoric? Why the insistence on the monument at the expense of the man? Why the premium on fiction, the circumvention of fact?

The research process expands in ever-widening circles. In search of a man, one looks first to his family.

Sam Goldfish's marriage to Blanche Lasky produced one child, Ruth, whose own daughter (her grandmother's namesake) was a schoolmate of mine at Hollywood High. Presuming on that flimsy, long-ago friendship, I called Blanche Capps; would she contribute her recollections of her grandfather to a biography? She seemed astonished that anyone would be writing a book about him. "I really can't tell you anything useful," she said. "I hardly knew him. And my grandmother died before I was born." She doubted that her mother would talk with me. "She feels it's a personal matter."

A friend of a friend of mine, long acquainted with the Goldwyn family, suggested I contact Blanche's brother Alan. He also seemed surprised by my project and asked some intelligent questions. "People have been trying to get a handle on the guy for years," he said. "His private life was very private. He felt it was his own goddamn business." Did anybody know him, really know him? "His wife—maybe. My mother understood him pretty well. I was always away at boarding school, and he was always making a movie. I never knew him well. I think he liked me. When I did see him, it was one of those family trips, where you have dinner and talk about whatever you talk about and shuffle home." Had he ever heard his grandfather talk about his early years, his family? "No. My mother never talked about her childhood, either." Alan agreed to see me and tell me whatever he could. He seemed casual and candid. I could hear light jazz piano music in the background. I liked him.

A few hours later, he called me back. He sounded unhappy and cautious, and there was no music. "I'm afraid I'm not going to be able to see you after all," he said. "It would really make waves for me with my family. My mother feels very strongly that it's a personal thing. I'm really sorry." He sounded sincerely apologetic. "It's a sticky wicket you've got yourself into," he said. Then: "Why don't you call my mother directly? Why *shouldn't* you write a book about him! He was a myth in his own time. All they can tell you is to fuck off."

In less direct terms, they did.

I wrote to Ruth Capps, telling her that while I could appreciate her desire for privacy, I was committed to doing this book and wanted to tell an accurate story. "Accounts of the circumstances of your parents' marriage and divorce are inconsistent and foggy," I wrote, "and my research has uncovered more gossip and speculation than facts. I feel that in all fairness I should offer you an opportunity to set the record straight. Could we at least meet and discuss the possibility?"

Mrs. Capps answered promptly, in less than twenty-five words. She was sorry. She did not wish to discuss her parents. She was "unable," she said, to help me.

Sam Goldfish's younger brothers, Ben and Bernard, truncated their surname to Fish when they came to this country.

Bernard Fish became a Christian Science practitioner and died—or, as Christian Scientists say, made the transition—in 1946, at a relatively young sixty. Ben Fish was a meek man who feared and admired his brother the tycoon. Sam, who despised weakness in anyone, gave him a marginal public relations job calling on theater owners and exchanges that distributed Goldwyn pictures, and rewarded him with a small interest in the company, a good salary and considerable contempt. When Ben Fish died in 1962, Goldwyn settled a substantial sum on his widow and reclaimed the company's stock. Ben Fish's son, Richard, is a photographer living in the San Fernando Valley. Over the phone, I asked if he could provide any information about his father's—and Uncle Sam's—childhood. "I'm afraid I can't be much help to you on that," he said. "Those early years were painful . . . difficult. My father didn't talk about them." Did he know anything about the cousins in England with whom Sam had lived before coming to America? "No, nothing. Maybe the family could tell you. Have you contacted the family?" I told him that Jack Foreman, the present manager of the studio and family spokesman, had informed me that the Goldwyns were saving their material, possibly for an authorized biography. Mr. Fish grew wary. "How did you know where to find me?" he asked.

"I went through all the Fishes in the phone book," I answered.

"Who is your publisher?" I told him. "Can you prove it?" I offered to show him the contract. "Well," he said, "I'll have to check with the family. I'll get back to you." I heard no more from Mr. Fish.

"I'll have to check with the family" became a familiar refrain—from friends and former employees as well as relatives. Initial caution in dealing with an unknown biographer is understandable, even admirable; I expected questions about my competence and credentials, but I was scarcely prepared to encounter an armed fortress. I made a plane reservation to New York, hoping to interview sources there. I wrote numerous letters explaining that I was working on an unauthorized biography, that my hope was to gather impressions and recollections of Goldwyn from as wide a spectrum of people as possible in order to create a dimensional portrait. I tried to make it clear that I had no axe to grind, no point to prove; that my only concern was accuracy.

Max Wilkinson, a onetime Goldwyn story editor, replied: "I would like to help you but I can't talk about Goldwyn . . . I have buried that part of my life and I am not interested in exhuming it." A man who was known as Jock Lawrence when he headed Goldwyn's publicity department wrote, on a letterhead bearing the name Justus Baldwin Lawrence and a Park Avenue address: "So far as I am concerned, Sam Goldwyn was one of the great experiences of my life and I would not be a party, at this stage of life, to anything that would not more fully be reflective of his greatness than some of the things published in the past. I suggest that, if Mrs. Goldwyn would wish me to assist in any way, it should be up to her to decide."

Letters to producer Arthur Hornblow, Jr., publicist Ben Sonnenberg, writer Budd Schulberg, writer-director Joseph Mankiewicz and two surviving Goldwyn cousins in England were unanswered. Lillian Hellman wrote that she was on her way to "months of work" and it would be impossible for us to meet. Otto Preminger, whom I telephoned in New York, said "I don't like to speak ill of the dead," then said he *would* talk with me, but not over the phone. I agreed that a personal interview would be preferable and told him I planned to come to New York. But Mr. Preminger was leaving the very next day to direct a picture in Paris, and would not be back for at least six months.

Myrna Loy, who starred in *The Best Years of Our Lives* and is said to have known the Goldwyn's socially, lives in New York. Two months after I wrote to her, a telephone caller identified herself as an employee of Miss Loy's. "Miss Loy is having a lot of dental work done," was the message, "and she's very busy preparing to tour with *Don Juan in Hell.*" Might I talk with her over the phone? "No, that wouldn't be possible. She's having a lot of dental work done, and she's very busy. . . ."

I asked a New York friend to check out the availability of Robert Sherwood-Sam Goldwyn correspondence with the law firm representing Sherwood's estate. The friend made innumerable phone calls, reached a dead end and suggested I hire a researcher.

I cancelled my reservation.

Two of the most comprehensive sources of motion picture history in the world are The American Film Institute at Greystone Mansion, in Beverly Hills, where taped interviews with leading film figures are available to researchers; and the Academy of Motion Picture Arts and Sciences, the Fort Knox of reference material on the movies.

Academy members, motion picture and television personnel, teachers, students, gossip columnists, movie fans and freelancers jam the little Academy every day of the week. Three professional librarians and three assistants provide information on subjects of varying degrees of density, from mushy (When did Liz Taylor divorce Eddie Fisher?) to gritty (What were the jail sentences of the Hollywood Ten?). Space limitations sometimes make it necessary to perch on a windowsill.* But the material is there, tons of paper, much of it yellowing—over 8,000 books (many out of print), scripts, pamphlets and periodicals on motion picture history, production, criticism, techniques, biography. There are credits, reviews, photographs and other pertinent information about 35,000 films, nearly every motion picture made in this country since 1915. Its trade-paper files begin with "Views and Film Index" of 1906, the first industry trade paper. There is some gossip (fan magazines dating back to 1920) and a dizzying mass of fact. References to Goldwyn range from worshipful to cryptic to irreverent to fanciful. The Goldwyn clipping file, items culled from worldwide sources, occupies three massive accordion files. It was a beginning.

* A new building is under construction. When the Academy moved into its present quarters twenty years ago, no one could have predicted that film would become the most obsessively studied art of the century.

3. The Goldfish Touch

A full-page ad in a March, 1914, issue of *The Moving Picture World* announced the second production of the Lasky Feature Play Company: *Brewster's Millions,* based on another successful Broadway play. With standard Goldfish hyperbole, the ad proclaimed Jesse Lasky "America's Most Artistic Director," Oscar Apfel "Acknowledged Peer of Directors and Genius of Innovators," and De Mille "Master Playwright, Director and Author of Numerous Dramatic Successes." In hindsight, De Mille found the omission of Goldfish's name "a tiny cloud, a portent of coming storms." *

"There was jubilation in the barn," wrote De Mille, "when I returned to Hollywood to plunge into the company's ambitious program of turning out one picture a month." * During the next twelve months they produced not twelve but twenty-one pictures!—the majority of them directed by Oscar Apfel, who ground them out like sausages. To accommodate this feverish activity, the studio was improved and expanded; roads were built and orange trees felled to make way for new buildings that went up with the speed of a fast-action movie. By the end of 1914, the Lasky Feature Play Company had on its payroll five directors, five cameramen and a stock company of eighty players.

Goldfish and Lasky bought the screen rights to every hit play they could get their hands on. Stage actors were reluctant

* Cecil B. De Mille, *Autobiography.* (Englewood Cliffs, Prentice-Hall, 1959).

to risk their reputations on the untried, undignified new medium, but Goldfish wanted the publicity value of the original cast whenever possible, and he was not unaware of the time- and money-saving value of their familiarity with the play. Money talked. A stream of actors began, with great trepidation, to join the westward migration.

In 1914, Lasky moved his family—including Blanche Goldfish—to California. Jesse bought a tiny house where he and his wife lived without in-laws for the first time in their five years of marriage. Sam's wife and mother-in-law settled into the Hollywood Hotel. Goldfish remained peripatetic, overseeing the sales, distribution and exploitation of the pictures. Lasky's major activity was buying properties and signing talent.

The Warrens of Virginia, written by William De Mille, marked the metamorphosis of his brother, Cecil, from administrator to actual director. A few months' observation of Oscar Apfel in action had convinced De Mille that he could do better. His shooting schedules ran twice as long as Apfel's—seven, even eight weeks—but his pictures were more ambitious. For *The Warrens of Virginia,* he and Lasky enticed Blanche Sweet away from D. W. Griffith with $2,000 a week (against Griffith's $85 a week) to play the feminine lead. In this picture, De Mille experimented with "naturalistic" lighting. Until then, the sole criterion of motion picture photography had been sharpness of detail. De Mille realized that light meant more than visibility: "If an actor was sitting beside a lamp, it was crudely unrealistic to show both sides of his face in equal light." He borrowed spotlights from the Los Angeles Opera House and "began to make shadows where shadows would appear in nature." * He became the first director to dim the intensity of the light when lamps were turned down or knocked over in a fight scene. He also introduced backlighting and sidelighting of his actors, thus creating some imaginative and dramatic effects and moods.

When Sam Goldfish received the finished picture in New York, he wired Lasky asking how he was supposed to sell a picture in which the lighting was too lousy even to show the characters' faces half the time. For this, he said, exhibitors would

* *Ibid.*

pay only half price! Lasky conferred with De Mille and replied that the shadows were art, not carelessness, and that if the exhibitors were too stupid to recognize "Rembrandt lighting" when they saw it, it was their loss. Reassured, Goldfish incorporated "Rembrandt lighting" into his sales pitch and raised the rental fee for the picture.

In the spring of 1914, Goldfish made a whirlwind sales trip through England, Scandinavia, Germany, Belgium, Switzerland and France, selling distribution rights in each country for from $3,000 to $4,000 per film until the bomb at Sarajevo exploded all commitments. The war made it difficult to deliver the films as contracted, and nearly impossible to collect moneys due. Goldwyn's memoirs make no reference to his personal feelings about the war, or its effect on his European relatives. Shortly after the war began, Lasky optimistically told a reporter, "The war holds no fears for us. We are now preparing for peace, and it is keeping us pretty busy, too."

In 1915, *The Birth of a Nation* established the legitimacy of the feature-length film as an art form. That year, the Lasky Company produced thirty-six pictures, a record number. William De Mille, anxious to upgrade the construction of photoplays, persuaded a former collaborator named Margaret Turnbull to join him on the Lasky lot. The two of them cranked out scenarios all summer, working in a little wooden house with screen doors to keep the flies out. De Mille hung a sign on the door saying SCENARIO DEPARTMENT—the first time the phrase appeared in Hollywood. In a few months they were joined by some local writers and by Margaret's brother, Hector Turnbull, drama critic for the New York *Tribune*. When DeMille was promoted to director, Turnbull became head of the story department (and, later, Blanche Lasky Goldfish's second husband).

As the supply of available plays diminished, their prices soared. Lasky offered a bonus of $250 to any staff writer who could come up with an original scenario; heretofore they had only done adaptations. This offer—modest in comparison with the $5,000–$10,000 he'd been paying for plays—quickly netted him two good properties: *The Golden Chance*, by Jeanie MacPherson; and *The Cheat*, by Hector Turnbull. *The Cheat* starred Fanny Ward, an established stage actress, and introduced Japanese pantomimist Sessue Hayakawa to the screen. Goldfish considered it the company's most prestigious, most talked-about production to date.

In 1915, when the war silenced Europe's opera houses, Lasky persuaded Metropolitan opera star Geraldine Farrar that her performance as Carmen should be immortalized on film. *Silent* film. In popularity, though not in temperament, Farrar was the Maria Callas of her day. Among her enthusiastic fans were thousands of teen-age girls who called themselves Gerry-flappers and stormed stage doors for a glimpse of their idol.

If there was irony in the great Farrar playing a silent Carmen, it apparently escaped everybody including Miss Farrar, who looked upon pantomime as a challenge for her talent and a "vacation" for her voice. And Goldfish by now craved more than popularity for his films. He wanted prestige.

Farrar contracted to make three films in eight weeks for $20,000. *Moving Picture World* called it "the greatest step in advancing the dignity of the motion picture." Her salary, unprecedented for films but still less than she might have earned concertizing, was sweetened by a two-story house-*cum*-servants, a limousine and chauffeur, a private bungalow and grand piano at the studio, an augmented orchestra on the set for mood music, living expenses for herself and her entourage, and billing as *Miss* Geraldine Farrar.

Her train was met at Union Station by the mayor, hundreds of extras in cowboy costumes, thousands of the local populace, a band, and five thousand schoolchildren strewing flowers along a red carpet laid from train platform to limousine.

Farrar's leading man in *Carmen* was the handsome young (twenty-three) Wallace Reid. The scenario, by William De Mille, was based on the original story, rather than the opera libretto—a decision motivated not by foresight but by copyright problems. The story is, after all, romantic and action-filled, and it played surprisingly well as a silent film.

Cast, crew and management found "Gerry" no prima donna but a warm, friendly, tireless worker and all-around good sport; Goldfish could not praise her enough. Farrar willingly applied her own makeup, arranged her own hair and objected only when the crude Klieg lights inflamed her eyes.

She finished out her contract with *Temptation*, but returned to the studio the following year, 1916, to star in *Joan the Woman*, again with Wallace Reid, again with De Mille. Farrar's and De Mille's mutual admiration knew no bounds. She thought him a genius; his ambition (happily never realized) was to direct her in a silent version of Wagner's *The Ring*. *Joan the Woman* was Farrar's favorite film, certainly her most arduous. When De Mille suggested that a scene in Joan's prison cell would be more realistic with white mice, painted brown, running over the star, she said, "He was so nice about it, I couldn't refuse." She cheerfully endured wearing eighty pounds of armor through a summer heat wave, and never complained when her nostrils were stuffed with ammonia-soaked cotton for the burning-at-the-stake sequences.

While Farrar was burning at the stake in Hollywood, Goldfish was smoldering with frustration in New York. His partners insisted on offering opinions and advice, and sometimes even had the temerity to tell him what to do! The partnership had been a turbulent one since its inception, and had held together for three years only because events had moved forward too rapidly for anybody to get off the speeding express to success. But Goldfish's limited vocabulary never included the word "consult," and his partners, while enjoying the fruits of his ceaseless activity, resented his high-handed abrogation of their supposedly equal authority. At one point, Lasky, De Mille and Arthur Friend actually voted him out of the corporation; but Goldfish simply refused to accept their decision, and the issue was tabled.

Even as the partnership soured, it was business as usual—booming. Goldfish, Lasky and De Mille were each drawing $1,000 a week. But the costs of production, plays, stars and directors were steadily rising; and although the old Trust had been dissolved by court order, a new one was taking shape in the form of Paramount Pictures, the first organization with a national distribution setup. The combine used the rivalry between the Lasky company and its chief competitor, Adolph Zukor's Famous Players, as leverage in dictating terms. Early in 1916, Zukor proposed a merger.

While the Lasky company had been making its enormous gains in the industry, Zukor, thanks largely to his long-term contract with Mary Pickford, had maintained his lead. Zukor's ambition was as ferocious as Goldfish's, but where Goldfish was fire, Zukor was ice. He was a tiny, ferretlike figure barely five feet tall; seated in a standard-sized chair, his feet dangled above the floor. His manner was deceptively mild, his voice moderate, his style subdued. His sudden silent appearances caused some employees to call him Creepy behind his back; but to his face, everyone, even Cecil De Mille, deferentially called him Mr. Zukor.

The combined clout of the two companies would create the most powerful force in the industry, with unprecedented control over to whom and for how much it would rent its pictures. No competitor would be able to match its roster of stars, including Pauline Frederick, Marie Doro, Marguerite Clark and, of course, America's Sweetheart. In view of the substantially greater assets of Zukor's company, his terms were generous. He proposed himself as president of the new corporation, to be known as Famous Players-Lasky, and offered to split the stock fifty-fifty. Jesse Lasky would be Vice-President; Goldfish, Chairman of the Board. On June 28, 1916, the merger became official.

Goldfish had been surrounded by turmoil all his life; he could not function without it. His approach to business was instinctive, often impulsive. Zukor's was logical and carefully planned. In *The Public Is Never Wrong*, Zukor wrote: "Every hour on the hour, and sometimes the half hour, Sam Goldfish sent a shock through the organization in the manner of those pneumatic drills. . . . Before long I was convinced that Goldfish disagreed many times only for the sake of argument."

A Chairman of the Board is not expected to participate in a corporation's day-by-day decisions; but as Zukor points out with masterful understatement, "Sam was not a believer, one might say, in parliamentary procedure . . . rules meant little to Sam when he was excited." Which was, of course, most of the time.

Goldfish was democratic in his contentiousness; he fought with everyone. The inevitable explosion was set off in August, at a conference in the company's New York office between Lasky and Pickford about the star's next picture. Goldfish dashed in and out of the meeting offering unsolicited advice and objections that raised the participants' temperatures and eyebrows. Finally Goldfish blurted out, "Jesse, don't let Zukor butt in on this picture. He's okay as an executive, but we've always made better movies than Famous Players, so see that you keep the production reins in your hands!"

Zukor had made Mary Pickford a star. Like a loyal and dutiful daughter, she reported the incident to her mentor. The next day, Zukor presented Lasky with an ultimatum. "I'm sorry to tell you this," said Zukor, "but Famous Players-Lasky is not large enough to hold Mr. Goldfish and myself. You brought him into the company and therefore I don't want to ask him to leave. But you'll have to choose between Mr. Goldfish and me." Zukor then left for a weekend in the country, there to await Lasky's decision.

The company's board of directors consisted of six "Lasky people" and six "Zukor people," so Lasky believed his would be the deciding vote.* Lasky, despite his personal dislike for Sam, tried hard to be objective. "I had tremendous respect for Zukor's courage and qualities of leadership. . . . But Sam was my sister's husband, and while he lacked Zukor's experience, he also was a brilliant strategist." After agonizing for two days over his decision, he concluded that "Sam was not geared to take a back seat for anyone," and sided with Zukor.

Lasky went to the Knickerbocker Hotel, where Goldfish was staying, to break the news. "He turned pale as death. It was a terrible blow. 'The company will buy your stock at the proper price,' I told him. 'Zukor has gone. He will come back after you have resigned.' After two or three days, Sam came around." Goldfish was hurt and embittered by what he considered to be treachery on Lasky's part; for the rest of Lasky's life, the two spoke only when social occasions demanded. But although the Goldfish ego was bruised, there was some comfort. The corporation paid him $900,000 for his stock. At thirty-four, Sam Goldfish was a millionaire.

* As it turned out, every director sided with Zukor.

4. *Good-bye, Mr. Goldfish*

Sam was not about to rest on his million. "I was accustomed," his (ghostwritten) memoirs relate, "to a life where every working hour was inspired by the one thought, 'How can I make the Lasky Company more significant?' You can imagine, therefore, the terrible blankness of those days following my resignation. Feverishly I cast about me for a new outlet for my organizing energy." *

Nineteen sixteen was a transitional period for the industry; actors, producers, distributors and theater owners were all scrambling for the largest possible piece of the action. Substantal businessmen were beginning to invest tentatively in the new medium, and Goldfish soon persuaded theatrical producers Archie and Edgar Selwyn to join forces with him. Borrowing from the names of its major investors, the new company was called Goldwyn Pictures. The major contribution of the Selwyns was the motion picture rights to their valuable portfolio of stage hits.

Goldfish immediately launched an unprecedented national publicity campaign. In a full-page announcement in *The Saturday Evening Post,* the snob in Goldfish made a blatant appeal to the snob in Everyman:

* Samuel Goldwyn, *Behind the Screen* (George H. Doran Co., 1923).

GOLDWYN PICTURES

Brains *write* them. Brains *direct* them.
Brains are *responsible* for their
wonderful perfection.

There followed a list of "Great Stars" (all women!—Mae Marsh, Mabel Normand, Jane Cowl, Mary Garden, Madge Kennedy, Maxine Elliott); "The ablest and most popular authors in the world"; and "Skilled screen and theatrical producers," including "Samuel Goldfish, the pioneer in the movement for better films."

The company leased a glass-domed studio in Fort Lee, New Jersey, across the Hudson from Manhattan. Goldfish's initial roster of stars was an attempt to copy the Famous Players formula: Maxine Elliott was his answer to Bernhardt, Zukor's first star; Mae Marsh was to be Mary Pickford's counterpart; Mary Garden would be the Goldwyn Company's Farrar; and Madge Kennedy and Jane Cowl were to contribute to the overall image of class. Mabel Normand, the Keystone Comedy queen, was their concession to the masses.

The company's first production, released in September of 1917, was *Polly of the Circus,* a romantic play by Margaret Mayo (Mrs. Edgar Selwyn). Mae Marsh, as Polly, was a disappointment to Goldfish; he attributed the success of the picture to a good story, not to her performance. She was the second actress he had lured away from D. W. Griffith—Blanche Sweet was the first, during his Lasky days—and he found both women "incapable of any notable achievement when removed from the galvanising influence of Griffith."

In an attempt to repeat the Lasky Company's success with Geraldine Farrar, Goldfish attempted to sign the woman he now called "the most consummate of singing actresses." Mary Garden was a statuesque, straight-talking, cold-blooded, well-established soprano whose best-known popular operatic role was *Thaïs,* based on the Anatole France story of a martyred saint. In 1917, motion picture acting still carried some stigma of illegitimacy, but Garden and Goldfish spoke the same language: money. Garden drove a hard bargain, and they finally settled on $125,000 for ten weeks' work.

Mary Garden in the movie version of *Thaïs* was the prototype for Imogene Coca's operatic numbers on *Your Show of Shows*. Nobody in the company knew anything about opera but Miss Garden, and Miss Garden knew nothing about motion pictures. Uncertainty compounded the confusion. Nobody listened, nobody learned. Up to a point, Miss Garden attempted to follow direction; when instructed to walk along a garden path lined with thirty parrots on perches and to scratch the head of every parrot, she dutifully complied, commenting that for $125,000 she would have scratched the heads of all the parrots in the world. But for the most part, she resisted direction and played the role exactly as she had on the stage.

The Fort Lee studio afforded Goldfish his first opportunity to involve himself in the details of moviemaking. He soon found himself mediating between Miss Garden and her floundering director. And although it was obvious to everyone concerned that the picture's death was as inevitable as its heroine's, not even Goldfish could bring himself to tell this forty-year-old prima donna how to play a part she had created on the stage.

"In the silent days," wrote Miss Garden in her autobiography (*My Story*), "we didn't say anything; we just looked. That's why there was no place for a woman like me. I had to talk. Just marching around and moving my hands smothered me as an artist. . . . A great actress had no place in the motion pictures during the silent days. . . . In those days you could do nothing but walk around."

But Miss Garden did considerably more than walk around. In the classic operatic tradition, she violently rolled her eyes, beat her breast and postured with such exaggeration that audiences were convulsed. Critics found the picture dull and stagy; one wrote that Garden died like an acrobat, instead of a saint.

It was an expensive failure for Goldfish, but he managed to snatch ersatz prestige from the jaws of defeat by finding something positive to publicize. He let it be known that *Thaïs*, although unanimously panned by reviewers, was the first movie in history to be shown inside the Vatican. A non sequitur, perhaps. The Goldfish touch, indubitably.

In order to fulfill her contract, wrote Miss Garden, "I

made *The Splendid Sinner* in three weeks, and I hope nobody in God's world will ever see it again. I have heard many films called the worst ever made; I am sure those who make such judgments never saw *The Splendid Sinner.*"

Having completed her ten weeks of work, Miss Garden said good-bye to the movies for good.

The corporate rivalry between Goldwyn Pictures and Famous Players (Goldfish relished nothing so much as outbidding or outsmarting his former associates) was matched by the company's intramural rivalry among actresses. Every actress believed that every other actress received preferential treatment in matters of scripts, directors, wardrobe, even the size of the ensemble that provided mood music during shooting. Mabel Normand required a jazz accompaniment for her comedy; Pauline Frederick was partial to soulful waltzes; and Geraldine Farrar, who signed with Goldfish when her contract with Lasky expired, felt that nothing but three classically trained string players could attract her muse.

Nineteen eighteen marked the official, legal metamorphosis of Sam Goldfish, immigrant, into Samuel Goldwyn, producer. It was not uncommon for immigrants to Anglicize their names; and Goldfish, an irresistible target for the puns of gossip columnists, had long been a source of embarrassment to Sam. Having gained the industry's attention, he wanted its respect. Too, anti-Semitism was widespread at the time, and a Jewish-sounding name could be a definite handicap. It was a time when Jewish secretaries wrote "Christian Scientist" on their job applications, hoping thus to avoid rejection by Gentile, and often even Jewish, employers. And while his ineradicable accent would never allow Goldfish to pass for anything other than what he was, his name would now be projecting an image to a mass audience. A Jewish image was not advantageous.

Without consulting his partners, Goldfish went into court one day with his lawyers and came out Goldwyn. Prophetically, the newspapers announced that the late Sam Goldfish was "not dead but legally annihilated." While the Goldwyn public relations staff labored to create a new image to fit the new name, their efforts were systematically sabotaged by Goldfish, who merely went underground—from whence, like some unexorcisable dybbuk, he periodically emerged, kicking and screaming, to blow Goldwyn's cover.

America's entry into the war in 1917 coincided with the release of the Goldwyn Company's first picture, *Polly of the Circus.* In 1918 transportation difficulties worsened; labor grew scarcer, and so did coal, their source of electricity for shooting. That summer the company followed the sun and the industry west.*

Goldwyn leased space in the Triangle Studio and, eight months later, bought the place outright. Built in 1915 by Thomas Ince, a director of William S. Hart westerns, Triangle was situated on sixteen acres in the wilds of Culver City, ten miles southwest of Hollywood. Its five glass-enclosed stages, offices, workshops and dressing rooms made it the Tiffany's of the movie industry.

Goldwyn easily enlisted Abe Lehr, his old glove bench partner, as his studio manager, but other personnel were less than enthusiastic about the move. Pauline Frederick refused to go unless Goldwyn provided a job for her husband, actor-director-writer Willard Mack; Goldwyn acquiesced. Rod LaRocque, the leading man in Mabel Normand's comedies and Mae Marsh's tragedies, stayed in New York. "He always held it against me that I turned him down," said LaRocque years later, "although I did so politely. 'If you don't recognize an opportunity when it comes, that's okay,' he said. I felt that I had unintentionally hurt him a little bit."

Geraldine Farrar was delighted with the move; she had enjoyed her previous film work in California and much preferred it to Fort Lee, where she found the summer months stifling and the ferry journey to and from New Jersey "a smelly pilgrimage that wore everyone's nerves to a frazzle." † Unlike the haughty Mary Garden, Miss Farrar refused to take her movies seriously.

The company's solvency was in large part the result of the comedies of Mabel Normand, whose following was large

* By 1919, 80 percent of the world's motion pictures were being made in Southern California.

† Geraldine Farrar, *The Autobiography of Geraldine Farrar* (New York, The Greystone Press, 1938).

and devoted. No love was lost between Goldwyn and the free-wheeling comedienne. He objected to what he considered her unladylike language and postures (sitting with her legs apart and striding about like a man); she called him a stuck-up bastard and performed devastating impressions of him at parties. In her four years with the Goldwyn Company, Normand made eighteen pictures—all low-budget, high-profit productions.

The only profits derived from the actresses Goldwyn imported from the theater, opera and concert stage were publicity and a sort of quasi-prestige. Their presence gave the Goldwyn lot the nickname within the trade of "the old ladies' home."

Jesse Lasky had given Farrar the benefit of some relatively good scripts by William De Mille, and the discriminating direction of his brother, Cecil. Goldwyn cast her in schmaltzy melodramas. One memorable hot summer morning at Fort Lee, Willard Mack dramatically presented an unintentionally hilarious scenario entitled *The Hell Cat* to a spellbound captive audience of two: Farrar and Goldwyn. Farrar was to play an Irish-Mexican heroine, Pancha O'Brien, who would be the object of a Perils-of-Pauline type rescue by a squad of U. S. Cavalry. Mack was especially proud of one "surefire" effect that involved Pancha's theft of an American flag, which she was to cut up and deposit in a dung heap. In another inspired scene, she was to cut the ropes binding a man's wrists, at the same time slashing his veins.

To Miss Farrar's intense relief, cooler heads, including Goldwyn's, prevailed; by the time the company reached its location site in Wyoming, only the title was unchanged; Miss Farrar had become the heroine of a Western feud between cattle men and shop owners.

In the California summer of 1919, the professional romance between Goldwyn and Farrar withered irrevocably. Goldwyn attributed the reversal to her marriage to Lou Tellegen, a handsome French actor who had been Bernhardt's leading man. Goldwyn considered Tellegen an unregenerate bounder who cared only for the advancement of his career, and who humiliated and exploited his adoring wife. In their first picture together—a story about the Russian Revolution called, inexplicably, *The World and Its Women*—Tellegen consistently tried to upstage his wife. Farrar, however, remained the star, and was billed as such on the advertising posters. Tellegen objected violently, and demanded equal billing. When Goldwyn refused, Farrar drove around Hollywood ripping up the offending posters! Years later, she admitted, "I was quite wrong. He was paying me a huge salary for a name that warranted it, and I was mistakenly trying to force him to rate Tellegen's value to that par. . . . One never knows what fools women will make of themselves when they place heart loyalty above pride and monetary interests." *

Halfway through the filming of her second picture with her husband, Farrar's "heart loyalty" drove her to threaten Goldwyn that she would not complete the picture unless Tellegen received equal billing. Goldwyn, adept at handling such situations by this time, replied that if she made good on her threat, he would exhibit the first part of the picture followed by the announcement, on screen, that at this point Madame Farrar would not proceed because the producer did not feature Lou Tellegen's name.

Farrar completed the picture, and one more—*The Woman and the Puppet*, a variation on the Carmen theme—before leaving Hollywood "with the happy anticipation of returning the following summer. . . . As I pulled out of Los Angeles, I could still hear the cheers of farewells and good wishes for a happy opera winter and my return to true and tried comrades of the silver sheet. . . ." † But one evening that winter, Goldwyn appeared unexpectedly at Farrar's door, telling the butler that his mission was urgent. Goldwyn was embarrassed but direct in stating his dilemma: his company was steadily losing money on Farrar's pictures; her contract still had two years to run—twelve weeks' work each year, for which she was guaranteed $250,000; and the financial position of Goldwyn Pictures was extremely shaky. Miss Farrar, aside from her Tellegen blind spot, was shrewd and realistic. Although her success in films had been greater than that of any other opera star, including Caruso, she knew that the medium never would be her forte. With a grand, if not entirely self-sacrificial gesture, she removed

* Geraldine Farrar, *op. cit.*
† *Ibid.*

her copy of her contract from a drawer and, with glorious panache and what Goldwyn described as "the most gallant look in the world," tore it up.

So ended Sam Goldwyn's association with opera.

Process Shot

Blanche Lasky's account of her marriage to Sam Goldfish is buried in her brother Jesse's papers—scrapbooks, correspondence, photographs, scripts, clippings and other assorted memorabilia—now the property of the City of Los Angeles. The papers were bequeathed to the city for its Hollywood Museum, which subsequently became a political football and went out of play, inextricably tangled in bureaucratic red tape. For the past seven years the city has stored the Lasky collection, along with an estimated three million dollars' worth of unduplicatable artifacts of the civilization known as Hollywood: original motion picture equipment, including the projector used for the first (1913) Los Angeles showing of *The Squaw Man* at Tally's Theater, a coal-burning projector and some of Edison's first talking-picture inventions, costumes and original costume sketches; thirty-five thousand still photographs, props, sound-effect devices from radio shows, personal letters and notes, recordings, movie and radio scripts, trade magazines, and a variety of miscellaneous relics including Valentino's serpent-shaped radiator cap and the head of the Lux Radio Theater kettledrum, autographed by all the stars who appeared on that show. The collection could provide the basis of a first-rate museum complete with library. It is almost, but not quite, inaccessible.

Researchers may visit by appointment on one evening a week, the only time that the curator and his little band of volunteer cataloguers are on the premises. Walt Dougherty, the curator, showed me a clip from *The Great Train Robbery* in which his father appeared as an extra. I asked him how he estimates the chances that the museum will ever be built. He shrugged. "These millionaire moguls are all dying off. If just one of 'em would donate the money . . . even if he specified that the museum had to be named after him! The Samuel Goldwyn Hollywood Museum, that'd be okay. But people are funny about money. Seems like the more they've got, the harder it is to pry it away from 'em."

It appears that the Hollywood Museum is an idea whose time came . . . and passed. So while tourists annually shell out millions of dollars for the heavily hyped tour of Universal Studios (featuring Raymond Burr's empty parking space, Dyan Cannon's empty dressing room, the Marcus Welby set and some flashy special effects), the genuine articles moulder in three immense cell blocks at the long-abandoned, rapidly deteriorating, oppressively dismal Lincoln Heights jail.

The jail abuts the railroad tracks in the crotch of Los Angeles—a smelly, smoggy wasteland of a neighborhood forsaken except by a few impoverished Mexican-Americans. The only structures near the jail—a bail bonds establishment and a TOPLESSBOTTOMLESS bar—are boarded up. Inside the jail, a five-story structure, the walls are adorned with Spanish graffiti, more exotic and creative to the eye than the familiar English. The ceilings are low, the air and lighting insufficient, the cell toilets stuffed with trash, the paint curling away from the walls. On the humid July evening of my visit there, it was all too easy to imagine the mood of its onetime inmates.

Three big cartons on a dusty shelf contain the Lasky papers—records of matters once of tremendous import and urgency—turning to dust. There, in and between the lines of letters exchanged between Jesse and Blanche Lasky, I found the obituary of Sam Goldfish's first marriage.

The closest, most enduring relationship of Jesse Lasky's life was with his sister; no spouse could displace or intrude on the siblings' devotion to each other. Jesse, the naïve, gentle dreamer, relied on his sister's clearheaded judgment and business sense. Blanche relished her role, and played it well. Both their marriages were disastrous mistakes. Jesse's became an arrangement, maintained for the sake of appearances. Blanche, displaying considerable courage for 1915, filed for divorce after five impossible years as Mrs. Goldfish.

Living in close quarters with his in-laws in the Broadway apartment, Sam, who may have found the situation reminiscent of his ghetto childhood, exhibited the emotional stability of a two-year-old. His wife's and mother-in-law's refusal to cater to or consult him about everything infuriated him, and his screaming rages kept the household in constant turmoil. The idea that other people had needs and feelings was inconceivable to him; he found intolerable their refusal to comprehend that their sole purpose in life was to satisfy his demands.

His reaction to the birth of his daughter, Ruth, about a year after his marriage, must remain a mystery; if he took any joy or pride in the child, he hid it well. Until very late in his life, he never publicly acknowledged her existence. Articles, interviews, press releases, entries in biographical reference books, even Goldwyn's own memoirs contain not one mention of his only daughter. After Blanche married Hector Turnbull in 1919, the childless Turnbull adopted Ruth. Such a procedure is legally possible only when the natural father gives his consent and/or fails to support his child.

Blanche could not rid herself of the name Goldfish quickly enough. Even during her marriage she had signed herself Blanche Lasky on some legal documents, and after the divorce she continued to use her maiden name. Ruth, who lived with her grandmother Lasky for portions of her childhood, was known to her schoolmates as Ruth Lasky. Whatever the terms of Goldwyn's financial settlement with Blanche—at the time of the divorce, his annual income was estimated at $20,000—she made no attempt to disguise her bitterness toward him. She was a strong, no-nonsense woman—it's easy to imagine her telling Sam what he could do with his money.

In the spring of 1932, Blanche Lasky died suddenly of pneumonia. She was 49. Her brother Jesse, already reeling from having been forced out of Paramount and to the edge of bankruptcy only weeks before, never fully recovered from that shattering spring.

In the thirties and forties, Lasky produced a few motion pictures (notably *Sergeant York* and *Rhapsody in Blue*) and hosted a radio talent show series, but he never regained his prominence, and remained heavily in debt. In the early fifties, his friends passed the hat to enable him to pay his back taxes. His old friend Cecil De Mille approached Goldwyn for a contribution. Goldwyn thought about it overnight, then agreed. Lasky was grateful; bitterness was not in his nature. In 1958, still in debt, he was, according to De Mille, "buoyant and bubbling as ever," looking forward to producing a long-contemplated picture. His autobiography, written with care over a ten-year period, had just been published. He gave a promotional talk for the book at a Beverly Hills hotel and on his way to his car, in the hotel parking lot, collapsed and died. At his funeral, five hundred of Hollywood's finest paid hypocritical tribute to a man they had written off as too soft. As at many Hollywood funerals, the sentiment rivaled that of Goldwyn's most banal movies. When John Raitt sang "I'll See You Again" to the crowd, there wasn't a dry eye in the house.

5. *Eminent Authors*

In 1919, Goldwyn's passion for gilt by association manifested itself in a new experiment: Eminent Authors.

The quality of motion picture directing and photography had gradually improved since the one- and two-reeler days, but scenario writing remained primitive. Most of the early feature films were based on well-known plays or novels to which, in his Sam Goldfish days, Goldwyn had acquired screen rights which entitled him to remake the same story an unlimited number of times. But the movie rarely did justice to the originals. Most scenarios were stiff and static, with superficial, stereotypical characters. No serious writer took screenwriting seriously. It was a joke, a lark—a game played with real money, dominated by hacks proficient in technique but lacking in imagination and artistic sensibility. Novelists and playwrights who did possess these qualities were ignorant of how to apply them to the scope and mobility of the film. Goldwyn was not the first to notice this gap, but his was the first all-out effort to exploit it.

Double-page spreads in the trades announced the news with Goldwynesque fanfare:

> Eminent Authors Pictures, Inc., organized by Rex Beach and Samuel Goldwyn, unites in one producing organization the greatest American novelists of today. It insures the exclusive presentation of their stories on the screen and each author's cooperation in production. These authors are—

Rex Beach	Gertrude Atherton	Mary Roberts Rinehart
Rupert Hughes	Governeur Morris	Basil King
Leroy Scott		

This was merely the first contingent of Eminent Authors, all of whom believed Goldwyn's assurances that they would have the unprecedented right to approve their pictures before release. The ads proclaimed that "The picture must first pass the severest critic that it will ever meet—the author of the story."

It was more than coincidental that the increasingly exorbitant salary demands of the stars were rising beyond the always shaky budget of the Goldwyn Company. Unable to afford the current box office attractions, Goldwyn decided to create his own. He would put the writers' billing above that of his actors!

The Eminent Authors caper launched Goldwyn's reputation, quickly incorporated into the burgeoning Goldwyn Legend, for respecting the story above every other element in his pictures. In time, Goldwyn, like the politician who comes to believe his own rhetoric, undoubtedly came to see himself as a patron of the art of writing. A borderline illiterate himself, his awe of the written word—a medium of communication he dimly sensed but never mastered—would have been pathetic, had it not been for the dues he exacted from the scores of talented writers who contributed to his pictures. The collective experience of Goldwyn's Eminent Authors set the stage on which was later played out endless variations of the confused, frustrated, compromised, disillusioned—and rich—Hollywood writer.

"Eminent" meant exploitable. Rex Beach, for example, had acquired a large and loyal following with such adventure novels as *The Spoilers, Jungle Gold, Masked Women* and dozens of other literary masterpieces. Beach and Goldwyn were soulmates; with their common lack of artistic discrimination and finely honed instincts for what would sell, they understood each other perfectly.

Beach's most memorable contribution to motion pictures was his casting of a cowboy monologist appearing in the Ziegfeld *Follies* in the title role of "Laughing Bill Hyde," a Beach adaptation of a short story. The role of a shy, awkward, whimsical character with a Western drawl was tailor-made for Will

Rogers, and when the picture made money, Goldwyn signed Rogers to a two-year contract at double his *Follies* salary. Goldwyn was in the process of relocating his studio from Fort Lee to Culver City. "We were overcome by our good fortune," said Mrs. Rogers of the family's move to California. An old building on the lot was converted into a stable, and the Rogers children rode every afternoon in the ample space around the studio, accompanied by their father whenever he could escape from the set.

Rogers' first picture under his new contract was *Almost a Husband,* with Peggy Wood. Next came *Jubilo,* based on a story by Ben Ames Williams (*not* an Eminent Author) about a happy-go-lucky tramp. In a classic example of the transmogrification of truth later raised to an art in Hollywood, the late Richard Griffith, curator of the Museum of Modern Art's film library, wrote: "*Jubilo* is characteristic of the Eminent Authors at their best: carefully developed story-line, a consistent effort to make plot stem from character, and to give the characters themselves individuality." Griffith called *Jubilo* "a little masterpiece of filmcraft." In fact, the Eminent Author who adapted Williams' story had botched it so badly that Rogers refused to proceed with the picture. Ultimately, it was shot without *any* scenario, paragraph by paragraph from the original story as it had appeared in *The Saturday Evening Post.*

Rogers made a total of twelve pictures for Goldwyn. They were reasonably successful, but when his contract ran out in 1921 and he asked for a raise, Goldwyn let him go.

Rex Beach deplored Hollywood's congenital plagiarism, pointing out that "the director who did one of my early stories liked the main idea of it so well that he changed the locale from Alaska to Dixie, made my half-breed Indians into mulattoes and did it over with only minor alterations in the plot." *

Beach's artistic grasp exceeded his reach; he was tough and pragmatic, and enjoyed the Hollywood game. Other Eminent Authors were less fortunate. In *Adventures of a Novelist,* Gertrude Atherton wrote: "Remuneration was extremely generous and equally assured. And we were to be paid a certain stipulated sum during the term of our contracts, whether our work were

* Rex Beach, *Personal Exposures* (New York, Harper & Bros., 1940).

acceptable or not. As far as I am concerned, this agreement was faithfully kept. And that is the only good thing I have to say about the life of a helpless author on a Hollywood lot."

The generous remuneration ranged from $150 to $300 a week—hardly lavish in Hollywood even then, when actors were receiving ten and twenty times that amount. But authors tend to be curious as well as impecunious, and Goldwyn's flattery warmed their egos. Elmer Rice, a young but already seasoned playwright, was initially skeptical but finally convinced himself that "if Goldwyn really wanted new ideas and fresh material there might be opportunities to use the motion picture medium creatively. . . . Moreover, the prospect of seeing the Far West appealed strongly to my appetite for travel. Finally, there was the economic situation. Another baby was expected. . . ."

Rice soon grasped the implications of the relationship between the Eminent Authors and Goldwyn's existing scenario department. "Jack Hawks, head of the department and a veteran of the infant industry, was an energetic, unlettered, likable, alcoholic extrovert, well-versed in all the routines and clichés of film making, and not without a certain instinct for dramatic construction." * Hawks' veto power over suggested story material was supreme; his standard response to anything new or different was, "Will Lizzie like it?" This was in reference to a hypothetical small town waitress to whose mentality the industry geared its product.

The other six or eight members of the old staff were former newspapermen, or youngsters whose writing experience was limited to a few years or months in pictures. This group, itself divided by an ongoing status struggle, reacted to the higher-paid interlopers with thinly disguised hostility. They were not only jealous, they were afraid of losing their jobs. One of these scenarists candidly told Rex Beach that if his story treatments were faithful to the plays and books on which they were based, there wouldn't be any sense in keeping him on the payroll.

Stars and directors, bedeviled by insecurities of their own, did their bit to make the Eminent Authors feel unwelcome. Although Goldwyn had encouraged the writers to move freely about the studio in order to familiarize themselves with the

* Elmer Rice, *Minority Report* (New York, Simon & Schuster, 1963).

picture-making process in all its aspects, shooting frequently halted when they appeared on a set and resumed only after they were told, often rudely, to leave.

The difference between visual, cinematic writing and purely literary writing was beyond some of the Eminent Authors; one submitted a scenario that contained the line "Words fail to describe the scene that follows." But even those who could think in visual terms could not withstand the inexorable erosion of the integrity of their work by heavy-handed continuity writers, directors and even title writers who had the power to change the entire meaning of a film simply by substituting, at a crucial point, a title card reading Yes! for one reading No!

The one legitimately eminent author in the group (and, predictably, its first casualty) was Maurice Maeterlinck, the Nobel Prize-winning Belgian poet and author of the hit play, *The Blue Bird.* If the other Eminent Authors were visitors to an intellectually foreign country, Maeterlinck, who spoke no English, was on a foreign planet. Goldwyn's publicist arranged Maeterlinck's transportation from New York to Hollywood in President Wilson's private railroad car, outfitted with every luxury including the publicist, who regularly issued statements, attributed to Maeterlinck, glorifying America and Goldwyn, not necessarily in that order.

Through his interpreters, Maeterlinck held out for $100,000 a year, plus the use of a house in Brentwood. Goldwyn argued that his other Eminent Authors had settled for considerably less, but Maeterlinck was unimpressed; in fact, he had never *heard* of any of the other Eminent Authors (an admission that prompted Goldwyn to ask his publicist, "What is he, a dumbbell?").

The poet's first offering concerned a small boy with blue feathers and involved a feather bed, presumably the villain. He was informed that fairy stories didn't sell. He then submitted a one-and-a-half-page abstraction called *The Power of Light,* also unusable. It was suggested that he write a love story; he turned in some pages involving a married heroine, much too torrid for the screen.

Maeterlinck was then subjected to a sort of cinematic brainwashing, spending long days in projection rooms where moneymaking films were screened for his edification. The technique boomeranged. The scenarios he eventually wrote were *too* trite, banal and crammed with clichés to be used; Elmer Rice found them "shocking evidence of the corrupting influence of Hollywood."

Adherents of the transmigration-of-souls theory could make great capital of the fact that P. T. Barnum died the year before Goldwyn was born. Certainly Goldwyn was Barnum's spiritual successor. In the tradition of the shrewd showman, Goldwyn knew that credibility came not through truth, but through repetition and gimmickry. His Eminent Authors experiment turned out to be a rare exception to his success-through-ballyhoo record—but not for lack of effort. On the train bearing her west to begin a three-year contract with Goldwyn, Mary Roberts Rinehart, the Mary Stewart of her day, received a telegram informing her that a blimp ("safer than a taxicab," said the wire) would meet her at the station. When she protested, Goldwyn compromised with an open taxi filled with flowers.

Mrs. Rinehart was no wide-eyed innocent. A shrewd businesswoman, she had driven ambulances and nursed the wounded in Mexico during the Pershing campaign, packed through thousands of miles of wilderness on horseback, written and produced numerous plays, helpmated her doctor husband and raised a family of three boys, all the while cranking out best seller after best seller. Yet this formidable, sophisticated woman was unprepared for the shock of realizing that her primary function in Hollywood was not to write, but to provide publicity for Goldwyn pictures. Her first assignment was to report not to the scenario department but to makeup, where her complexion was yellowed, her generous mouth transformed into a tiny cupid's bow, her eyebrows raised to give her an expression of perpetual surprise, her lashes beaded so heavily she could scarcely open her eyes. When her face had been rendered virtually unrecognizable, she was transported around the lot and the countryside like a mannequin, photographed on horseback, in airplanes, on the beach, in the studio garden. Finally she was taken onto the set where "her" picture was being filmed. "My hopes rose; perhaps now I would see my picture being made. I might even make suggestions that they use my story! I had been seeing 'rushes,' the footage shot the day before, but none of them had seemed to resemble my story.

"But it was a vain hope. I was carefully posed with the scenario on my knee and the cast about me, and a half dozen men with cameras took a number of 'still' photographs." Goldwyn's publicity department released the photos with the caption "Mary Roberts Rinehart discussing her new picture with the director and the cast." Mrs. Rinehart had never talked the picture over with director *or* cast; indeed, that was the only occasion on which she ever even *saw* the director. "I was charmingly treated, I was always welcome at the offices, but I was precisely as useful as a fifth leg to a calf."

When she protested, "I was told of the vast gulf between the picture audience and the reading public; I was assured, politely, that I knew nothing of this new art; and when I threatened to become violent I received a box of flowers!"

After two months of this insanity, Mrs. Rinehart returned to her Pittsburgh home to complete *The Bat,* later a stupendously successful play. But soon Goldwyn beckoned again, and she returned to the Coast to find, to her dismay, that a novel of hers had been mutilated into a motion picture.

"It was then that I evolved a plan to beat the game. . . . I asked to be allowed a scenario writer of the studio's selection to work with me in Pittsburgh and to produce a technically correct scenario for my next picture. It was so arranged, and I started East, not with one continuity writer, but with two!

"I now began to have some hope. In the guest room they set up their typewriters, and each morning opened with a discussion of the day's work. Then they would retire, and in my study below I could hear the machines clicking overhead. For some weeks this went on. . . . At last they started West. They had a good and consistent story in thoroughly technical form. To my utter astonishment, the scenario department threw it out entirely." *

The natural resource of a writer is his/her experience, and in that sense, as well as financially, Mrs. Rinehart and her colleagues profited by their time in Hollywood. But the town's caste system was already well on its way to becoming as strati-

* Mary Roberts Rinehart, *My Story* (New York, Farrar & Rinehart, 1931).

fied as Calcutta's. Los Angeles society, such as there was, snubbed the picture people; and the movie colony—a self-absorbed cultural wilderness containing no art galleries, few bookshops, no legitimate theaters or museums and no concert halls—snubbed the writers. By necessity and temperament, the Eminent Authors were spectators. Their observations were always perceptive, often caustic, sometimes witty—but they never passed through the looking glass; they never belonged.

In Hollywood, always a company town, conversation consisted exclusively of shoptalk: movie business and movie gossip. A few dozen twentieth-century Kublai Khans dominated Hollywood's aristocracy; Goldwyn was in the vanguard. The life style was quintessential *nouveau.* Graduates of the bastard school of architecture sowed the seeds of camp across the landscape—commercial and residential structures that were strangely appealing in their nuttiness. If a mansion, car, servant, wardrobe, jewel or *objet d'art* was hideously expensive, it was In; status symbols were zealously acquired and tastelessly displayed. Thus it was that the Eminent Authors, most of them, found the Hollywood scene as shadowy and insubstantial as the life it presented on the screen. Small wonder that they gradually drifted back East feeling thoroughly thwarted, battered and misunderstood, muttering with tolerant superiority of Philistines and phonies. Only Rupert Hughes, who later became a director, managed to turn out a profitable script; his *The Old Nest* grossed close to a million dollars. The Eminent Authors experiment was a qualified failure, a necessary stage in the evolution of Goldwyn's merchandising techniques. And if the results were satisfactory neither as literature nor as screenplay, nobody noticed but the Eminent Authors.

6. *Behind* Behind the Screen

Catastrophe was Goldwyn's muse. Never a drinker, he got high on chaos. When external events provided a hook on which to hang his free-floating anxieties, he was at his finest. 1919 was such a time.

During the war, costs had skyrocketed while the European market shrank. Threatened with bankruptcy, Goldwyn maneuvered his way through a minefield of creditors, meeting a weekly payroll of $90,000 by a series of eleventh-hour machinations that left his partners breathless. Exhausted and exasperated by his brinkmanship, they voted him out of the corporation; he wheeled and wangled his way back into their good graces and they apprehensively rescinded their vote.

When international hostilities ceased, a civil war ensued in Hollywood. Competition for an expanding market became more frenzied than ever. Those who hesitated went under. Those who survived did so by ignoring the rules and risking everything on their instincts.

Goldwyn persuaded a group of financiers to invest $4,000,000 in his company and, by agreeing to use only Dupont raw film, secured an additional $3,000,000 from two of the Du-Pont brothers. He poured it all into the frantic production of solidly commercial comedies, melodramas, westerns and adventure pictures.

In 1920, the Goldwyn Company released twenty-three pictures, memorable only for the aggressiveness with which they were promoted. Ads in national magazines strained for dignity, often drifting into absurdity or downright incoherence. Goldwyn's staff regarded him as a slave driver; perhaps exhaustion prompted a copywriter to write, under the headline IF IT'S GOLDWYN IT'S A WINNER!: "You can see a motion picture any old time! Goldwyn is worth seeing all the time!" One Goldwyn picture was advertised as "the envy of the motion picture world and the everlasting delight of the motion picture public." And who could resist this enticement: "When you see a Goldwyn picture you forget your troubles—you forget the baby's croup and the cook's leaving."

Although Goldwyn had an office at the studio, where he tried to familiarize himself with the mechanics of making pictures, and another in New York, the organization had mushroomed beyond his direct control. By 1922, enough intrigue was going on to justify even Goldwyn's congenital paranoia. The villain was Frank Joseph ("Joe") Godsol, a Raffles-type character who insinuated his way into the company when Goldwyn installed three theatrical producers, Lee and J. J. Shubert and Al Woods, on his Board of Directors, hoping that their reputations would attract new capital. Woods and Godsol were related. Godsol was elected a vice-president and a member of the executive committee.

The Cleveland-born Godsol, good-looking, athletic and suave, had cut quite a swath through European society. Goldwyn, impressed by his style and his contacts, was probably unaware of his reputation as a high-class swindler; his most spectacular venture had involved the sale of fake jewelry. With dissension already rampant in the ranks, Godsol's aim was nothing less than to take over the company.

Godsol became Goldwyn's severest critic, egging on all other challengers to Goldwyn's hegemony. Lee Shubert was a willing ally, probably because he and Goldwyn were much alike; the Shuberts' immigrant background approximated Sam's, and so did their difficulties with the English language. Lee Shubert never referred to Goldwyn as anything other than Mr. Goldfish.

Imagining a meeting of this improbable board of directors—the theatrical producers, the DuPonts, the conservative financiers, the flashy, Machiavellian Godsol and the volatile, inarticulate Goldwyn—the mind bends. The board members insisted on having some say in how their money was spent. They asked annoying questions about the myriad expenditures involved in producing and distributing motion pictures, of which they knew nothing. Goldwyn considered this unreasonable. The Board's demands impinged on his other activities, and the explanations he reluctantly gave them, filtered through his ego and his abridged vocabulary, clarified nothing and aggravated the collective frustration.

Goldwyn's first serious error was in overexpanding his distribution outlets. He personally opened sales offices in England, France, Germany and other countries where American films had been scarce; but the production end of his company was incapable of providing enough pictures to support the sales end. The result was that distribution costs, normally around 20 percent, soared to 50 percent.

Late in 1920, the DuPonts, concerned for their $3,000,000, urged some restructuring of the organization. Their audacity so enraged Goldwyn that he resigned, a decision he immediately regretted—and reversed. The corporate tower of babel continued.

In 1921, Goldwyn made his second—and fatal—error. He imported *The Cabinet of Dr. Caligari,* a stylized, surrealistic, experimental film so "advanced" that when Goldwyn screened it in his projection room for his staff, they were all rendered speechless. The picture was controversial enough to attract widespread publicity, and "artistic" enough to add prestige to Goldwyn's name (even though his only connection with *Caligari* was in making the German film available to American audiences). But theatres that showed the picture became disaster areas. People booed and demanded their money back, then avoided the scene of the crime for weeks afterward. Theaters lost so much business that they filed lawsuits. The ultimate beneficiary was Joe Godsol, who seized upon the debacle as conclusive proof that Goldwyn was ruining the corporation. In March, 1922, the stockholders paid Goldwyn $1,000,000 for his stock and forced him to resign; it was at this juncture that he was said to have angrily uttered his "immortal" command, "Include me out!"

Godsol's triumph bruised Goldwyn's ego, but freedom

from meddling partners and directors was some compensation—along with, of course, his million. He secured an advance of $100,000 on his "memoirs," rented a beach house in Great Neck, Long Island, and spent the summer "dictating" to ghostwriter Corinne Lowe.

Miss Lowe, a fan magazine writer, made no attempt to convey Goldwyn's idiom or vocabulary. Undoubtedly making the best of a sticky assignment, she simply told a glamorized, highly selective version of Goldwyn's story in the same glossy, gushy, gossipy style with which she wrote for *Photoplay*.

Behind the Screen appeared first in *Pictorial Review* and in 1923 was published as a book. It is a fascinating document, unintentionally revealing in its omissions, distortions, and reflections of the values of its subject. Goldwyn was then forty years old. The story he could have told, but never chose to, had all the elements of high drama: oppression, adventure, power struggles, a cast of colorful, complex characters in conflict with themselves and each other, all set in chromatic locales. It would be unfair to say that Miss Lowe was not up to her material; she was a professional, in her fashion, fulfilling an assignment. What Goldwyn wanted, and what he got, was essentially a 263-page puff, superficial and sentimental in the worst sense of the word. He dispensed with his pre-*Squaw Man* life, all thirty years of it, in a few cliché-studded paragraphs. There is not one reference to his marriage or his child. With the cold efficiency of a hit man, he rubbed that chapter out of his life.

Behind the Screen tells us that Mary Pickford "goes to the heart much as does a Foster melody." Fanny Ward had a fetish for frankfurters: "I can see her now as she sat before one of her famous gold platters heaped high with the incongruous fare." Mae Murray "could not have saved many nickels from her allowance. . . . One evening at the Hollywood Hotel the charming little actress changed her evening wrap four times." De Mille was "courteous, self-controlled, kindly . . . who, indeed, could dislike him?"

Fan magazine stuff, assuredly. Goldwyn loved it; fan magazines sell. The revelations continued: Harold Lloyd "has all the old-fashioned reverences. 'I can't understand how any man could ever dissect his own mother's character,' he once said . . .

'After all—whatever she does, whatever her faults—she is your mother.' "

Pola Negri "has every fashion magazine published in Europe and in America, and pores over them for hours."

There is a detailed account of Mack Sennett's discovery of Chaplin, gratuitous in that it had nothing whatever to do with Goldwyn. One passing remark about Chaplin does, however, give one pause; it concerns his "horror of old age. With a kind of fierce rebellion he looks into a neighbouring glass at the streaks of grey in his hair. 'Ugh!' he will shiver. 'To think the time is coming when I shan't be young any more!' "

In this collection of name-dropping nonsense, one passage stands out. The style is Lowe's, but the feeling is indisputably Goldwyn's. The subject is Chaplin, but Goldwyn is clearly projecting when he speculates on the source of Chaplin's obsession with power. "Those early years of his in London when, the son of poor vaudeville artists, he experienced hunger and tragedy and the constant terror of the next day, have driven far into his brain. No prosperity can quite rid him of fear. That is why he wants to assure himself in every way of his present strength. For what is it but fear which makes a man conscious always of the thickness of his armour, the sharpness of his weapons?"

However rarefied the atmosphere Goldwyn created around himself, there would always be whiffs of the stale, sour breath of the ghetto.

Process Shot

Hollywood, always an easy target for cheap shots, views journalists with a wariness bordering on paranoia. The only Hollywood personalities who exhibit any cordiality toward the press are either ambitious lightweights (irrelevant to this book) or well-established heavies with indestructible reputations. But this latter group is a rapidly diminishing one, and the recollections of the survivors have been strip-mined by students, writers and researchers.

Septuagenarians who haven't yet published books are writing them, or contemplating writing them, and have belatedly realized that if they are profligate with their recollections, their own books will contain only warmed-over material. A plethora of Hollywood books already gluts the market. One Hollywood bookstore, a mecca for movie freaks, caters to collectors. The catalog of its stock—books, scripts, scores and stills—requires 524 pages. What is the source of this bottomless fascination with the movies? It would seem that for some of us movies are the reality, life the illusion.

My phone calls, a couple of hundred of them, produced pleasant enough greetings, but my first mention of the fatal name evoked, at least half of the time, thudding silence—followed by tight questions. The handful of loyalists—relatives by blood and by marriage, and longtime employees mentioned in Goldwyn's will—asked immediately, "Does the family know about this? I'll have to check with them," and thereafter made themselves unavailable.

The people most willing to talk had the least to say about Goldwyn. They did talk endlessly about themselves, volunteering astonishingly irrelevant information. From a retired director, I heard the sordid details of his custody battle with his ex-wife; from an internationally known actor, of his childhood traumas and psychotherapy; from an art director, a twenty-minute anti-Nixon diatribe; from a producer, a twenty-five-minute *pro*-Nixon diatribe; from a top actress, of the difficulty of finding competent servants nowadays; from a writer in appalling physical and mental shape, of the miraculous benefits of Christian Science; from another director, a system of handicapping horses; from a production manager, a long list of guaranteed hangover remedies; from a publicist, an hour of name droppings; from an agent, the gory story of his alcoholism; and from a director of countless B pictures, the entire, unexpurgated story of his life.

These were the people who did not want me to leave—a desire that had nothing to do with me, only with my attention. Awkwardly, I declined drinks, dinners, lunches, dates with people desperate for some validation of their existence. Their unsolicited confidences were motivated only partly by ego. Victims of time, they had functioned where the action was for decades; their obsolescence was unplanned. Most of them were healthy and alert, their creative juices still on tap; but except for the university seminar circuit and an occasional film festival or retrospective, their existence is scarcely acknowledged. No wonder so many of them are trying to write books.

At seventy-eight, Henry King is planning his "greatest picture ever": *The Story of Guadalupe*. It'll be bigger, he says, than *The Song of Bernadette*. The scene of these preparations is an eleventh-floor office near Hollywood and Vine, a building I had last visited on VJ-Day; from the vantage point of its top floor, the famous intersection had resembled Times Square on New Year's Eve. Today, nothing could provoke a celebration on that spot. The flow of traffic remains steady, but since my generation grew up and moved to the suburbs to raise our children, the streets have been inhabited by losers of every description: drifters, freaks, hustlers and an appallingly large number of the aged shuffle along streets nearly as filthy as Times Square's.

The sign on Henry King's door reads PLEASE KNOCK *LOUDLY* OR RATTLE THE MAIL SLOT, and his hearing aid is another reminder to speak up. The ambience is unpretentious, functional, bleak. In the summer of 1974, the place reeked with an acrid smell, the source of which stood next to King's desk: three battered, badly charred filing cabinets, relics of the fire that devastated the Goldwyn studio just weeks after the old man's death. These burnt-out hulks were the property of Billy Wilder, who had been renting space at Goldwyn's at the time of the fire; exactly what they were doing in Henry King's office was not clear. Interviewing the director of the 1925 version of *Stella Dallas* in that small, rather shabby room, dominated by the overpowering stink of that fire, was one of the more surreal moments of my search.

Dressed like a proud anachronism in blue and white pinstriped seersucker suit and oversized plaid bow tie, and sounding like a mellow C. B. De Mille ("Lux presents . . . Hollywood!") with catarrh, King discoursed, nonstop, for two hours.

His relationship with Goldwyn began with *Stella Dallas*, followed by *The Winning of Barbara Worth*. Both pictures were made in 1925. The prop man assigned to *Barbara Worth* (and most subsequent Goldwyn pictures) was Irving Sindler, who still lives, with his wife Della, in the old neighborhood a few blocks from the studio. Sindler is a short, stocky, hearty man who speaks East Side New Yorkese in a hoarse, gravelly voice. He struggled up the stairs from his storeroom under an armload of scrapbooks that meticulously chronicle the life and times of Irving Sindler. Sindler made good copy for Goldwyn's ever-vigilant publicists; his trademark appeared in a hundred of the 250 pictures he worked on, beginning with Pickford's *Little Annie Rooney*.

Mamoulian's trademark is a cat; Hitchcock's, his person. Irving Sindler's was his name. In *Hurricane*, set in a French-speaking locale, one of a row of stores bore the name I. Sindlere. In *The Westerner*, a cook shack on the range had a makeshift sign, "Ma Sindler's Home Cooking." During the shooting of

Dead End, Sindler announced the birth of his son by stenciling "Sindler & Son" on a delivery truck. Sindler's name appeared on a sewing machine label in *The North Star,* a street sign (Sindler Avenue) in *The Kid From Brooklyn,* a furniture store in *The Best Years of Our Lives,* a milk truck in *Up in Arms,* a library book ("The Life and Works of I. Sindler") in *Ball of Fire.* In *The Adventures of Marco Polo* it appeared, in Chinese, on a pennant; in *Hans Christian Andersen,* on the side of a sunken ship. "In *Wuthering Heights,*" says Sindler, "there was no place to put it. So I had it put on a tombstone. 'Here lies Irving Sindler. He was a very good man.' "

Sindler had been kicking around the studio as a laborer and a double for Douglas Fairbanks ("In those days, honey, you did everything!") when he was hired as a prop man for *A Thief in Paradise,* with Ronald Colman and Vilma Banky. "There were no property masters then—just prop men. They wanted prop men who could get along with George Fitzmaurice, the director. "Fitzmaurice smoked big cigars and had a bad temper. You'd say Good Morning to him, he'd say 'What's good about it?' We had a gold derby; whoever got in trouble with Fitzmaurice had to wear it."

The pride Sindler took in his work is evident in the care with which he's preserved his mementos and the tone with which he recalls the details of meeting assorted challenges. "On *They Got Me Covered,* we had a gag, I had to hit Bob Hope with a raw tomato so that a clay pipe would explode in his mouth. He said he was afraid. I took a real tomato and filled it with colored whipped cream. I tried it on me first. For the pipe, we had wires specially made; when he opened his mouth it released a spring and exploded, just very thin clay. . . .

"In *Pride of the Yankees,* celebrating the homecoming on the train, Walter Abel had to eat a straw hat. I got a caterer to make it out of dough. He even flavored it for him!

"In *The Princess and the Pirate,* we had a big spread; the color had to be perfect. Color was new then; consultants came out from New York. Mr. Goldwyn said, 'I'm gonna call in Chasen's.' Dave Butler [the director] said, 'Why don't you let Irving do it?' Chasen's would have charged thousands. I said, 'I'll give you change from five hundred dollars.' And I did! I went out and bought real fruit, so it would photograph right.

They were very happy. I'm always in favor of the real thing, honey, if it's a close-up—even flowers.

"Mr. Goldwyn was like a father to me. In those early years I did everything for him: drove him around, picked up the mail, answered fan mail. We were like a family. Abe Lehr used to give everybody ten dollars at Christmastime—but after the unions came in, they discontinued that. Mr. Goldwyn was always fighting the unions. They couldn't decide whether they were independent or a major. If you were a major studio, you had to pay the scale. Independents, you didn't have to. There was so much commotion about that, tryin' to classify what side of the fence he was on. It wound up, he hadda pay scale.

"You didn't make mistakes with Mr. Goldwyn. His life was time and money. But one time he called me into the office. He says, 'Irving, I know I'm gonna close down for a little while. Any time I can advance you some money, I'll be glad to do it. Don't forget, you're one of the family.'

"He was just like a father to me."

After several hours with the Sindlers, I took a walking tour of the old neighborhood—a mistake. The site of the Mom & Pop grocery store my mother patronized is now occupied by The Pussycat Theater, advertising in huge Dayglo letters "DEEP THROAT—THE 100% GULP!" Poinsettia Playground, my childhood hangout across the street from the studio, is deserted; the wading pool that was drained during polio epidemics is permanently dry. The house next door to the one in which I grew up has been replaced by the Villa Poinsettia, a convalescent home. My old house serves as the annex.

The west side of Hollywood is dotted with hideously overpriced geriatrics wards. Landmarks include the Beverly-Sinai Towers for Retirement Living, Eden Guest Home, Garden of Eden Rest Home, Golden State Retirement Hotel, Villa Stanley Senior Citizens Home and Tel Aviv Rest Home, guaranteed "Kosher, all diets including diabetic, 24-hour supervision, kind care."

At a prestigious address on the Sunset Strip, the unpretentious bungalow that housed my father's agency for twenty years still stands. The present lessee is THE PLEASURE DOME MASSAGE PARLOR.

7. Free at Last

In 1922, having been voted out of two companies, Goldwyn formed a third: Samuel Goldwyn Productions, Inc., a totally independent venture with no stockholders, no partners and no board of directors. The Goldwyn Company immediately filed an action in the United States District Court to enjoin him from releasing pictures under the legend "Samuel Goldwyn presents," on the grounds that the name had been used by the company since its incorporation in 1916, before Goldfish became Goldwyn. Sam was, of course, outraged. He fought the injunction and a hilarious legal battle ensued, culminating in a compromise: he could use the name if the qualifying "Not Now Connected With Goldwyn Pictures" appeared on the screen and in advertisements in letters as large as those of "Goldwyn."

Joe Godsol's was a Pyrrhic victory. His takeover of the company was followed by a cyclical recession in the industry, and the Goldwyn Company soon faced bankruptcy once again. In 1924, Marcus Loew, owner of a huge theater chain with an insatiable appetite for pictures, acquired three independent companies whose combined product would supply his theaters with a new picture each week. One of the companies belonged to Louis B. Mayer; another, called Metro, to Joe Engel. The third was the failing Goldwyn Company.

Although Sam Goldwyn was never associated with Metro-Goldwyn-Mayer,* he relished the fact that the public, under-

* He reportedly once was invited to join MGM, but when he insisted that the company be renamed Metro-Goldwyn-Mayer & Goldwyn, negotiations ceased.

standably confused, always believed he was; characteristically twisting the truth, he always referred to it as "the company that bears my name." Loew was not amused, and now *he* took legal action to prevent Goldwyn's use of the name. The final compromise gave Sam the right to use "Goldwyn" with the provision that "Samuel" would always precede it.

Abe Lehr's last official act as studio manager of the Goldwyn Company was to present Louis B. Mayer with a large key, symbolic of handing over the property, at the ceremony observing the merger. In Goldwyn's new company he resumed his role as aide-de-camp. Lehr was the prototype for all Goldwyn loyalists to come: trustworthy, unquestioning, totally dedicated, well paid and worshipful. Lehr was a nervous little man who wanted to be liked and succeeded. Unhampered by any noticeable personality, he became that rarest of creatures, a Hollywood executive without enemies.

Goldwyn rented space in the United Artists studio, owned by Douglas Fairbanks, Sr., Mary Pickford and Charlie Chaplin, and hired what he considered the best talents available for his first production, *The Eternal City*. The adventure-melodrama was a remake, with political overtones added to update it. As director Goldwyn hired George Fitzmaurice, a foppish former window dresser whose forte was romantic and exotic tales. He had a window dresser's eye for composition which sometimes detracted from the drama. Fitzmaurice made bad pictures beautifully. Every shot was a picture. *The Eternal City*, released in 1923, starred Lionel Barrymore, Bert Lytell, Barbara La Marr and Montagu Love.

Goldwyn's former associates at the Goldwyn Company had repeatedly resisted his suggestions to film the popular *Potash and Perlmutter* stories by Montague Glass. His second production as an independent, also released in 1923, was *Potash and Perlmutter*—followed by two sequels, *Partners Again* and *In Hollywood With Potash and Perlmutter*. All three were examples of heavy-handed ethnic humor—the *Bridget Loves Bernie* of their time—and all were enormously successful. The rising salaries of stars, compounded by the rising cost of just about everything else, were a continuing problem. Where *The Squaw Man* (1913) had cost $47,000, two (non-Goldwyn) 1923 pictures, *The Hunchback of Notre Dame* and *Robin Hood,* cost nearly a million.

Panicky producers, caught in the financial squeeze, found that stars, by virtue of their conspicuous high salaries, made convenient scapegoats and began to regard them as necessary evils. From the very inception of the star system, producers had tried to build stars out of unknowns who gratefully signed long term contracts at token wages. As their popularity grew, so did their demands. In the short run, everybody profited; ultimately, everybody suffered from the industry's collective greed.

Goldwyn liked to think of himself as a starmaker. He attempted to fashion stars out of cardboard, paste, glitter and publicity—with disastrous results. In his early years he applied this technique to Mary Garden and Anna Sten; later, to Virginia Mayo, Farley Granger, Vera-Ellen and Joan Evans. He publicly appropriated the credit for "discovering" Gary Cooper, whose potential was perceived not by Goldwyn but by Henry King, then in Goldwyn's employ; Dana Andrews, who had paid nine years' dues in Hollywood before Goldwyn, at the suggestion of his vice-president, tested him; Laurence Olivier, whose casting in *Wuthering Heights* was William Wyler's idea; and Ronald Colman.

Colman had had a brief, unsatisfactory career in English films before Henry King noticed him in a small part in a New York play. "I went backstage. Colman told me he felt he was no good in pictures. He'd been told he didn't photograph well because of two small scars on his face, above his lip and his eyebrow. I made a test. I got him over being camera shy, to where he could sit and talk without being conscious of the camera. I had him put pomade on his pompadour—it made his face too long—and told him to grow a mustache. Then I put him in *The White Sister,* and he was terrific. After that, he was the most sought-after actor in the country. When Goldwyn saw *The White Sister,* he wanted me, and he wanted Colman."

Goldwyn signed Colman in 1923, gave him a bit in *The Eternal City,* then starred him in a string of adventure stories and soap operatic melodramas. In *The Dark Angel,* Colman's costar was an authentic Goldwyn discovery, the smolderingly sexy Hungarian, Vilma Banky. The heavily embroidered story handed out by Goldwyn's publicists tells of the producer's spotting her photograph in a Budapest shop window, launching a massive search and finding her at the very last moment before he boarded a train for Paris. At any rate, Goldwyn and Banky did meet in Budapest, and signed a contract there.

Colman and Banky became one of the great love teams of the twenties, but Banky was a shooting star, grounded by sound. When Goldwyn accepted the inevitability of the talkies, he hired a voice coach to work on smoothing out Banky's guttural Hungarian accent, but the results were not impressive. Rumor had it that Banky was lazy about her vocal exercises. Her contract still had two years to run—at $5,000 a week—when Goldwyn called her into his office one day and told her, "You go to the bank every week and get your money!" She followed his instructions faithfully; and she never saw Goldwyn, or the inside of his studio, again.

Stella Dallas was the archetypal four-handkerchief weeper —a syrupy story of sacrificial mother love. Goldwyn loved the novel and filmed it twice; Stella's last incarnation was, appropriately, as the heroine of a soap opera. The silent version was by far the best, thanks to Henry King's direction and an outstanding cast.

Frances Marion, who wrote the screenplay, suggested that Belle Bennett play Stella. Goldwyn himself discovered the fifteen-year-old who played the daughter. On a business trip to Paris he spotted Lois Moran, an American dance student, and cabled Henry King: I HAVE FOUND A GIRL WHO I THINK WOULD BE WONDERFUL FOR LAUREL—HAVE HAD TESTS MADE AND AM SHIPPING THEM ON TO YOU. LET ME KNOW WHAT YOU THINK.

It was immediately obvious to King that "Sam had never made a test in his life! He only shot her face! I got Sam on the phone. 'What kind of legs does this girl have? You say she's a dancer. Has she got those awful dancer's legs?' He said, 'For the first time in my life, I never looked! She's too young for me, anyway.' He was so enchanted by her face!"

Moran's legs turned out to be satisfactory, and shooting began. If King had any problems with Goldwyn, he has long forgotten them. "As far as Sam was concerned, I could do no wrong. *Stella Dallas* was going to be his first big United Artists release. He believed in the subject. Everything he'd done previously had been show pieces; this was his first 'serious' picture."

Although Goldwyn had seen the rushes every day with King, he was unprepared for the impact of the completed picture. He saw it for the first time in the studio projection room, with his secretary, Abe Lehr, and Lehr's wife. King arrived as the screening ended and found everyone too distraught to speak. Goldwyn put his hands on King's shoulders and burst into tears. "I can't stand it!" he sobbed. "You've ruined me! Look at Ann Lehr—she's in hysterics! An audience can't stand all this emotion!"

The confused King, whose intention had been to evoke precisely all that emotion, asked uncertainly, "Do you like it?"

"Nothing has ever been made like it!" said Goldwyn, blowing his nose. "I love it! But if it does this to four people, what will it do to a theater full?"

Goldwyn thought it over for a couple of days and then called King and Frances Marion into his office. "I've never made a picture that didn't have girls in bathing suits swinging or on horseback or some big show thing to sell. Never anything like this." Frances Marion reminded Goldwyn of a spectacular scene she had written into the original version of the script, showing Jean Hersholt, who played Stella's alcoholic friend, in the throes of delirium tremens. Feeling that the only purpose of the scene was sensationalism, King had left it out of the picture. Goldwyn instructed him to put it in. "I spent about $30,000 for all these special effects, putting it in for him. It was one of the most horrible horror scenes you could imagine—an elephant comes through the keyhole and walks around the ceiling molding, there's a monkey, a roomful of bees—all trick stuff. We took the picture to San Bernardino to preview. The manager of the theater said, 'I like everything in the picture except that horror scene.' Sam said, 'I agree! Take it out!' "

In *The Film Till Now,* critics Paul Rotha and Richard Griffith call *Stella Dallas* "a brilliant and deeply emotional film [which] was superficially destroyed in this country by the cheap and contemptible publicity that it received. It was diversely said to be 'the greatest mother-love picture ever made,' and that 'Mr.

King had focalised in it all the creative artistry of his great career.' "

Goldwyn, elated over the picture's financial success, wanted to sign King to a contract in perpetuity. He settled for three pictures: *Partners Again,* a comedy; *The Magic Flame,* a romantic melodrama; and *The Winning of Barbara Worth.* The last two starred Colman and Banky.

The elements of the *Barbara Worth* story, scripted by the prolific Frances Marion, were bandits, capitalists, engineers, settlers, land reclamation, desert and dams. Colman played an Eastern engineer in competition with a cowboy for the girl, Banky.

It was Henry King who noticed Gary Cooper sitting outside his office, waiting to audition for a bit part in the picture. Cooper had starred in some two-reelers but had never earned more than fifty dollars a week. Even after he financed his own screen test, he was unable to get any studio executives to look at it. But King was interested enough to run the test. "It was what we called Poverty Row. A man rides up on a horse, gets off, looks around and goes into the saloon. He was from Montana, and could ride. I offered him fifty dollars a week to go to Nevada to ride. He said, 'If some small part comes along, can I get it?' I said sure."

Before the company left for the location work, King shot the interior scenes at the studio—a reversal of standard procedure. When the actor who had been cast as the lead cowboy, a character named Joe Lee, turned out to be unavailable at the last minute, King used Coop in some of his minor scenes. The next day, Goldwyn, after seeing the rushes, called King off the set. "You're trying to put that damn cowboy in the biggest part in the picture? The rushes were all right, but what are you going to do when it comes to his *big* scene?"

"I'm rehearsing that scene right now," King explained patiently. "Our Joe Lee is tied up at Warner Brothers. This isn't costing us anything but the film."

"You're just teasing, Henry," said Goldwyn. "You just do everything to *tease* me." And walked away.

King, who was known to be many things to many people but never a tease, spent the whole morning rehearsing Cooper.

In the scene, Cooper, after a twenty-four-hour cross-desert ride, was supposed to drag himself up the stairs of a hotel, knock on the door and collapse in exhaustion when it was opened. King had Cooper walk up and down the stage all morning long. "I wet his face and smeared it with Fuller's Earth and let it dry, and I did that over and over again. We walk some more. More Fuller's Earth. More water.

"I told him that when Colman opened that door, I wanted him to fall flat on his face, and he said he would. Then I told Colman I wanted him to catch him. Well, there was pathos in his knock—if you can imagine that. He was the most forlorn-looking person I ever saw in my life. When Colman opened the door and saw him standing there, he was so startled, he didn't catch him until one shoulder had hit the floor. I wanted to get a close-up of his face right away—the way he looked could never have been duplicated. But Sam called me outside again! He said, 'Why are you trying to tease me?'

"I said, 'I'm not! I'm trying to make a scene with an amateur!' He said, 'That man is a great actor!'

" 'How do you know?'

" 'I was peeking through a hole in the curtain. That man is a great actor! Let's sign him up!' "

Goldwyn delegated the negotiating to Abe Lehr, who asked King what sort of contract he should offer Cooper. King, who was paying him fifty dollars a week, said, "He's just a youngster, but I think he's a comer. I think we should give him $100."

Lehr felt that exorbitant amount would "spoil" the young actor; he offered seventy-five dollars. While Cooper was considering it, his agent got him a contract with Paramount starting at $750 a week.

The location shooting for *Barbara Worth* took place in the barren Black Rock Desert of Nevada, near the Idaho border —6,000-foot elevation, nothing but grit. The company spent ten weeks there, living in tents. The encampment accommodated twelve hundred people, most of them crew members who constructed the exterior of an entire Western town, complete with railroad station. A well was drilled for showers, but drinking water had to be hauled in.

Vilma Banky played a dual role: a pioneer woman who

dies in a sandstorm; and her daughter, Barbara Worth. An unplanned sandstorm came along in the midst of shooting and blew everything away, including the sets, which had to be rebuilt. In the midst of the storm, the train pulled up with Goldwyn aboard. From the platform, he could see nothing but sand. The train went back down the mountain immediately, with Goldwyn still on board.

It was not usual for Goldwyn to visit his companies on location. He may have been showing off for his new bride, who accompanied him. After ten years of bachelorhood, Goldwyn had found the perfect wife.

On the surface, they seemed an unlikely couple. When Sam Goldwyn met Frances Howard McLaughlin he was forty-three, she was twenty-one. Frances Howard (her stage name) was blonde, blue-eyed, Catholic, with fragile, aristocratic looks that belied her purposefulness. Their backgrounds could hardly have been more dissimilar, but their values and ambitions dovetailed. Both were predators. Character is fate.

Frances Howard's professional career began when, at fifteen, she and her sister Connie toured as The Howard Sisters. She subsequently became a chorus girl and fashion model. In 1924, she landed a plum role as Broadway's first flapper in *The Intimate Stranger,* a comedy starring Billie Burke and Alfred Lunt. Miss Burke later recalled that "Miss Howard had unusually fine hair and was immensely distressed about it during the tryout period. She used to come to my dressing room and weep about it. 'Mr. Tarkington wants me to cut my hair short for the part,' she would say, 'and I'm afraid to do it, I may not be good enough, I may not get the part, and then I shall be *ruined.*' But Frances did cut her hair, did get the part, and played it wonderfully."

A Goldwyn subordinate, always on the lookout for new, inexpensive talent, summoned her to Goldwyn's New York office. Sam, who is said to have so detested bobbed hair that he once instructed his publicity office to try to enlist the Pope in a crusade against it, took one look at her, said curtly "I don't like bobbed hair," and turned away.

Her next role, again as a flapper, was in *The Best People.* Jesse Lasky caught her performance and thought her a promising actress with "sensitivity." He signed her to a five-year contract with Paramount and costarred her with Adolphe Menjou in *The Swan* (the same part—the Princess—was played in 1930 by Lillian Gish, and in 1956 by Grace Kelly). The picture was shot at Paramount's Long Island studio. Ernest Fegte, then one of the youngest art directors in the industry, was assigned to the picture.

"We got along awfully well," says Fegte, "and we dated. I was young and she was younger. One morning I came to the studio and she announced that she had married Goldwyn. She had never let on! We had been out to the theater, nightclubs and stuff about four or five times during the making of the movie, and I never knew that she even *knew* Goldwyn until she announced it to me that morning."

She had, in fact, known Goldwyn for only three weeks when they were married on April 23, 1925. They had met at a Manhattan party given by publisher Condé Nast. "I still remember my dress," Frances told a reporter thirty-four years later. "It was white crepe and it cost me the appalling sum of $310. It was my first big social affair."

Mrs. Goldwyn's recollection of that detail after so many years reflects her lifelong preoccupation with clothes, money and, above all, appearances. She was young and impressionable when she met Goldwyn. He was established, respected for his success, and a millionaire. He had a valet, and dressed and looked like a gentleman. Only when he spoke—or shouted—did he give himself away. But Frances may have found his inarticulateness appealing, an indication that he needed her. Which, indisputably, he did.

Goldwyn's ignorance of women was abysmal; he had learned nothing from his marriage, nothing from his divorce, nothing from the starlets he occasionally dated. The romantic stories he bought and filmed reflected his simplistic saint-or-sinner perception of women—and Frances Howard McLaughlin was, by his lights, a saint.

He proposed in a taxi a week after he met her; they were on their way to the opera. Neither of them enjoyed opera, but both considered it an advantageous place to be seen. Referring to her Catholicism, he asked, "What would our children be?"

"Catholic, of course," said the self-assured young woman. "And no nonsense about it."

Mrs. McLaughlin, a staid, whitehaired Irish lady, strongly opposed her daughter's marriage outside the faith. Had she known that during the Depression her prospective son-in-law would provide jobs for her son Charlie, her daughter Connie and Connie's husband, she might have given him a warmer reception into the family.

The hastily arranged wedding took place in Jersey City, across the river from New York. Goldwyn saw to it that the press outnumbered the guests. Mrs. McLaughlin attended, along with her daughter Connie, Sam's attorney, and director Henry King and his wife. There was a wedding luncheon and champagne, but no honeymoon; neither the bride's nor the bridegroom's schedule would permit it.

After her marriage, Frances Goldwyn denied having ever taken her acting seriously; "The stage was just a pleasant way of making a living for me," she told a *Collier's* interviewer. She moved immediately to California with her husband and her contract with Paramount was canceled—it is not clear at which party's request. Her motion picture debut in *The Swan* also turned out to be her swan song in pictures. If she had ever contracted a fever for stardom, it abated soon after her marriage. Blanche Lasky had merely been Mrs. Goldfish. Frances created the role of Mrs. Samuel Goldwyn. The casting was perfect. For nearly fifty years, she played the part for all it was worth.

The week of Goldwyn's wedding, *The New Yorker,* then in its second month of publication, published a profile of Sam Goldwyn—written by his press agent. The article described his philosophy as "outstripping the other fellow by any means possible that doesn't land one in jail," and generally depicted him as a colorful, refreshingly unsophisticated primitive with a vocabulary of ten words—"words used by a prizefighter who has gone into the cloak and suit business and upon whose nodular toes an expressman has let fall half a ton of goods. If after an interview . . . you are all in, he will look at you in astonishment and ask, 'Vat's the matter?' If you can shout louder than he does and have a vocabulary of five words, you win. . . .

"Almost everyone in the picture business has at one time worked for him. He has never been known to praise a man who has slaved for him except for purposes of publicity. There is nothing he likes better than to be photographed holding on to the arm of a celebrity. Nevertheless, Sam Goldwyn is a great man. His insensitivity to the feelings of others is a trait often found in genius."

The profile concluded that "Sam Goldwyn's characteristics—his mental makeup, his manners, his background, his lack of traditions—are so typical of the motion picture industry with its conceits, its gropings, its courage, its exciting achievements —that he stands out of all the people in it as the symbol, the epitome of the movies, and heir apparent to its great future achievements."

As always, Goldwyn loved seeing his name in print—but sentences more complex than "Sam Goldwyn is a great man" were beyond his comprehension. He called for his translators. They assured him that the description was complimentary, that it fit him perfectly.

(Like a glove.)

8. *Making* Whoopee

Although she was not to the manor born, Frances Goldwyn was, in the early days of her marriage, a passionate parvenu—a zealous student of the mores and manners that ruled the town. For in spite of its reputation for wildly flaunting convention, the *haut monde* of Hollywood was actually about as unconventional as the populace of Gopher Prairie. It was only in their conventions that they differed.

By the mid-twenties, Goldwyn had acquired a large home in Hollywood, not far from the studio, and a house at Santa Monica, where the industry's elite had established a beachhead. Lasky, Mayer, Pickford and Fairbanks, Shearer and Thalberg, Harold Lloyd, Billie Burke and Marion Davies (courtesy of W. R.) all owned elaborate homes within one short stretch of oceanfront. On weekends, they competed to see who could throw the biggest, most expensive, most publicized, most "original" parties, some of which took a full week to prepare. Conspicuous extravagance was the order of the day. Dance floors were built at the high tide line, orchestras engaged, elegant costumes designed; guest lists "starred" visiting nobility. The forced gaiety of these gatherings contributed to a colossal collective self-delusion that kept reality at bay and helped create a false bottom which sank imperceptibly while the party continued; the Grand Ballroom of the Titanic comes to mind. By tacit agreement, people reinforced each other's illusions.

At the same time, possibilities, opportunities, abounded.

Given sufficient style and nerve, most of the parties were crashable. But never the Goldwyns'. That would have been tantamount to crashing Buckingham Palace.

In September of 1926, Frances Goldwyn capped off her perfection in Sam's eyes by producing a living monument to his ego—named, inevitably, Samuel Goldwyn, Jr. "Junior" is never a comfortable handle for any boy. With the additional handicap of a rich, famous, egocentric father and a mother with a will of iron, can a Junior ever hope to play with a full deck?

Sammy was not, according to reports, a happy child. The sea breeze carried the shrieks of his temper tantrums up and down the Santa Monica shore. His mother disciplined; his father doted. Goldwyn called the boy "my Eagle Prince" and demonstrated his devotion, in the traditional manner of European Jews, with kisses on the lips—surely an embarrassment as the boy grew older. There is no reason to believe that Goldwyn ever perceived his only son as anything other than an extension of himself. Sammy's sporadic attempts to assert his independence seemed to his father a baffling tic, a disobedience on the part of his own body.

Goldwyn *père* and Goldwyn *fils* began as strangers and drifted further apart. Not one, but two generations separated them; Goldwyn was forty-five when Sammy was born. Even had they been able to bridge that gap—and even if Goldwyn had somehow been able to perceive the boy as a person in his own right—what common ground could there be for the refugee from the ghetto and the millionaire's indulged son?

Ever since motion pictures were invented, sound had been the inevitable but elusive next step; Edison conceived of sound pictures as early as 1889, long before the technological groundwork was laid. In 1909, Marcus Loew had placed live actors in nickelodeons, behind the screens, and had them recite dialogue at full yell, in sync with the actors on the screen. He called it Humanova. It did not catch on.

By the end of 1926, Vitaphone (owned by Warner Brothers) was producing primitive talkies, but only a dozen theaters in the country were equipped to project them.

The transition to sound lasted two years, during which Goldwyn continued to grind out silent romance and adventure flicks: Colman and Banky in *The Awakening* and *Two Lovers;* Colman and Lily Damita in *The Rescue;* and shimmy queen Gilda Gray in *The Devil Dancer*. In 1929, he cautiously inserted sound effects and some dialogue into *This Is Heaven,* costarring Vilma Banky and James Hall; that film prompted Banky's premature retirement (at age twenty-five). But statistics showed conclusively by then that sound was more than a fad (as many had insisted). In 1927, paid admissions per week were $60,000,000. Two years later, they had jumped to $110,000,000.

The casualties produced by the advent of sound in the ranks of silent movie idols have been well-documented; for a time, Hollywood was a shambles of wrecked careers. The two silent male stars who most successfully survived the revolution were Charlie Chaplin and Ronald Colman. One of the most phenomenal strokes of good fortune ever to befall Sam Goldwyn was his having signed Ronald Colman to a longterm contract before sound waves broke over Hollywood.

Colman had everything: terrific looks, masculine voice, authentic English accent, sex appeal. An experienced master of his craft, he understood the subtleties of the new medium and the importance of restraint. Most actors used the unaccustomed microphones like megaphones; Colman addressed his with the intimacy of a lover. So it seemed perfectly natural—foreordained, even—that the first talkie produced by the immigrant Jew with the outrageous accent would star the actor with the most cultured, sophisticated and romantic voice on the screen as Bulldog Drummond.

Playwright Sidney Howard was credited with the screenplay—although, as the Eminent Authors had unanimously pointed out, that credit meant only that the writer had at some time done some work on the script. As a matter of practicality, Goldwyn instructed his director, F. Richard Jones, to adopt D. W. Griffith's method of rehearsing the entire script before any film was shot, thus minimizing expensive last-minute changes. This became standard procedure in many subsequent Goldwyn pictures.

Bulldog Drummond was slick and successful; its impetus carried Goldwyn through the Crash that came shortly after the picture's release. By then, the phylogeny of the silent film was complete; the last great silents were novas, their brilliance signaling the end of the form.

Ironically, Hollywood's richest, most creative period began in 1929, while the rest of the country's economy was sinking. Escape from the grim reality of the Depression was eagerly welcomed, and it took no genius to divine this need, or the logical product to fill it. 1929 was the year of the filmed Broadway musical—but because early sound techniques immobilized the camera in a soundproof booth, these were essentially static, photographed stage plays. Just as their popularity appeared to be waning, Goldwyn decided to produce *his* first musical: *Whoopee.*

Enter Flo Ziegfeld.

Ziegfeld had been presenting his fabulously profitable *Follies* annually ever since 1907, along with a string of other smash Broadway hits. He represented everything Goldwyn thought of as Class, and was a natural object of admiration, possibly even a father figure, for the younger man. Goldwyn wanted to be known as the Ziegfeld of the movies. To that end, he established his Goldwyn Girls—a blatant knockoff of Ziegfeld's famed showgirls—and spent inordinate sums on lavish costumes and scenery; he bragged of spending forty-five dollars for a simple pair of sandals.

In his prime, Ziegfeld would have been more than a match for Sam at the bargaining table. But when Goldwyn approached him on the subject of *Whoopee,* the Great Ziegfeld was sixty-one, and his health was failing. Accounts of the deal they made vary, some saying they coproduced the picture with matching investments, others that Ziegfeld needed money and sold the screen rights outright, along with virtually the entire cast. At any rate, the picture went into production in 1930, with Ziegfeld on the set either as technical adviser or as coproducer.

Eddie Cantor, who had created the leading role (a hypochondriac who goes West) on the stage, was part of the package. Cantor had made a couple of obscure silent films; to the moviegoing masses, he was an unknown. He was impressed and flattered by Goldwyn's decision to star him in a major film (said to be budgeted at over a million dollars). Believing that the future of his movie career was at stake, Cantor, in a spirit of cooperation, suggested that Goldwyn hire as dance director a Broadway impresario, director and choreographer whose work he, Cantor, had admired in *Fine and Dandy*. Goldwyn agreed, and thus did Busby Berkeley come to Hollywood.

In 1930, it took five days on two trains to cross the country: the Twentieth Century Limited to Chicago, and the Santa Fe Super Chief to Los Angeles. Cantor and Berkeley spent the time adapting the show for the screen. Their traveling companions and collaborators were Goldwyn's screenwriter William Counselman (later distinguished for his comic strip, *Ella Cinders*) and director Thornton Freeland. According to Cantor, Counselman and Freeland knew so precisely what they were doing that they were able to shoot the entire movie in a mere thirty-six days. According to the critics, it looked like a thirty-six-day production. But audiences loved it. So did Goldwyn.

Ziegfeld hated it. According to his biographer, Charles Higham, he was depressed and bored at the studio and also at the Palm Springs location. "Ziegfeld watched his brilliant effects ruined one after another, in conditions similar to the Belgian Congo. The only area in which Goldwyn permitted him any influence was in the dance direction, [where] Busby Berkeley . . . copied many of Ziegfeld's concepts. But the film was a travesty of the stage show, and Ziegfeld loathed it even more than he hated most movies." *

Travesty or not, *Whoopee* served as a launching pad for the movie careers of Berkeley and Cantor. No other showman, not even Ziegfeld, ever approached the singleminded dedication with which Busby Berkeley presented his "girls" as delectable confection-commodities. His close-ups of their faces, legs and cleavage were worshipful; his manipulations of them into geometric formations and patterns created dizzying, dazzling effects.

Berkeley saw that the unique potential of the camera vis-à-vis dance numbers lay in its limitless angles. He lifted the audience out of its accustomed seat—beyond the proscenium—and gave it breathtaking new perspectives from above, beneath and inside, looking out. In *Whoopee*, he introduced his trademark, the overhead kaleidoscopic dance formation. He

* Charles Higham, *Ziegfeld* (New York, Regnery, 1974).

shocked everyone on the lot by dispensing with the standard four cameras, all shooting at different angles with their sequences later pieced together by the cutter. In all his career, Berkeley never used more than one camera, and he never shot a scene more than once. His ability to visualize entire routines in his head enabled him to cut, as he put it, "in the camera." His preparation was so minutely detailed that he could shoot complex five-, six-, seven-minute production numbers in one perfect, uninterrupted take.

Goldwyn's sense of comedy was as poor as his sense of sentimentality (evidenced by his reaction to *Stella Dallas*) was sure. His sense of humor was crude, juvenile, and frequently out of sync with those around him. When Berkeley, in a nonsensical mood one day, told him shooting had been held up because wardrobe had failed to send down the leotards for the horses, Goldwyn, deadly serious, called wardrobe and raised hell. The gags in the rushes similarly escaped him; in the projection room he would ask Cantor worriedly, "What happened to this scene? It was so funny on the stage." Cantor, who knew precisely where the laughs were by virtue of having played in the stage version for a year, would explain with diminishing patience the difference between the reaction of a theater audience and that of three professional filmmakers sitting in a studio screening room.

Goldwyn subsequently produced three more Cantor-Berkeley films. *Palmy Days* was a thoroughly mediocre picture, hastily thrown together to cash in on the success of *Whoopee*. *The Kid from Spain* was, said *Variety*, "a swell flicker. A glorified girl show in celluloid . . . tastefully presented in the now familiar school of Berkeley choreography which is bullish on the overhead camera shots." But *Variety's* reviewer took issue with the two-dollar ticket price, pointing out with irrefutable logic that "a two-dollar picture these days must also be considered in direct ratio to the proposition as to how many people have two dollars."

Lynn Farnol, Goldwyn's publicity head, labored to give the picture a two-dollar-ticket image. An expensive, four-color souvenir program boasted that the picture's seventy-six girls represented "a new type of showgirl. They are not waxy, cold, aloof, impersonal clotheshorses in towering headdresses, seen as part of a tableau across footlights. Instead they are seen intimately, beaming down warm and friendly through the eye of the camera. They have beauty and personality as well. By a wink, a nod or a smile, each one makes her bid to have you like her."

Farnol described the picture's opening number (the prototype for Berkeley's spectacular water ballets) in the language of a pimp with delusions of grandeur. "In a glistening hall of black and silver where the prettiest girls in the world sleep, daybreak streams in through the tall windows as the girls awaken. They open the story with a ditty and a dance that leads them up the spiral staircase in their flimsy lace nighties to the rooftop pool for their morning water drill."

In the more conventional cabaret sequences, Berkeley placed the Goldwyn Girls (he called them the Berkeley Girls) on two huge pedestals which he wanted to revolve. Goldwyn objected, saying, "Do it the way it is. If you must revolve them, do that at some other studio." Berkeley subsequently went to Warner Brothers, where he made history with the effect in *Forty-second Street.*

Berkeley's fourth and final film for Goldwyn was *Roman Scandals* (1933), a switch on *A Connecticut Yankee in King Arthur's Court.* The Yankee became a Jewish museum attendant; the Court, the Roman Empire.

Roman Scandals caused a $25,000 misunderstanding between its producer and its writers. George S. Kaufman and Robert Sherwood turned in a fresh, funny, perfectly respectable scenario; but Goldwyn, unable to leave well enough alone, subjected the script to rewrites by six other writers, including a number of Cantor's own gag writers. Adding insult to injury, he refused to pay Kaufman and Sherwood the remaining $25,000 of their fee, and paid up only after a protracted lawsuit.

In 1930 and 1931, while Cantor was developing into a full-fledged movie star, he was becoming even more firmly established in another new medium: radio. After *Palmy Days,* Goldwyn had signed him to a five-year contract, one picture a year. But Cantor's weekly radio show emanated from New York. It was agreed that the pictures would be made in the summers, during the radio show's hiatus. But Goldwyn knew nothing of radio, and cared less. He was constantly telling Cantor that he was wasting his time on the air. Why be seen or heard in anything but a Goldwyn vehicle? Every time the two men met, Goldwyn would say disgustedly, "You're still on the air, huh?" and shake his head. He never made the connection between the tremendous success of Cantor's pictures in the hinterlands and the fact that forty million people tuned in to hear Cantor plug those pictures over the radio every Sunday night. Out of ignorance or pure perversity, he began summoning Cantor west on all sorts of minor pretexts during the broadcasting season, thus making it necessary for the comedian to forfeit ten thousand dollars for every show he missed.

After Buzz Berkeley departed for Warner Brothers' greener fields, Cantor made two more pictures for Goldwyn: *Kid Millions* (1934) and *Strike Me Pink* (1936); both costarred Ethel Merman. During preparation for the latter production, Goldwyn kept Cantor on the Coast for two months during the radio season while he, Goldwyn, tinkered with the script and made other changes. Cantor begged to be released from his contract, but Goldwyn paid no attention. By the end of the filming of *Strike Me Pink,* Cantor was purple with rage; he refused to work if Goldwyn came on the set. Goldwyn, infuriated by what he considered Cantor's ingratitude, finally allowed Cantor to buy his way out of his contract. For years, the two men did not speak.

The pictures Cantor made for Goldwyn were all silly, funny, farcical fluff. They all made money. But money was no longer enough for Goldwyn. Now he wanted to be taken seriously.

Process Shot

Mervyn LeRoy's office is high up in the high-rent district, at the west end of the Sunset Strip in a towering complex of buildings in front of which liveried chauffeurs lean on their limousines. The view from LeRoy's desk is awesome, the spaciousness extravagant, the appointments plush. Trophies, plaques, scrolls and at least one Oscar linc the walls. Judging by the difficulty LeRoy's secretary had had fitting me into his schedule, I expected his office to be a scene of mad activity; but if this was the eye of a hurricane, it was cleverly disguised.

When I arrived, in midafternoon, LeRoy and his secretary were watching *Truth or Consequences* on the color TV. LeRoy explained that he had taped an appearance on the show to promote his autobiography, and it was scheduled to be shown that very afternoon. The three of us intently watched the entire thirty minutes of that sick and sorry show, but neither LeRoy nor his book ever appeared. "They must have changed the schedule," he murmured, sounding more hurt than annoyed, and turned his attention to me.

Mervyn LeRoy is a slight, dapper, vigorous seventy-four. When he gave me a healthy handshake and said, "I want to help you," I was awash with gratitude—until I realized the phrase was a formality that covered his uncertainty about who I was and what I was doing in his office. I repeated what I had told him over the phone: that I was collecting impressions of Sam Goldwyn. "I want to help you," he repeated. "I have a lot of antidotes [*sic*] about Sam in my book. Gags about how he got the words mixed up. But God knows those have been told a million times."

I agreed. "But you knew him for over forty years. You worked for him, you socialized with him; you were even related to him by marriage for a while."

"That's right. Blanche and Jesse Lasky were my cousins. But I was pretty young when they split up. I have no idea why that happened."

"But what about *your* relationship with Sam?"

"He borrowed me from Warner Brothers in 1931 to make *Tonight or Never*. When I went over there, he said, 'Mervyn, would you mind doing a couple of days retakes on a picture with Eddie Cantor called *Palmy Days*?' I looked at the picture. It wasn't very good, I might say. He said, 'I want you to do a couple days' retakes on the cafeteria scene.' It turned out to be three and a half weeks' work, which I wound up doing for nothing.

"Sam was one of the best-groomed men that was ever in this town. He was a very brilliant man. He wanted to do everything himself, and he did. He made his pictures, sold his pictures. He was a great showman."

LeRoy produced *The Wizard of Oz* for MGM. "Goldwyn owned that property; Mr. Mayer bought it from him for Metro." Did LeRoy know why Goldwyn hadn't produced it himself? "No. He didn't want to make it. It was a fairy story. Listen, we had a job selling it to Metro! You tell them you got a fairy story, they think it's just for kids!"

The director who guided the performances of Edward G. Robinson in *Little Caesar*, Paul Muni in *I Am a Fugitive From a Chain Gang* and Pat O'Brien in *Oil for the Lamps of China* is demonstrably not an insensitive man; but when it came to Goldwyn, familiarity induced astigmatism.

"My wife and I were at his home many times to run pictures on weekends. One thing about Sam Goldwyn—if he invited you for dinner at eight o'clock, he meant eight o'clock. And he'd sit down at eight o'clock.

"He would have people like Phil Berg, Lew Wasserman, good gin rummy players. Semiformal. Sam always had a tie and shirt on. Always. In those days, we all dressed to go up there. Not like nowadays, you can go to play cards or for dinner sometimes without a tie. Which I like."

LeRoy paused, dredging his memory. "I really want to help you," he reminded me. "When I was making *Quo Vadis* in Rome, Sam and Frances came over with the Sherwoods. We went to see the Pope together. Sam asked my wife, 'When we get to the Vatican, how do we find him?' I think His Holiness thought Sam had something to do with *Quo Vadis,* that he was part of MGM."

"You know who can tell you a lot about Goldwyn? Phil Berg. He was a great agent. He used to handle Gable." LeRoy buzzed for his secretary. "See if you can get Phil Berg on the phone for me, will you, dear?"

Berg is at home; pleasantries are exchanged. "Phil, there's a wonderful woman here in my office." Covering the receiver, he asks me my name. "Her name is Carol Easton, and she's writing a wonderful book about Sam Goldwyn. She'd like to talk to you . . . Oh. I see. You did. I see. No, Phil, she's not going to write anything mean! Yeah. Yeah, I see. I know, Phil, but she's not going to write anything mean about Goldwyn. She just wants to write a good book . . . Here, I'll let you talk to her." And Berg agrees to see me.

I had only one more question for LeRoy: When had he last seen Sam Goldwyn? "Oh, it was before he had his first stroke. In the sixties, after he had stopped making pictures, we still used to run pictures at his house. I think he was unhappy that he was no longer making pictures. But like a lot of the boys in the business today, including myself, if you can't find the right property with good taste, that you feel it'll be a success, don't make it! People think it's easy to find a great story. It's not. It's very tough. Some of these guys today have such bad taste, it's just awful."

LeRoy segued into a story about *The Wizard of Oz* then and I realized, belatedly, that Mervyn LeRoy was making a deliberate—or was it automatic?—effort to impress me. It was, of course, entirely unnecessary; I have been impressed with Mervyn LeRoy, or at least with his work, for as far back as I can remember. But here he was, surrounded by tokens of his considerable achievements, in this curiously quiet office where the phone rang only once during my visit, and that was a social call, knocking himself out to impress . . . me! Whose name he kept forgetting! For all the world as though . . . as though he had nothing better to do.

Phil Berg impresses not with his accomplishments, but with his wealth. He and his wife live in secluded splendor in a white Grecian palace on a private hill—it could pass for a nine-hole golf course, or a memorial park—behind the exclusive gates of Bel Air. The house, filled with a priceless collection of statuary, paintings and *objets d'art*, seems more museum than home.

Berg is shriveled but spry; like LeRoy, he was born with the century. He arrived in Hollywood at the age of twenty-six with an $800 stake, became a millionaire before he was thirty, and was one of the few who quit while ahead. After World War II, "I decided that I wasn't gonna spend the rest of my life wondering whether Loretta Young should wear a bustle, or taking an eighty-eighth of an inch off of Gable's mustache. We actually sat in the projection room and wasted two hours on that! Everybody thought I was crazy when I walked away from it. Never regretted it, not for a minute. I have my bus, a custom-made double-decker Greyhound. It has three showers, two heads. We take it all over the world. I have my yacht, my Master's sea captain papers. Anyway.

"Frances turned out even worse than Sam. Predators. I represented a young director named Irving Reis. He made a picture for Sam, who then assumed he had a mortagage on the rest of his life—although the guy was under no contractual obligation to him whatsoever. I made a deal with Zanuck for Reis to work at Fox. When I told Goldwyn about it, he hit the roof. He called Zanuck. Zanuck called me. He said, 'Did you have a deal with Goldwyn?' I said of course not! You have never heard such screaming! And you know who was the most outraged? Frances! *She* got into the act! He remolded her in his image!

"I was always fighting with Sam. I was always fighting with everybody. You can't be a good agent and win popularity contests. You can have very good friends among producers, if they respect you. But you can't always have love. Anyway.

"With Sam, you hadda be especially tough—because if you gave Sam that much, he'd grab your arm! When Bill Dozier was a young agent working for me, he made a deal with Goldwyn, sold him the rights to a book. Bill came back to the office and wrote a memo about the deal. He puts the price in it and as usual he writes at the bottom, 'Producer preparing contract.' A few days later the contract comes through, and the price is altogether different. Dozier wrote $50,000 in the memo; on the contract, it's $40,000. I called Goldwyn. He said, 'Phil, dot boy of yours, he's been up to tricks.' I said, 'I have great confidence in him. Isn't it possible that you made a mistake?'

" 'I know when I spend $40,000. I know when I spend $*50*,000.'

"Now, he's pulled stunts like this before. I thought, 'I'm gonna get him for this. So I said, 'Well, Sam, if you insist that you said forty, you'll get it for forty. But we're already told our author he's gonna get fifty, so of course my company will pay the difference. But I want to warn you, Sam, I am going to advise the Writers Guild of this whole circumstance.' "

Recalling that incident of decades ago, Phil Berg worked up a little retroactive anger. "Sam Goldwyn," he said emphatically, "is a venerated elder statesman today. You put that in your book, everybody'll be mad at me! I don't care, because it's true. And it's indicative! I wrote to the Writers Guild. There were editorials in *Variety*—Goldwyn was fit to be tied. In the end, he was hoist on his own petard, and there wasn't a damn thing he could do about it.

"Sam was not crass, as was Harry Cohn. I sued Harry Cohn seven times in one year. Didn't you ever hear about that? You never heard about that?" Berg filled me in on the details of all seven suits. "Anyway. Sam did not have any formal education but he dressed beautifully, he really did. Maybe *over*-meticulous. And he tried to get in with people that were a bit more cerebral than he was. This was sort of an Age of Pericles.

"Sam never lost the opportunity to cut a corner. He had a very nice man, Abe Lehr, who sort of was a business manager and ostensibly ran the administration part of the studio. Sam kept beating him up, gave him a very bad time. Sam didn't improve Abe Lehr's health any; he wore him down, is what he did.

"Sam didn't have peers. Either people fawned on him, and he'd stand on their necks—or he fawned on them a little. There were eight or nine of us who played bridge: Hunt Stromberg, Sam Wood, Jack Conway. Irving Thalberg, one of *my* dearest friends. Irving was *incredibly* helpful to Sam Goldwyn; he actually cut a lot of Sam's pictures. He was really frail; his hands were transparent.

"Chico Marx was the best bridge player, but he never won too much, or we would've thrown him out of the game. Sam was a *miserable* bridge player. We played for *enormous* stakes—$1, $2 a point. In the early thirties, that was an awful lot of money. If he was losing, he wouldn't let us leave. We'd play till one, two in the morning. But it wasn't the money, really. It was the game. He didn't want anyone to have any advantage.

"When we played cards—in those days, everybody had a chauffeur. We didn't want to keep chauffeurs up all night, so I'd let Earl go and we'd all use Sam's chauffeur. We all lived in the same neighborhood. One night we were playing up at Sam's and for once he was great! Phenomenal! Won everybody's money! And of course, he gets a headache and disappears! George Kaufman gets so mad he walks into the sunroom and went round the room and broke all the bamboo chairs. Kaufman and Goldwyn didn't even speak the same language. The guys used to imitate Goldwyn's accent when he wasn't there. One time, he *was* there and overheard us. Everyone was very embarrassed.

"We played a lot of backgammon for big stakes. I'm sure he had Sammy trained to rush in and knock the table over when he was losing." What was Berg's impression of that father-son relationship? "He never seemed to talk to Sammy."

Berg grew contemplative, drifting dangerously toward nostalgia. "Remember the Black and White Club?" I tried to look bright and comprehending as he dropped a string of names I'd never heard. "There's no graciousness these days," he said ruefully. "People only have two in help, instead of eight or ten."

Without break or transition, Berg returned to Goldwyn. "After I was retired, Sam called me up. He said, 'Nobody knows this, but I've been doing finger painting! I just wondered if you wouldn't like to be in a group I'm forming.' I said, 'Sam, are you serious?' But he spoke to me about it again. He even wrote me a letter about it!

"Finger painting!"

Berg paused reflectively. The museum-house was hushed. Occupied by one aging couple and a dwindling staff of servants, it scarcely seemed lived in. The Bergs are childless; I wondered idly who their heirs might be, and what it must cost to maintain such a place, even with only two servants. I asked Berg if he had anything else to tell me about Goldwyn, and he replied with the unmistakable self-satisfaction of a survivor. "The last time I saw him," said Phil Berg, "he was like a vegetable. After all those strokes."

H. Bruce ("Lucky") Humberstone lives in one of the hundreds of semiplush apartment buildings that comprise the eastern profile of Beverly Hills. The area is populated by people on the Up or Down Hollywood escalators; for that prestigious address, they pay a premium of fifty dollars to one hundred dollars a month more than the cost of a comparable pad just a couple of blocks away, in mundane Los Angeles. (The stigma of an unfashionable address can be partially overcome by renting a post office box in the enchanted city. There is, of course, a waiting list.)

When Lucky was earning $100,000 a year as a sought-after director of (mostly) B movies, he lived in luxury on the west side of Beverly Hills. He assured me emphatically that his present circumstances are no comedown, simply common sense; since his daughter married, one bedroom is all he needs. His place is modest, comfortable despite evidence of a decorator's heavy hand. Perhaps the second bathroom (in a one-bedroom bachelor) makes up for certain luxuries lost.

At seventy-one, Lucky is small and compact, an aging bantam cock—on the surface, all fanfaronade (a sign atop his color TV says IT'S HARD TO BE HUMBLE WHEN YOU'RE AS GREAT AS I AM). I spent two evenings with Lucky. The first was monopolized by his brittle boasting—how he "saved" every picture he worked on, and some to which he merely contributed invaluable advice. Before he would speak of Goldwyn, he led me into his bedroom to view autographed pictures of Doug and Mary, smiling beatifically down upon his monogrammed satin bedspread. It was Mary Pickford, for whom he worked as assistant director on *My Best Girl,* who recommended him to Goldwyn in 1925 when he, Lucky, was twenty-two years old.

"She told him I got four hundred dollars a week when she was only paying me three hundred dollars. Assistant directors in those days were getting eighty-five a week. I walked into Mr. Goldwyn's office and he said, 'So you're Humberstone, huh? Anybody that gets four hundred dollars a week has gotta be goddamn good.' He said, 'If you're good enough for Mary Pickford, you're good enough for me. You start tomorrow.'

"My first picture for him was *Two Lovers,* about 1926. Vilma Banky and Ronald Colman, he was my man. What a guy. I was on *Bulldog Drummond, Raffles, Condemned to Devil's Island, One Heavenly Night, The Greeks Had a Word for It* and *Whoopee.* And *Street Scene.* And *Arrowsmith.*

"After two or three pictures, I had my salary up to $500 a week and bonuses of $5,000, $6,000 a picture. I was the highest-paid assistant director in the business. When they started *Condemned to Devil's Island,* I was on something else. But it got out of hand—two weeks behind schedule in the first month, and Goldwyn replaced the assistant with me. He said, 'Take over and find out what's the trouble.' Wesley Ruggles was the director. I found out the problem was that Wes Ruggles was in love with a doll and the picture was being done at night for many weeks. Wes was taking two- or three-hour dinners, or two or three hours for a midnight lunch. I went to Wes. I said, 'I'll be very honest with you.' I told him I didn't want to do that to him or any other director. I said, 'Let's get going here.' He said, 'Thanks for the tip.' Within a week, we were on schedule."

Before Humberstone ever directed a film on his own, he assisted on thirty pictures, one of the last of which was *Whoopee.* The opening number of that picture was known as

The Stetson Hat Number. It featured twenty-two showgirls (Goldwyn did not use the term "Goldwyn Girls" until *The Kid from Spain*) wearing skimpy halters, G-strings, gun belts from which pistols dangled in their holsters, and Stetson hats. The lead girl, a blonde with remarkable legs, had never appeared in a picture before. Her name was Betty Grable.

Lucky Humberstone claims the credit for that felicitous bit of casting. "There was no Central Casting at that time. I ran ads in the paper for showgirls to come to the gate. Five hundred would come, and I'd pick out a few. They had to be really sensational. The face was the thing. They didn't have to dance or anything, they just posed. Out of that lineup I got Lucille Ball, Betty Grable (she was fourteen years old), Paulette Goddard (who had never been in a picture), Barbara Weeks, who was a star for a while, and Virginia Bruce. They were all in *Whoopee.* Thornton Freeland directed the story. I did all the musical numbers." If he remembers Busby Berkeley's having had anything to do with the picture, he doesn't mention it. As for the Ziegfeld-Goldwyn relationship, "They got along fine. There was not one word of dissension through that whole picture." Which is tantamount to claiming that nobody got bruised in the Super Bowl.

"Goldwyn," Humberstone stated, echoing Irving Sindler, "was like a father to me." What did that mean? That they were close friends? Well, no; as a matter of fact, Humberstone was never invited to the Goldwyn home. Had he taken his personal problems to Goldwyn for fatherly advice? He stared at me as though the question was too ridiculous to answer, and swiveled the conversation around to a series of Humberstone stories, all of which concluded with "But that's irrevelant [sic]. You want to know about Goldwyn." Apparently Lucky's definition of father was an older man who doled out an allowance. And Goldwyn, when he wanted something, paid generously indeed.

The day before our scheduled second meeting, Lucky telephoned. "This is Bruce Humberstone. Can we make it next week instead? I have to go to San Diego this weekend, something really hot. It means a lot to me. It isn't a dame." The dialogue was right out of one of his movies! I expressed my regret that it wasn't a dame, and we set another time. Meanwhile,

I began to wonder how Lucky Humberstone spends his time. I knew that to phone him earlier than two in the afternoon was to risk waking him. He is, he told me, a night person. But . . . how did he fill those nights?

At our second meeting, Lucky was noticeably more relaxed—expansive, even. We talked at some length about George Fitzmaurice ("He was Goldwyn's pet") and about *Wonder Man,* Lucky's only assignment as director (not assistant) for Goldwyn. It grew late. I had spent the morning at Phil Berg's and the afternoon at the Academy Library. I had a thirty-mile drive ahead of me, and my eyes were refusing to focus. But for Lucky, it was the shank of the evening. He grew garrulous. He produced clippings, conveniently stashed in the living room, that documented a sensational child custody battle. He spoke of his daughter, his father, his stepmother, Jack Warner. ("He has to be spoonfed, pureed foods. His housekeeper quit because she got tired of cooking for eleven servants.") He rambled.

Actors who have been directed by Humberstone contend that he hustled them so hard that they didn't know what they were doing. His pictures were assembly-line productions from start to finish. Which is precisely why he was in such demand. There was an enormous market for low-budget B pictures, companion features for the biggies, and *somebody* had to direct them. Who? John Ford wasn't about to, not for any amount of money—nor was Willy Wyler or King Vidor or any other aesthetically oriented director. But more often than anyone cares to admit, artistic talent was subsidized by the commercially profitable hack work of the Lucky Humberstones, who could turn out a feature-length picture using less than 200,000 feet of film, retakes and all—as opposed to a George Stevens, whose artistic discrimination might require a million.

"I don't know why they call him Lucky," a producer said to me. "He's always been such a loser." The nickname took hold after Humberstone miraculously survived a horrendous car accident. But on reflection, it's not at all inappropriate. For a man of average intelligence, without noticeable talent or charm, to have directed six-figure productions starring Betty Grable and other household words—what better name than Lucky?

I began by seeing H. Bruce Humberstone as a comic

figure, absurd in his pretensions and self-delusion. But a look in Lucky's eyes got to me. He seemed . . . bewildered, perhaps as much by his disproportionate success as by his abrupt separation from it. (In the forties, he directed fifteen pictures; in the fifties, seven; his last picture, something called *Madison Avenue*, was released in 1960.) "Hack" is a withering word. But what other word is there for the director of *Charlie Chan at the Olympics, Merry Wives of Reno, I Wake Up Screaming, Tarzan and the Lost Safari*?

The major studio system, along with the mass audience's insatiable appetite for Hostess Twinkies entertainment (now fed by television; Lucky told me that during the week preceding our first meeting, three of his pictures had been shown on TV) produced legions of Lucky Humberstones and rewarded them with high salaries and higher contempt. Many are dead now; most, like Lucky, retired—and retirement is always a private judgment day. Lucky followed me down the hall to the elevator, apologizing for not having given me more "dope" on Goldwyn. "If there's anything else you want to ask me . . ." he offered. The damned elevator was at another floor. We waited.

I did not have the courage to ask H. Bruce Humberstone whether he considers himself a success, or what he did with all that money, or even how he spends his time. I did ask, as he stood there expectantly with that terrible two-o'clock-in-the-morning look in his eyes, what the H stands for.

It stands for Harry.

9. Selling "The Goldwyn Touch"

Goldwyn followed the success of *Whoopee* with three more light, entertaining pictures, all directed by the prolific George Fitzmaurice, all photographed by George Barnes, all released in 1930. *One Heavenly Night* starred Evelyn Laye, John Boles and Leon Errol. *Raffles* and *The Devil To Pay* starred Ronald Colman with, respectively, Kay Francis and Loretta Young.

Raffles had already been filmed several times—one silent version starred John Barrymore—but the part might have been written to order for Colman, who played the gentleman thief with his usual panache. Colman had received an Oscar nomination for *Bulldog Drummond,* and his (and Goldwyn's) second talkie, *Condemned to Devil's Island,* had also been a tremendous hit. *The Devil To Pay* was still another enjoyable, forgettable trifle. By virtue of such trifles, however, Colman had become the most popular star of the early talkies, both in America and abroad. In 1931, Goldwyn cast him in the title role of *Arrowsmith,* the idealistic young doctor-hero of Sinclair Lewis' best-selling novel.

As the cycle of musicals ended, a cycle of "message" pictures began. Sound had added a new dimension to pictures just as the Depression was adding one to real life, and these two factors contributed to what was quickly labeled "the new realism." Motion picture stories, dialogue, acting and sets became naturalistic. Goldwyn, wanting desperately to upgrade his reputation into the heavyweight class, produced his first two "important" pictures in 1931: *Street Scene,* adapted from Elmer Rice's Pulitzer Prize-winning play, and *Arrowsmith,* adapted from Lewis' Pulitzer Prize-winning novel.

Critiquing *Arrowsmith* in a forty-eight-page panegyric called *Samuel Goldwyn, the Producer and His Films,* Richard Griffith, the late curator of the Museum of Modern Art's film library, lavishly praised Sidney Howard's screenplay which, said Griffith, "exemplified the meaning of 'the Goldwyn touch' . . . in its elision of the incidental and highlighting of the genuinely thematic elements of the plot, an editorial task which was the joint responsibility of producer and writer."

Richard Griffith was a gentleman and a scholar who took his work seriously—if anything, too seriously—and his veneration of Goldwyn's pictures was sincere. But a steady bombardment of publicity, calculated to produce blind spots in the vision of Griffith and his colleagues, took its toll. The catchphrase "the Goldwyn touch," fortuitously tossed off on a publicist's typewriter and perpetuated by all the considerable resources at Goldwyn's command, became the magic carpet upon which the naked emperor was to be magically wafted to the land of respectability. "The Goldwyn touch" was an inspired, immensely profitable hoax that harmed no one; the propagators of the myth partook of its benefits for decades.

Arrowsmith was deserving of praise, but it was hardly the courageous landmark that critic Griffith made it out to be. The heart of Lewis' polemic was an exposé of the medical profession, told episodically in terms of dramatic but one-dimensional characters and situations. What worked well novelistically did not lend itself gracefully to cinematic terms, and the film was fatally flawed by Goldwyn's fear that controversy would poison the box office. "The Goldwyn touch" really represented his desire for the best of both worlds. The formula by which he hoped to achieve this—one he was to follow for the rest of his career—was to hire the best (too often equated with most expensive) talents he could buy and assign them to a property with a "serious" subject. If Goldwyn had limited his interference to budgetary and other administrative matters, this formula might have produced the immortal classics he craved. But Goldwyn wanted it all: profits, power *and* prestige. In overreaching, he compromised his creative people, and he watered down his subjects to insure their palatability to the masses. All this was business as usual in Hollywood, where compromise was the name of the game. What made Goldwyn exceptional were his pretensions, his insistence that he was above the game. In the thirties and forties, America had an apparently bottomless appetite for kitsch, and certainly there was nothing reprehensible about filling that demand. But nobody ever matched Goldwyn's ability to serve up kitsch, call it culture, and sell it to standing room only.

John Ford, who directed *Arrowsmith,* was canny and cool; he edited his films in his head, before shooting. With no extraneous scenes—never a close-up to have on hand just in case—Ford's pictures could be cut only one way. Goldwyn relished his producer's prerogative of final cut and would never have relinquished it to any director. But when John Ford agreed to do *Arrowsmith,* he had already been widely acclaimed for his direction of *The Informer.* That prestige, along with Ford's Irish stubbornness and taciturn demeanor, intimidated the producer to the extent that he allowed Ford more leeway than he had given any director except Henry King.

Ford's direction, along with Ray June's photography and Helen Hayes' performance as Colman's wife, received unanimous praise. But the script, emasculated by the removal of the novel's exposé aspect, received mixed reviews. So did Colman's acting; *Variety* found it "all on one plane and quite colorless." Colman's popularity was more than strong enough to withstand a few bad notices, however, and Colman himself considered *Arrowsmith* one of the best of his Goldwyn pictures. (The absolute worst, in everyone's opinion, was *The Unholy Garden,* a love story set in the Sahara and costarring Fay Wray. Ben Hecht bragged of having written the screenplay "in a pet" in one night.)

Goldwyn next starred Colman in *Cynara,* a soap-operatic "woman's picture" in which Kay Francis forgives her unfaithful husband after his inamorata kills herself. But in 1932, Goldwyn's long, lucky roll of the dice with Colman—nine silents and eight talkies—had run its course. It was probably time for Colman to move on, anyhow—but the means by which Goldwyn forced the

Blanche, Sarah, and Jesse Lasky
From the Jesse Lasky Memorabilia Collection

Blanche and Jesse in Vaudeville
From the Jesse Lasky Memorabilia Collection

Sam Goldfish, *c.* 1918

Sam Goldfish with Abe Lehr, 1919

Eminent Authors Rupert Hughes, Mary Roberts Rinehart, Basil King, Rex Beach, and Goldwyn

Why do women weep? Why do men chuckle?

Why does the whole audience clutch their hands and strain their eyes?

REMEMBER, how the fat man ha ha'd right out and got the audience giggling and the old lady laughed until the tears ran down her cheeks. What a wonderful picture that was!

And last week even the gruff old bachelor had red eyes when the lights went on. You felt as though you had lost your own sister when Melissy died.

All the way home you discussed the story.

Why do you enjoy this picture or that one so much? Have you ever stopped to think why?

First it was such a human story.

And the star was so sweet in the part. You always *did* like her. All the characters seemed just like the real people.

And the scenes—real rooms in real houses. The outdoor pictures were like a vacation for you—out in the open—daisy fields, sunshine, mountains, deserts.

Perhaps you didn't notice the photography, you were so interested in the story, but you will remember how clear it was—how beautiful the lighting.

These are the things you will always find in a Goldwyn picture. Interesting stories—your favorite star—beautiful settings—perfect photography. Goldwyn combines them all. When you see a Goldwyn picture you forget your troubles—you forget the baby's croup and the cook's leaving.

You come home feeling as fine as though you'd had an outing.

Never miss a Goldwyn picture. They are the ones you know you will enjoy.

GOLDWYN PICTURES

Sam Goldfish, A.K.A. Goldwyn, *c.* 1920

Eddie Cantor with Goldwyn Girls in *Roman Scandals*

Ronald Colman as Dr. Arrowsmith

split provided a distasteful finish to an association that had substantially sweetened the fortunes of both men.

In *The Masquerader*, the last film Colman would make for Goldwyn, he played a dual role: a journalist, and a member of Parliament who is addicted to drugs. The plot was based on a best-selling novel of 1905; several versions had previously been filmed. Perhaps it was in the hope of stirring up interest in this antiquated story that Goldwyn's publicity department issued a statement, purporting to quote Goldwyn directly, to the effect that Colman looked better on screen when mildly dissipated, and that he played his love scenes better after several drinks. Colman *had* looked dissipated in *The Masquerader*, but only because he was playing a junkie. He was never a drunk, as Goldwyn implied, nor was he ever drunk on the set. He *was* late on at least one occasion; perhaps that offense triggered Goldwyn's charges. Or perhaps it was all a colossal blunder. At any rate, Colman sued for libel and $2,000,000 in damages, claiming that Goldwyn's statements reflected upon his character and his ability as an actor. The case was settled out of court, but Colman refused to work for Goldwyn again, even though his contract still had two years to run. Goldwyn countered with the cliché that was his standard threat with recalcitrant actors: "You'll never work in pictures again!" Colman didn't care. He had plenty of money, and he was single. He set off on a round-the-world odyssey, and when he reached Madrid he told the press, "I shall never again make pictures in Hollywood again. I have reached the age where a man should work at what interests him." But a year later, after the dust had settled, both men reconsidered. Goldwyn accepted the inevitable and released Colman from his contract, and Colman signed with another studio, where he found greener pastures and greater roles. But Goldwyn never apologized, and Colman never got over his bitterness. As it turned out, the beneficiaries of this unfortunate episode were the moviegoers. Had Colman remained with Goldwyn, what actor would have played Sidney Carton in *Tale of Two Cities?* Or Conway in *Lost Horizon?*

Street Scene—Goldwyn's other contribution to culture in 1931—had everything going for it, including the original New

York cast and the playwright. The play, a melodramatic story of tenement life culminating with one character's murder of his adulterous wife, had won the Pulitzer and succeeded commercially, as well. Goldwyn bid high for the motion picture rights; but the playwright was the same Elmer Rice who had observed the Eminent Authors fiasco at close hand, and who had fled East after that experience in a state of disenchantment and emotional disarray. Rice was neither awed nor dazzled by Goldwyn, and he was determined to preserve the integrity of his play. He wanted written assurance that the play would be transferred to the screen with no changes except those absolutely required by the change of medium. He knew that the way to negotiate with Goldwyn was directly, and when the producer arrived in New York, Rice arranged a meeting.

The playwright pointed out that Goldwyn had offered one of the highest prices ever paid for motion picture rights. "If you have some other story in mind, why don't you hire someone to write it, instead of wasting your money on *Street Scene?*"

"What are you talking about?" said Goldwyn irritably. "I don't want to make some other story. I want to make *Street Scene.*"

"That's all I'm asking you to do," Rice argued, with a logic not even Goldwyn could dispute. On the spot, he hired Rice to do the screenplay, thus insuring the movie's faithfulness to the play.

Goldwyn then engaged King Vidor to direct, thereby realizing an ambition of long standing. He had first approached Vidor in the early twenties, after the young director had created a sensation with his first picture. Summoned to Goldwyn's New York office, Vidor recalls being told, not asked, to go immediately to California to work on a picture. "Without even saying Are you busy, Are you under contract, Are you tied up? He just plunged right in. I was young and I was flattered. I was in my early twenties; I never will forget his positive, aggressive approach." But Vidor withstood the flattery and declined the offer. "I couldn't do it. I was loyal to the people who financed my first film, and I had promised to make three more films for them."

By the time Goldwyn borrowed Vidor from MGM for *Street Scene,* the director—still young, and remarkably handsome

—was one of the most prominent in the business. Vidor and Rice were in agreement about keeping the action on the street, as it had been on the stage.

Vidor rehearsed the cast for a week before he started shooting. "At the end of the week's rehearsal, on Saturday, we gave a performance on the set, because everything was available. Goldwyn came, and Frances, and quite a few other people. Helen Hayes was there, and Goldwyn told her, 'This is gonna be a great film! A wonderful film! One of the best! If you don't believe me, come up to my office and I'll show you the letter I wrote to New York this morning!' "

Vidor compensated for the static setting—a street lined with brownstone tenements—with unusual camera angles that created an illusion of motion. The camera was constantly moving, often shooting down from high above the set. *Street Scene* was praised for its imaginative camera work by George Barnes, for its realistic depiction of tenement life and people, and for the haunting theme music by Alfred Newman. Vidor says today that he's proud of the picture. "I think it has a great style. It was a very compatible staff and crew. George Barnes, the cameraman, was on some of my earliest films. I would crank the hand-cranked camera, and he would play the violin."

Street Scene and *Arrowsmith,* abetted by aggressive publicity campaigns, accomplished their joint purpose. By the end of 1931, Goldwyn was indeed being taken seriously—by himself, no less than by the industry. In his rare moments of self-consciousness, his speech became slower, approaching ponderousness—befitting, he thought, a man of prestige. He adopted the habit of referring to himself, lovingly, as Mr. Goldwyn. Thanks in large measure to Frances' tactful guidance, his clothes were a little less glossy now, his shoes less pointed. His valet, he often boasted, had formerly worked for Valentino. He still swooned over celebrities.

1931 was also the year of Laurel Lane. The Goldwyns had been living in Hollywood, less than three miles from the studio. Walking was a lifelong discipline with Goldwyn, and he enjoyed the daily walk to and from work, with his chauffeured limousine trailing behind (not that enjoyment was his motive; he did it for his health). The house was on West Franklin Avenue, in an eminently respectable neighborhood; but there were certain drawbacks, especially when it came to entertaining on the grand scale Goldwyn felt befitted his position. For one thing, there was no screening room. In order to show pictures, projectors had to be set up in the hall. In the thirties, even as now, Beverly Hills was an infinitely more desirable address than West Hollywood. And in Beverly Hills, the sanctum sanctorum was Coldwater Canyon, in the hills behind the swanky Beverly Hills Hotel.

Laurel Lane rises sharply up the west side of the canyon for a few hundred yards and ends at the top of a hill. Goldwyn bought the hilltop—five wooded acres with a spectacular view—and it became his Mt. Olympus. The demands of the studio being what they were, he assigned the planning and supervising of the construction of a suitable house to Frances. He gave her carte blanche; his only specification was that the house be white. But after six years of marriage, Frances had developed an unerring sense of her husband's taste. She knew better than anyone that for Sam, the ultimate criterion was Respectability. How could it have been otherwise? As an illiterate immigrant, he had instinctively groped for the rules he believed would, when mastered, bring him the status and recognition he craved. In his business dealings, Goldwyn felt free to play it by ear, as necessity dictated. But in his personal life, the rules, and the means with which to follow them—the right clothes, the right automobiles, the right address, the right guest list—were his security blanket. The insecurities that bedeviled him, despite all his success, made informality, the mere thought of disregarding convention, intolerable. Here was the heart of his snobbery, the key to his aggressiveness.

The insecurity was only one side of Goldwyn's nature. The other, paradoxical (and paranoid) ingredient in the Goldwyn gestalt was the monumental ego that perceived itself as the center of a hostile universe. That combination of paranoia, egomania and insecurity produced the steamroller drive, the insistence on propriety, the emphasis on outward appearances, the lust for both power *and* prestige.

Frances Goldwyn knew her husband perhaps better than he knew himself. The palatial, two-story, sixteen-room Georgian showplace/fortress she had built was, by his lights, perfection.

Outside, it was the obligatory white, stately and formal. Inside, it was also formal. The silver, the china, the linen, the paintings, all were understated, conservative. The kitchen, designed with an eye to entertaining on the grand scale, was "modern" and efficient. The projection room was luxurious. Sam's private domain, considered by Frances to be "the heart of the house," consisted of his bedroom, bathroom, dressing room, office (he called it his study) and gym. Had Goldwyn ever made a picture about a very important producer, the set would undoubtedly have been modeled after Twelve Hundred Laurel Lane.

When the Goldwyn family took up residence in the splendor of their new home, Sam Goldfish was not invited to accompany them; but Goldfish needed no invitation to move uptown. Schlepping all the embarrassing baggage of Goldwyn's past along with him, Goldfish installed himself in the "heart of the house." There he remained for more than forty years, to everyone's annoyance, until the death of his alter ego. Even then, Sam Goldfish had the last laugh.

10. *Goldwyn's Garbo*

Hollywood underwent a delayed reaction to the Depression; not until 1933 did the industry bite the bullet. Attendance dropped to half of the 1931 figure, when 50 percent of the population had gone to the movies every week. In the most frantic scramble for survival since 1919, salaries were cut to the bone. Early in 1933, two major studios went into receivership while two others trembled on the brink. The false bottom was dissolving. Producers contemplated the abyss, and panicked.

Paradoxically, the demand for product continued to grow. Movies, which had begun as "chasers" to clear the house for the vaudeville acts, had ended by chasing vaudeville itself out of the theater. The public's appetite for live entertainment had been superseded by the hypnotic appeal of the moving, talking shadows on the screen. Theater owners, for their part, found movies cheaper and infinitely more reliable than vaudeville acts. Their sensible solution to the economic squeeze was to abandon the long-standing policy of combining movies with vaudeville in favor of the more practical policy of combining movies with movies. Double, even triple features were the result.

Goldwyn could scarcely have chosen a less opportune time to take a flyer on an unknown European actress; but when he saw Anna Sten in a German version of *The Brothers Karamazov,* he was smitten by her classic blonde beauty (which bore a startling resemblance to that of Frances Howard when Sam had met her) and her ability to act, as he put it, "like a sonofabitch!"

Miss Sten's mother was Swedish, her father a Russian ballet master. When she was fifteen, the great Stanislavski had spotted her in an amateur production and sponsored her at the Moscow Film Academy. She had made silent pictures in her native Russia and talkies in Berlin. She spoke no English—but this detail, which had proved fatal in Banky's case, Goldwyn nonchalantly brushed off.

Garbo and Dietrich were the reigning goddesses of the day, and all the studios had imported imitations—none of whose names are remembered. Goldwyn expected Sten to eclipse not only Garbo and Dietrich, but Bernhardt, as well. It was Mary Garden, all over again—on a vastly more expensive scale.

Sten had just divorced Fedor Ozep, who had directed *Karamazov,* and married Eugene Frenke, who had *produced* it, when Goldwyn made arrangements to bring her and her new husband to Hollywood. He announced his intention to star her in his own production of *Karamazov,* opposite Ronald Colman. When Colman's law suit aborted that plan, Goldwyn launched a widely publicized search for a property worthy of Sten's talent and beauty. Only a classic, he believed, would do. He finally settled on *Nana,* Zola's story of the Parisian courtesan who meets a tragic end.

Two years elapsed between Sten's arrival in Hollywood, in 1932, and the release of her first picture. First of all, she required dialogue coaching. *Extensive* dialogue coaching. Then the voluptuous Miss Sten, a Rubensesque earth-mother type, was put on a strict diet and pounded daily by a masseuse. She shed some pounds, but not her accent. Meanwhile, a heavy publicity campaign was saturating the country. Famed press agent Pete Smith, then on the Goldwyn payroll, is credited with the release that described Sten as "an actress whose beauty seems to have sprung from the soil, and whose intelligence is that of the instinctive artist and the earnest student of life."

Goldwyn tried, unsuccessfully, to get Josef von Sternberg, Dietrich's director, to direct *Nana.* His second choice was George Fitzmaurice, who accepted the assignment; but after $440,000 had been invested in Fitzmaurice's work, Goldwyn scrapped everything that had been filmed, fired Fitzmaurice and asked Dorothy Arzner, the first (and, at that time, the only) woman director in Hollywood, to take over. "I sort of salvaged the thing," is Arzner's appraisal.

Arzner had begun her directorial career in 1926. She had directed Clara Bow in her first talkie, and Katharine Hepburn and Ruth Chatterton in their first starring roles. Only an exceptional woman could have infiltrated the all-male directorial preserve; striding about the set in her tweeds and brogans, Arzner was a commanding presence. She found Goldwyn to be "not conspicuously better or worse than other producers. He challenged expenditures, but he did provide me with the best of everything. Julie Heron, the set dresser. Gregg Toland, the cameraman. Adrian's beautiful costumes. I wish it could have been in color. There was one pink dress with ostrich plumes . . ."

For all the lavishness of the production, Arzner shot the final version in just seven weeks. "He had been in the hole when I took it over, but I think I brought it in under budget, even so. He would blow his top, jump up and down—then I would explain why it was important to the story, and he would calm down and acquiesce.

"He was not courteous. He was bad-mannered and crude. I had a little trouble with Sten at first, and he told her to do what I wanted or go back to Russia. He sent a lot of writers to the hospital with stomach trouble. There were something like twenty-five scripts for *Nana;* he finally had to decide on one because he'd spent so much. After the picture was finished, I asked to see the first script. It was by Edwin Justus Mayer, a fine playwright. It had some *magnificent* scenes, which Goldwyn discarded."

Thanks to Goldwyn's exploitation, which reportedly cost $47,000 and would have done justice to the Second Coming, *Nana* was a big hit—for one night. George Oppenheimer, who, as Goldwyn's story editor, attended the grand opening at Radio City Music Hall with his boss, wrote in a memoir, "The country was Sten-conscious and eagerly awaited news of the opening. For days before the event, newspaper advertisements featured large photographs of Sten in seductive poses. . . . New York responded pantingly. The opening day broke all existing box-office records at the Music Hall.

"Then came the reviews. They were bad; the word-of-mouth was worse. Sten was a bomb. She was admittedly lovely to look at, but her accent and her acting were something else again. It seemed to me, who watched her in three pictures, that the trouble lay in her inability to assimilate the words given her. It was as if she had memorized them with little regard for their meaning." *

There were almost as many theories about the cause of the picture's failure as there were theorizers. Alva Johnston, in his 1937 biography of Goldwyn, wrote: "The morale of the studio broke under the terrific grind of imprinting the Goldwyn touch on Miss Sten. Nervous wrecks directed nervous wrecks." Some of the critics called Sten a rank amateur. Others praised her performance, but criticized the mutilation of Zola's story. (Goldwyn later admitted that when the censors wouldn't allow him to film the story the way it had been written, he should have abandoned the project.)

A clear-eyed present-day viewing of *Nana* reveals it to be undeserving of anyone's serious consideration. Sten, whose performance was a decidedly second-rate imitation of Dietrich, evokes sympathy—not for the character she played, but for herself, when forced to deliver such lines as "It's men who make women whatever they are." The magnificent costumes and sets, the fine photography, even the theme song by Rodgers and Hart, could have enhanced the story and the acting. They could not, however, replace them.

Even if the picture had had some merit, Goldwyn's overkill exploitation might have doomed it. "He had such illusions of greatness," recalls Dorothy Arzner. "He said Sten would be greater than Garbo, greater than Dietrich. You have to let the *audience* decide those things.

"When the picture was finished, he gave a big party. He served caviar and vodka, and he did the Russian dances with Anna Sten. Then after the picture was released, he sent me a telegram of how good it was. I don't think it made a lot of money, but Frances did tell me once that it did better than Sten's other pictures."

Undaunted, Goldwyn chose another classic for Sten's next picture. Having attributed the failure of *Nana* to the adulteration

* George Oppenheimer, *A View From the Sixties* (New York, McKay, 1966).

of the original story, Goldwyn proceeded to perpetrate the identical crime upon Tolstoy's *Resurrection.* He assigned a covey of writers to the property and changed the title, which he considered beyond the public's ability to understand or even pronounce, to *We Live Again.* He asked Dorothy Arzner to direct, but "I told him I just couldn't face up to it. He left a contract on my desk for quite a while. It was for quite a sum. But finally one day it was gone and I heard he'd hired Mamoulian."

Rouben Mamoulian was the premiere "ladies' director" of the day. He had directed Helen Morgan in *Applause,* Miriam Hopkins in *Dr. Jekyll and Mr. Hyde,* and when Goldwyn signed him he had just finished directing Garbo in *Queen Christina.* Like Sten and Tolstoy, Mamoulian was Russian-born; thus, *Resurrection* turned out to be a very Russian picture—moody, scornful, artful in its set design (also by a Russian) and photography, but ponderous and *heavy.* Sten played a servant girl seduced by a prince. He goes off with his regiment. She buries her baby. Years later, she is unjustly sent to prison. The belatedly remorseful prince follows her to Siberia, where they are reunited at the falsely happy ending. The picture *was* a classic—a classic example of Hollywood's ability to transmute gold into lead.

Fredric March played opposite Sten as Prince Dmitri. For Goldwyn, this was a casting coup. March never liked the part or the picture, and grumped about the set until one day Goldwyn noticed his long face and said, "Cheer up, Freddie. You got the best part in the picture." As he finished speaking, he noticed that Sten was within earshot, looking bewildered. "And you, Anna," he added without missing a beat, "you got the best part, too!"

The advertising campaign proclaimed that in *Resurrection,* "The directorial skill of Mamoulian, the radiance of Anna Sten and the genius of Goldwyn have united to make the world's greatest entertainment." ("That's the kind of ad I like," said Sam. "Facts, not exaggeration.") A few critics agreed, with reservations; but once again, the public found Miss Sten's charms resistible. It was time for Goldwyn to cut his losses; but by now, the stardom of Sten had become an obsession. He began work on what someone unkindly called "Goldwyn's last Sten"—another "two-different-worlds" love story called *The Wedding Night.* This time, instead of peasant and prince, the lovers were an unsophisticated country girl and a disenchanted married city feller. The story was by Edwin Knopf, who reportedly had based the character of the man—a writer, played by Gary Cooper—on his friend F. Scott Fitzgerald. Sten played the daughter in a Polish-American family of Connecticut tobacco farmers (!) with three expressions: happy, sad and thoughtful. The ending (Sten dies—with every hair in place—from a phony fall down some stairs) was so contrived as to be laughable. King Vidor was the unlucky director.

Vidor found Sten's accent impenetrable and, ultimately, insurmountable. "Her pantomime flowed quite easily and freely, but her dialogue was quite a different matter. Her words and syllables were never quite synchronized with her gestures. Rather than a director, I began to feel like a dentist trying to pull the syllables out of her mouth before the accompanying gesture had passed by."

Goldwyn had a habit of unexpectedly appearing on the set. When a director heard the rat-tat-tat of his heels on the wooden sound stage floor, shooting invariably was halted. Vidor recalls one such interruption which took place during the filming of a love scene for *Wedding Night*. "He plunked a chair close to the camera and peered anxiously at the two embarrassed lovers, making them so self-conscious that they could hardly remember their lines." Vidor wanted to simplify the dialogue (which Sten could not pronounce intelligibly) and slow the pace of the scene, but Goldwyn insisted that Anna could master the kind of rapid-fire delivery Claudette Colbert had popularized in *It Happened One Night*. Cooper and Sten continued to struggle with the lines. "Finally," says Vidor, "Goldwyn got impatient and gave them a pep talk. He made an eloquent plea for co-operation. He told, as is usual at these moments, of the dwindling receipts at the box office. He told them his whole career depended on the success of this picture. Then, reaching a grand climax, he said, 'And I tell you, if this scene isn't the greatest love scene ever put on film, the whole goddamn picture will go right up out of the sewer!' With that, he turned and walked off the stage."

Goldwyn reportedly spent two million dollars on *The Wedding Night*. It was one of his worst investments. The film had a handful of devotees, but only the most pedantic critics found it even worth discussing. Sam cared little for the opinions of critics ("Do you know what a reviewer makes? Two hundred fifty dollars a week!"), but box office receipts were another matter. Distribution figures were his native tongue, and keeping in touch with his sales representatives around the world was always his top priority. In order to accomplish this, he arose every morning at dawn and trained himself not to sleep more than six hours a night. When the results came in on Sten's third strike in a row, Goldwyn saw that the handwriting on the wall was in red ink. Sten saw it, too. By mutual agreement, her contract was dissolved.

Process Shot

The search for Sam Goldwyn became a scavenger hunt. In five months of rummaging through the refuse of people's minds and writings, I had accumulated a bewildering mass of fragmentary and contradictory facts; the framework remained maddeningly out of reach. The elusiveness of the people I believed might fill in the framework made it impossible for me to get a handle on what really drove Goldwyn, what kept him competing until time forced him out of the game. My research led into a hall of mirrors. Which one reflected the real Sam? *Was* there a real Sam? His secret—if, indeed, he had a secret—seemed locked inside a hostile conspiracy of silence. My ears rang with rejections. I believed I was getting an ulcer. I knew I was having migraines. I contemplated breaches of journalistic ethics I would normally have found unthinkable, and fantasized acts of violence against the amorphous Them that was causing me such undue (I felt) frustration. My enthusiasm, buoyant when I undertook the project (anticipating a sentimental journey home), was draining away. Worst of all, I saw, finally, that the person most responsible for my predicament was myself.

Having bragged with supreme vanity of possessing total recall, it was humiliating to realize that not only did the Hollywood in my head no longer exist, but it never *had* existed. When I was a child, I saw as a child. As an adult, with no Daddy to open doors, I was an outsider—the equivalent, in Hollywood, of a leper wearing a bell. My approach was greeted by doors slamming shut. Wallowing in nostalgia for a time that never was, reality fell in on me.

Once, years ago, in Las Vegas, I fed my last quarter to a slot machine, perfunctorily pulled the handle and was halfway to the door of the casino before I heard the bells and buzzers going off and dashed back to collect my jackpot. In June of 1974, I had the same feeling. On the verge of calling the whole thing off, I took a last random long shot. A writer friend had casually suggested, back in January, that I contact the man I shall call Mr. Helpful. "He worked for Goldwyn, and he's known the whole family for years." I put the name on my low-priority list, but I finally did call him and, to my surprise, he invited me to his home. It never occurred to him to check with the family. An honorable man, all he intended to tell me was the truth. Who could possibly object to that?

It was Mr. Helpful who, indirectly, pointed the way to Sam Goldwyn. Charmed by his warmth, disarmed by his candor, I listened all morning while he filled in some gaps and gave Goldwyn that extra dimension—humanity—I'd been searching for.

He began by making it clear that he respected Goldwyn—"not as an intellectual, which he was not at all, but one must say he was one of the great inspirations of the film business. He lost as much as he made. He would be on top, and lose it on some picture that didn't work out. He considered it a Mad Adventure."

Mr. Helpful has known Goldwyn's daughter for many years. "When I met Ruth, she hated her father. She spoke very badly about him; she seemed very much biased by whatever her mother must have told her, or other people. Then later, I was at his house two or three times for dinner, and she was there. So somebody, maybe Frances, must have patched things up somewhat between them. Although the Cappses were not thought of as being on the 'A' list of families. I was always surprised that although Mac Capps worked for his father-in-law, it was only in a technical capacity, as an assistant. Never in a creative capacity.

"When Ruth's son, Alan Capps, became a human being, not just a baby, Goldwyn started being interested in him. As he grew up, Alan was invited there, to play tennis, and to observe the formalities of being a grandson. And Sam Goldwyn gave him advice. He was very good at that. He liked to play the part of the experienced, marvelous grandfather who would dole out advice which ultimately would influence other people's lives—his son's, his grandson's, my own at some limited times. He was, however, not able to get Alan into the cameraman's union. Alan felt that he, as the grandson of Sam Goldwyn, shouldn't have to start at the bottom, and he was bitter. Ruth is still rather bitter about this; she feels he could have done more, though I don't think he could have. Then when Sammy became a producer, Alan thought he could work for him—that *he* could push him into becoming a cameraman. But although Alan is a brilliant photographer, Sammy was totally unapproachable. Have you talked to Sammy yet?"

I explained that I had also found Sammy to be totally unapproachable, and Mr. Helpful said something I was to hear, in different forms, from a half-dozen people. "I find," he said thoughtfully, "that Sammy is under a strange power of his father. Or was . . . " Instead of elaborating, he changed direction. As Goldwyn's employee, he had found Sam "not generous with his emotions. However, when one wants to be wanted, one misconstrues certain gestures. I had just come out from New York and was rather lonely working with Wyler, who is not a very talkative person. Also, I had difficulties with the art director, a Californian who resented me because I was from New York. I sent Goldwyn a message saying that I did not have the authority to do what I was supposed to do, and I went to his office, intending to say good-bye. He said, 'You can't leave. What you're doing is invaluable.' He got up from his desk and walked over to me. He put his arm around me. Very confidentially. He said, 'You know, my relationship with you is a different one than with anybody else. I want you to think of me as an uncle. Call me Uncle Sam.'

"Well! I'm his nephew now! I calmed down; I realized I was *needed!* A week later, I wanted to talk to him again. I had a marvelous idea. Wyler liked it. But throughout the entire rest of the production, I couldn't see him any more. My uncle! He was not available! I wrote him little notes. I wrote, 'Uncle Sam:

When are you going to see your nephew?' Later, I was invited to dinner and I told him that. He thought it was not funny at all. He said, 'I want to tell you something. I've been watching you, and you are making a terrible mistake with your life.'

"At that time, I had left my original field and I had directed some films. Goldwyn said I shouldn't direct—because there wasn't enough money in it. He measured the quality of a person in terms of how much money you had. When he saw that I wasn't going to take his advice, that was the beginning of the end of our relationship."

Almost as an afterthought, Mr. Helpful provided a poignant glimpse into the declining years of the failing mortal behind the myth, the legend, the PR flackery. "At the end, when he was very ill, he started to be senile. There were, however, lucid moments in which he did not respond to Frances, who suddenly became a kind of strange intruder into his life. Ruth, who had never been close to him, suddenly became a confidante. She mellowed. She said, 'Well, the old man, he's not so bad.' There she was, his daughter, and they discovered each other. With her playing almost the role of his mother! She was there every day, but not all day; he would talk to her and she would tell her friends about it with a little kind of sheepishness. Not what they talked about, but that suddenly there was a new relationship, and she was happy about it. At the very end, Frances, I think, was reinstated again. But by then, he was three-quarters dead—except for those few moments when he would awaken out of his smiling sleep. . . ."

Later that day, at the suggestion of Mr. Helpful and, with his permission, using his name as a reference, I called Jennifer Coleman. Mrs. Coleman is the former wife of Sam Goldwyn, Jr., and the daughter of playwright Sidney Howard, who frequently worked on screenplays for Sam Senior. Mrs. Coleman was cordial but cautious; she'd be glad to talk to me about her former father-in-law, whom she loved dearly, but of course she would have to check with her ex-husband first. She promised to call me back, and the residue of the morning's cooperative vibes made me believe there was a good chance that she would.

Instead came a call from a distraught Mr. Helpful, apologetically begging off from further involvement in my project.

What had happened? "It's absolutely ridiculous! Sammy called me. He was furious, absolutely livid, that I had the 'audacity' to suggest that you call Jennifer. He apparently considers himself the guardian of the reputation of his father. He said Jennifer might say something less than worshipful about the old man. He said that Frances will not allow a book to be published about Goldwyn in her lifetime."

(Will not *allow* . . . ?)

"He wanted to know what I told you, so I told him. He said I was 'disrespectful'!"

(*Disrespectful?*)

"I don't know why they are so fearful. On the surface, they are concerned that there will be a bad picture presented. Money may be involved, I don't know. Sammy was so ridiculous, so irrational, *shouting*, that I finally had to hang up on him. This is all absolutely ridiculous and I am terribly sorry, but I will have to ask you now not to use my name."

I apologized for the waves I had made in his life, and that was the last I heard from Mr. Helpful.

Confronted with a kind of arrogance new to my experience, I headed instinctively for the ocean, a reliable source of perspective. Stretched out on the sand, trying to make some sense of what had happened, I was soothed by the surf into a half-sleep. Incredibly, I heard someone yell, "ROLL 'EM!" I opened my eyes. Less than fifty yards away, through waves of heat that added a Fellini effect, a film crew was at work! Actors! Director! Script girl! Grips! Electricians! At least thirty people! The camera was panning the beach! I was in their movie!

The title of the picture, I learned later on, was *Lifeguard*—but that was irrelevant. The point, for me, was that I had stumbled into a movie. Not the one on the beach. *Sam's* movie. Bad as it might be, however corny, B movie or C, I couldn't walk out in the middle. I had to know how it ended. For the first time in weeks, I laughed out loud. What had I been so upset about? What had I been making myself sick over? It was a *movie!*

That week, as though some signal had been given, a curse rescinded, resistance began to erode. People to whom I had written months before responded. King Vidor, whose answering service had learned to recognize my voice before I identified myself, called to apologize profusely for the delay, explaining that he had been out of town, at his ranch. Dave Butler, director of the two Bob Hope pictures Goldwyn made, invited me to spend an afternoon with him at Malibu, then another at Hollywood Park. Dana Andrews, back home after months of touring the dinner-theater circuit, called and offered his cooperation. Thanks to the intercession of Mervyn LeRoy, Walter Brennan agreed to see me at his Simi Valley ranch, where he gave me what may have been the final interview of his life.

The librarian at the Academy put me in touch with two of Jesse Lasky's children, both of whom turned out to be willing and knowledgeable informants. Marguerite Courtney, Goldwyn's story editor in the late thirties, invited me to visit her in Idyllwild, a mountain retreat east of Los Angeles. Writer-producer Sam Marx contributed insights and anecdotes—an especially generous gesture, inasmuch as he was writing his own Hollywood book.

The peripatetic Danny Kaye, who had been telling me for months (over the phone) that he'd be happy to see me as soon as he got back from New York/Hong Kong/Cleveland/San Francisco/Washington, D.C., et cetera, remained inaccessible —but his wife invited me to their home, where I spent two surreal and enlightening hours. During one hectic week, I had productive meetings with film editor Danny Mandell, director Lewis Milestone, attorney George Slaff, writers Niven Busch and N. Richard Nash, art director George Jenkins, costume designer Mary Wills, director George Marshall, and Dana Andrews.

The sudden reversal was undoubtedly the result of sheer persistence. The timing could not have been more fortuitous. As my paranoia subsided, I began to get a fix on *Goldwyn's* paranoia, which had infected his family and some of his associates and been bequeathed, apparently, to his son. Find a man's fear, and you find his secret. Goldwyn's "secret" was merely that Sam Goldfish, whom he had attempted to bury under a mountain of press agentry, lived! Lived, and for the sole purpose of taunting Goldwyn!

Goldwyn, who bragged of hobnobbing with presidents,

was Hollywood's quintessential snob; Goldfish tugged mercilessly at his pretensions. YOU'RE A PHONY, was Goldfish's refrain. YOU'RE AN IMPOSTER, AND YOU'LL WIND UP HUNGRY AND BROKE LIKE YOU STARTED. YOU CAN'T EVEN SPEAK GOOD ENGLISH. YOU CAN'T EVEN READ IT OR WRITE IT. YOU'RE NOTHING BUT AN IGNORANT PEASANT, AND YOU'RE NOT FOOLING ANYBODY.

True. Goldwyn's fear of exposure was pathetic for that very reason. His position made him respected and feared, but *the pretensions fooled no one*. But Goldwyn had created a role for himself, and was compelled to play it out. His family still has a heavy investment in the image. No wonder they refused to talk to me! Goldwyn himself never (with one exception, which he regretted) gave an interview over which he did not have approval. The image is too fragile to withstand examination by some nosy journalist, huffing and puffing on the house of cards.

There was another group of unwilling subjects. At first, they seemed to be protecting Goldwyn; in fact, they were protecting themselves. These were the yes-men, the sycophants who, for a price, allowed themselves to be bullied, compromised, humiliated and dictated to, all in the cause of feeding the insatiable Goldwyn ego. Of course they'd rather not talk about it! Of course they'd rather not *think* about it! Their silence was not conspiratorial, but merely a defense mechanism, concealing a sad episode in their own past.

If I wanted a true picture of Sam, I would have to look to the people whose self-interest was not threatened by recollections of their relationships with him. This list was headed by the craftsmen (and women) and technicians who were genuinely, justifiably proud of their work. They produced the elements in his pictures—the sets, costumes, props, editing—that were frequently fine in themselves, whatever the value of the picture as a whole. Goldwyn was famous for using people, but these people used the opportunities he gave them to practice and perfect their crafts, and they came out ahead.

None of these realizations came to me fullblown. They roiled around in my head for months, revised with each new input of data. Sam began to make cameo appearances in my dreams, speaking words I could never remember in the high, reedy, heavily accented voice that I came to know after five different people, all sounding startlingly alike, imitated it for me. The impulse to give up had been fleeting and futile; it was too late for that now. I decided to travel light, and divested myself of my preconceptions—about Sam, and about Hollywood. The destination would be a surprise. The trip would be . . . the trip.

11. Gilding "The Goldwyn Touch"

In 1935, after a painful year of assorted bankruptcies, reorganizations and economies, the motion picture industry pulled itself together and hovered on the brink of what would come to be called its Golden Age. The major studios staked claims to carefully defined segments of the mass audience. MGM's output, averaging forty productions a year, was consistently aimed at the middle class. Paramount pictures were somewhat more sophisticated, while Warner Brothers offered working-class musicals and melodramas. In comparison with the number of pictures produced by these giants, Goldwyn's four or five releases a year were negligible; but his relentless repetition of the quality-not-quantity theme in his advertising campaigns and his constant barrage of publicity releases was paying off. The opening of a Goldwyn picture, heralded nationwide as a special event, miraculously *became* a special event, a self-fulfilling prophecy. The public was buying the Goldwyn touch.

It was the era of long-term contracts; but for Goldwyn, with his limited production schedule, the cost of keeping a large roster of talent under long-term contract was prohibitive. As a matter of practicality, he had always signed actors he considered promising to seven-year contracts, with options—*his* options; thus had he parlayed his initial successes with Cantor and Colman into enormously profitable long-term investments. But most of Goldwyn's contract players worked more on loan-out than they did for Sam. With directors, he usually made one-picture deals. The "career" people in Goldwyn's employ were the technicians and craftsmen who gilded the Goldwyn touch.

A film is a mountain of minute details—the contributions of writers, researchers, wardrobe men and women, tailors, costume designers, casting directors, musical directors, set designers and decorators, sound men, property men, editors (of stories and of film), Technicolor consultants, carpenters, makeup women and male hairdressers (the sexist classifications were traditional), publicists, grips, electricians and so on. Each department includes numerous assistants, most of whom have assistants of their own.

Goldwyn had a phenomenal ability to retain and manipulate financial details; but his ignorance of the technical end of picturemaking was abysmal. The common term "process shot" confused him, and he always had trouble remembering the difference between "montage" and "pan"—a distinction understood by many laymen, let alone any first-year film student. But Goldwyn went to great lengths to establish his reputation for expertise in every minute phase of production. That way, he could take all the credit for his successes. And when, as with Anna Sten, there was no credit to take, he was perfectly capable of shrugging his broad shoulders and walking away, a total innocent, from the scene of the disaster.

Over the years, he acquired some exceedingly capable technical people—masters of their crafts who took enormous pride in their work.

In the mid-1930's, the nucleus of Goldwyn's technical staff consisted of photographer Gregg Toland, cutter Danny Mandell, art director Richard Day, set decorator Julia Heron, property master Irving Sindler, sound engineer Gordon Sawyer, costume designer Omar Kiam, researcher Lelia Alexander, musical director Alfred Newman, makeup artist Blagoe "Bob" Stephanoff, and casting director Bob McIntyre. They thought of themselves as a family. Some of them worked for Goldwyn for decades.

Julia Heron entered the picture business in 1914, as an actress. "I was lousy. And De Mille wouldn't use me because he said I looked too much like Geraldine Farrar. So I went to work in the prop room. Edith Head worked there, too. She used to wash out the stockings of the stars.

"In those days, we used to do three or four pictures at a time. The first picture I worked on for Goldwyn was with Ronald Colman, just before sound. Vilma Banky was in it. They tried to put sound in, but Goldwyn got very upset because you couldn't understand her."

When Miss Heron retired in 1960, she was past sixty-five. "*Long* past. I don't tell my age, because I've lied so much about it." Simple arithmetic places her age in the eighties. She is fragile now, and failing; but the passion she felt for her work flickers in her gray eyes as she peers intently into your face, confessing, "I'm a little hard of hearing," as you shout yourself hoarse. As set decorator, it was her responsibility to select furniture, hardware, appliances, pictures—anything (except for hand props and food, which came under Irving Sindler's jurisdiction) that wasn't nailed down. Her impossible task of pleasing producer, director, art director and actors was, she says, "sheer hell. But I found out through channels that Goldwyn didn't like anything on the wall behind the actors, and after that I seldom had any trouble with him. I never talked to him very much. He never stopped and talked to his people, like De Mille did. His mind was on something else. He just didn't see you. I was up at his house just once. He had all the people there like Dick Day and his wife. Formal dress. But I never even got a Christmas card from them. *Or* a bonus."

Miss Heron's was a grueling job. If shooting was scheduled to begin at eight, she was on hand at five, sometimes three A.M., to supervise preparation of the set. On the lot, her diminutive figure was in perpetual motion, marching from office to research library to set on her spike-heeled shoes. She was formidable, tough and competent, and has an Academy Award (although not for a Goldwyn picture) to prove it. Her memory is selective but accurate; after all the years, disconnected fragments surface. "Wyler and I had a row about Merle Oberon's bedroom [in Wuthering Heights]. He wanted oak furniture, which is what they used in those days, but he wanted it all fallen to pieces and broken down. But oak doesn't *do* that. It lasts forever! I told him I'd put cobwebs on it if he wanted that effect, but that that furniture *never* goes to pieces! Then he wanted fur rugs on the floor. Goldwyn *hated* fur rugs. . . .

"*Marco Polo* was a flop because the Georgian street wasn't a Georgian street. I always looked up stuff. I had a terrific library—Goldwyn insured it for $5,000. You couldn't beat me on an English set in those days. . . .

"Dick Day left Goldwyn and went with Twentieth, and I sold Goldwyn on the idea of getting him back. That was after he'd left his wife and married a Goldwyn Girl. She died of cancer. . . ."

Richard Day died in 1972, at the age of seventy-eight, after an extraordinarily full life. Born a Canadian, he was a high school dropout who flew with the RAF in World War I. Day was a self-taught designer when he began his apprenticeship at MGM. Tall and charming, he looked the part of a dashing RAF pilot, and was considered by his peers to be one of the great art directors of all time. He first worked for Goldwyn on *Whoopee.* After his outstanding work on *Arrowsmith, Street Scene* and *Dodsworth* (for which he won that picture's only Oscar), Goldwyn came to rely on him more and more. The same was true of the taciturn Gordon Sawyer, one of the first and finest sound men in the business. Sawyer mixed the sound on practically every Goldwyn talkie from *Bulldog Drummond* to *Porgy and Bess,* despite attempts by every other studio to lure him away.

Costume designer Omar Kiam (a member of the Gimbel family!) was indisputably the most colorful of Goldwyn's "team." Kiam reported for work each day in a chauffeured Rolls Royce, wearing an opera cloak and carrying a gold-headed cane. Although Kiam designed clothes for some of Goldwyn's most contemporary pictures (*Dodsworth, Dead End, Stella Dallas*), period clothes, the more exotic the better, were his forte. His costumes for *The Adventures of Marco Polo* were the best thing in the picture. But Kiam's career with Goldwyn ended abruptly when the elegant designer, then working on *Wuthering Heights,* attended an elegant party at the Goldwyns'. According to another of the guests, Kiam "got so drunk that he picked up a goldfish bowl and fell on top of the Goldwyns with it."

Gregg Toland went to work as an office boy at Fox in

1919, when he was fifteen years old. Crossing the lot one day, he happened to glance up and notice a cameraman on a parallel, cranking away. "It seemed exciting," he told an interviewer years later, "to sling a tripod over your shoulder, and it seemed exciting to be able to go into a darkroom and load film." Toland was not a naïve man, but he never lost that initial feeling of excitement about photography. Discovering the secrets of light and mastering its mysteries became his lifelong obsession, and Sam Goldwyn provided him with the means with which to pursue it.

When Toland signed on with Goldwyn in 1929, he had already served a decade of apprenticeship as assistant cameraman on two-reelers, Tom Mix westerns and Theda Bara melodramas. After the other assistants went home at night, Toland hung around to polish the camera. His industriousness soon earned him double the going salary (thirty dollars a week) for assistant cameraman. At Goldwyn's he graduated to co-cameraman, sharing credits on half a dozen pictures (including *Bulldog Drummond*) with George Barnes, who would later become Hitchcock's cameraman. Toland's first solo efforts were the Eddie Cantor epics *Palmy Days* and *The Kid From Spain.* His early work was conventional, but he was learning. On his own, he continued to experiment—with lenses, with light values, with techniques pioneered by his predecessors in the field.

Unlike some photographers who took pains to develop recognizable individual styles, Toland believed that photographic style should be dictated by the mood of the scene. That philosophy, taken for granted in present-day filmmaking, was revolutionary in the early thirties. Film itself was comparatively insensitive to subtle gradations of light, and lenses were so primitive that it was impossible to focus simultaneously on background and foreground. Audiences were not aware of this handicap, but it was a constant source of frustration to directors and cameramen.

Toland's first opportunity to swing with his concepts came when Goldwyn assigned him to the Anna Sten pictures. His cinematography on *We Live Again* was the only element of that picture to receive unanimous praise. Goldwyn, sensing the valuable contribution Toland could make to the "Goldwyn touch," kept the cameraman under contract for nearly twenty years by giving him what he wanted most: the freedom and facilities to conduct his optical experiments. Toland developed into a camera wizard, creating effects so subtle that they escaped the notice of the audience, but which critically affected the mood and meaning of a scene. His work was painstaking, but the results seemed magical. If a scene called for an unearthly glow, a romantic glow, a demonic glow, Toland knew how to achieve it. He could light and photograph a set in such a way as to make it appears that the entire room was illuminated by the flame from one flickering candle. When existing lenses proved inadequate to his purpose, he ground his own lenses and coated them (a process now done automatically) to achieve the effect he wanted. With some notable exceptions (Goldwyn loaned him to Orson Welles for *Citizen Kane*), the beneficiary of Toland's ceaseless experimentation was Sam Goldwyn. And although, on the surface, the introverted Midwesterner and the volatile refugee could not have been more different, they had in common the obsessive preoccupation with their work beside which all else in life was insignificant. That was the basis of their mutual respect and, on one limited but basic level, a kind of understanding.

Goldwyn maintained a similar relationship with Danny Mandell, the only living film editor with three Academy Awards.* Mandell went to work for Goldwyn in 1935, at $150 a week. "Even then," says Mandell, "he was called The Great Goldwyn. I had a lot more responsibility, working for him, than I would have had working for a big studio. The major studios, they had their own optical departments and insert departments and title departments. Goldwyn had to hire outside companies to do all that work, and I had to supervise it all, go over all the details with them and make sure they followed through.

"He was always very fair with me. But he was not an easy person to work for. When he got excited, sometimes he wouldn't know what he was saying, he wouldn't make sense. You almost needed a crystal ball to know what he meant."

When the cast and crew of a film gather together to view

* For *The Pride of the Yankees, The Best Years of Our Lives* and Billy Wilder's *The Apartment*.

that film, no two of them sees the same movie. To each individual, his or her contribution is dominant. In the case of the film editor, however, his contribution very often *is* dominant. *The man who cuts the film has the power to hide other people's mistakes.* "For example," says Danny Mandell, "when an actor is bad, you always play on his back if you can. If his lines are bad, you pick out lines that are better from other takes." What a great editor needs most of all is, according to Mandell, "an instinct for showmanship. The ability to put things in their proper order, to know what a viewer would want to see . . . and then make sure they have enough time to *look* at it.

"At the outset of a production, they used to have what they called a budget meeting. I'd be given a script, I'd read it. Then Goldwyn would ask me for my comments. I'd tell him what I thought was wrong, what I thought should be rewritten. A lot of writers would cop out, you might say, by saying, 'Here we have a terrific fight in which so-and-so wins.' Leaving the director, and the cutter, to figure out the details.

"The next step was, just wait for the first day's rushes. If there was something I wasn't satisfied with, I'd go out on the set and tell the director. Or if I thought I needed a close-up of somebody, or another angle, or if something was badly timed so it didn't cut together well, I'd complain to the director. Sometimes they'd listen, sometimes they wouldn't.

"When I first started working for Goldwyn, he kept very, very close to what was going on—sometimes, too close for comfort. You'd wish he would leave you alone so you could get some work done. His comments would be general. 'I think this scene moves too slowly,' or 'I think you're featuring the wrong person.' He always had excellent taste in the way people were dressed, I'd say, and there were never any off-color jokes in a Goldwyn picture. He wouldn't stand for it. And he wouldn't stand for brutality, or anything gory." Asked whether that summed up Goldwyn's creative contributions to his films, Mandell shrugs. "I can't say for sure, because he used to hold story conferences with the writers and directors which I wasn't in on.

"A lot of my time, and my assistant's time, was taken up with what I used to call the Entertainment Committee. While a picture was still shooting, he would bring people in, potential exhibitors, owners of theater chains, and give them a sales pitch. And he'd want me to show them thirty minutes, or forty-five minutes, of the picture.

"The most common frustration for an editor," he explains, "is when the director wants one thing and the producer wants something else. You don't know which way to turn, whose side to be on. I was always very honest. I didn't Yes anybody. I'd get mad and get up and walk out of the screening room. Goldwyn would say, 'Look, I don't know why you're getting so excited! If *I* got so excited, where would we be?' But I never really found him unreasonable. If you had some good points, you could sell him. He wasn't stubborn. He said *I* was stubborn. But I think he respected me for it."

Irving Sindler, Julia Heron, Richard Day, Omar Kiam, Gregg Toland, Danny Mandell—they and their counterparts in other departments earned Goldwyn's respect by delivering what they promised and by refusing to be bullied. Goldwyn was wise enough to hire and hold them; this made him unique among independent producers, and the vaunted "Goldwyn touch" was the product of their efforts. To these elements was added, in 1935, the catalyst called William Wyler.

12. Willy Wyler: The Finishing "Touch"

Wyler, like Goldwyn, emigrated from Europe in his teens—but a generation later in time (1920), and under comparatively luxurious circumstances. His father was an Alsatian haberdasher who would have welcomed his son into the family business. Instead, Willy turned to his mother's cousin, Carl Laemmle, a generous nepotist who imported scores of his relatives to America, where he gave them jobs in his motion picture company.

When Laemmle obligingly hired him as a messenger boy in his Hollywood studio (Universal), Wyler delightedly recognized that he was in the right place at the right time. By 1924, he was an assistant director. Between 1925 and 1935, he directed twenty-one two-reelers, ten westerns and ten feature-length pictures, four of which were considered major films. The last of these caught Goldwyn's attention just as he was searching for a director for a property he had been snookered into buying by Lillian Hellman. It was one of the few occasions when a writer got the best of Goldwyn, and Hellman had done it with panache.

To flash back briefly, Goldwyn had originally hired Hellman in 1935, after the phenomenal success of her first Broadway play, *The Children's Hour.* Miss Hellman, still in her twenties, had already worked as a story editor at MGM, and the experience had given her a clear-eyed, unworshipful view of Hollywood and its personages. The Hellman–Goldwyn relationship was a stormy love–hate affair. Both were difficult people, forever hurling gauntlets at each other. From the beginning, Hellman made it clear that nobody, not even Sam Goldwyn, was going to push her around. She was independent and insistent on her terms, take it or leave it. She held out for an exorbitant $2,000 a week. Sam took it.

The first assignment he gave her was *The Dark Angel*, a remake of one of his biggest Colman-Banky hits. Mordaunt Shairp, an English playwright, was to collaborate on the screenplay, and Sidney Franklin was to direct.

Hellman arrived in Hollywood willing and able to work, but studio protocol dictated that writers and directors engage in weeks of circular discussions, euphemistically designated story conferences. After six or seven weeks of this nonsense, Hellman grew restless and bored. She returned to New York, neglecting to bid Goldwyn good-bye. Baffled by her defection, Goldwyn offered what he believed she wanted: more money. She declined. Finally, he offered a long-term contract "with fine clauses," said Hellman in *An Unfinished Woman*, "about doing nothing but stories I liked and doing them where and when I liked."

She returned to the studio and *The Dark Angel*, which had fared infinitely better in its first incarnation. In this version, Fredric March was terrific, Merle Oberon terrible, Hellman's shamelessly trite dialogue embarrassing, Gregg Toland's photography outstanding, Dick Day's sets Academy Award-winning, critical reviews devastating and box-office receipts huge.

With Goldwyn's carte blanche as to choice of story, Hellman decided that her next effort would be an adaptation of her own play, *The Children's Hour*. Although the plot (a disturbed child wrecks three lives by charging, untruthfully, that two of her teachers are lesbians) posed potential censorship problems, Hellman managed to convince Goldwyn that the play was *really* about the damage a lie can do, and that the lesbian aspect could be excised and the title changed (as the Hays office insisted) without hurting the story. In fact, she convinced him it would be even better that way! To clinch her argument, she pointed out that three of his contract players—Joel McCrea, Miriam Hopkins and Merle Oberon—would be perfect in the leading roles.

Goldwyn, having uncharacteristically painted himself into a corner with his contract with Hellman, bought the film rights for $50,000. He decided to call the picture *Women Can Be Wrong,* and he began, as was his habit, picking every brain within earshot about potential directors. In due course, and with Hellman's approval, he offered the picture to Willy Wyler.

Until 1935, Goldwyn's studio gate was a revolving door for directors. His twenty-four talkies had been directed by nineteen different men and one woman. If he was to continue to upgrade his image, Sam needed a captain for his team, one who would hang around long enough to establish some continuity. Perhaps he even sensed that he needed Wyler as much as Wyler needed him. At any rate, he made Wyler an irresistible offer: three years, forty weeks a year at $2,500 a week (with options), and freedom to make pictures elsewhere between Goldwyn projects. Wyler saw this as his chance to make "important" pictures without the restrictions of time and budget which had, he felt, hamstrung his talent at Universal.

The differences between Wyler and Goldwyn were deep, yet they were evenly matched. Goldwyn had power and physical stature; the diminutive Wyler had presence and charm. Goldwyn's style was hot; Wyler's, icy. Each man considered the other an ingrate; only rarely, and grudgingly, did they acknowledge their mutual indebtedness. Both were stubborn, combative, single-minded men, past masters at the art of advantageous compromise. Their egos clashed violently. The fact that their association endured for nearly a decade was due in large measure to Gregg Toland, who functioned as mediator and interpreter as well as cameraman.

These Three (Goldwyn's final title for *The Children's Hour*) was the first of eight pictures Toland and Wyler did together. If any of the scores of pictures Goldwyn produced ultimately survive as significant cinema, they will be among this group of Wyler-Toland collaborations. Through no fault of theirs, *These Three* was not one of their better efforts. Like *Nana,* the script was diluted, mangled and hopelessly compromised by a falsely happy ending. But the direction and photography were virtually faultless, and they were highly—in some cases, gushingly—praised by reviewers. The picture also served as a shakedown cruise, an opportunity for each man to acquire an appreciation for the other's perfectionism and to develop the kind of shorthand communication essential to an intimate working relationship.

Wyler already had a reputation for being a sadistic bastard, insisting on record numbers of "takes" that enraged some actors and demoralized others. His direction was intuitive, rather than intellectual; his thirty or forty takes were his way of allowing happy accidents to occur—little, unrehearsed touches. A fumble, a stumble, a blink of an eye. All those takes (the record for one scene was said to be sixty) were his way of keeping his options open in order to conduct a highly selective process of elimination.

Wyler's approach to his work was validated by his results; and although the toll it took on the actors was prodigious, nobody ever forced an actor to work for Wyler against his will. There was always a long line of replacements available, eager to submit themselves to his punishment. Occasionally, driven by a fleeting feeling of financial panic (or simply to demonstrate to Wyler who was running the studio), Goldwyn would complain about the squandering of his money and restrict Wyler to two takes per scene. Wyler would continue to shoot all the film he desired, but he would make sure that Goldwyn saw only two takes—and Goldwyn, who surely was wise to what was going on, went along with the game. But for the most part, Goldwyn, with his costlier-is-classier mentality, approved of Wyler's methods. From the beginning, Wyler tested the limits of his authority.

Danny Mandell was present when Goldwyn saw the first cut of *These Three*. "Wyler and I," says Mandell, "had shortened the sequence at the graduation exercises and we had completely cut a scene in a railroad station, without consulting Goldwyn. All through the running of the picture, Goldwyn never said a word. When the lights went up he said, very quietly, 'I'm very disappointed.' We waited to see why he was disappointed. He says, 'I'm very disappointed. TERRIBLY DISAPPOINTED!' He pointed his finger at me and he said, 'How anybody could bitch a picture up like this! You loused this picture up. You ran this for me a week ago, and it was all very lovely!'

He was quite strong with me, and Wyler, who had recommended me for the job, jumped in and said, 'I will not stand by and let you abuse this man. He's done a wonderful job, and you're being very unfair!' That was all Goldwyn needed! I didn't realize it at the time, but he wanted an excuse to get into a fight with Wyler! He was mad at Wyler about something else, I don't know what. Well, this went on until two, three in the morning. Finally, he said, 'All right, all right, cutter—' at times like that, he wouldn't remember my name—'I'll tell you what you do. You come in first thing in the morning, and you put that scene back the way it was.'

"I put the scenes back the way he wanted, and when we previewed the picture that week, it was a big success. Outside the theater, Goldwyn came up to me, all excited, and he said, 'Whaddya think? It went very well, didn't it?' I said, 'Yeah, I think it went *very* well.' He said, 'But tell me—why did you have to put back all that dull graduation scene, and that stinkin' scene in the railroad station?'

"Sometimes he got confused about things like that."

These Three was received with such enthusiasm that Goldwyn assigned Wyler to his next picture, which was to be, as usual, the biggest and best of his career. In this case, however, the picture lived up to its advance billing. *Dodsworth* was a rare gem, with every facet expertly crafted and polished. It was nominated for Academy Awards in seven categories: best picture, director, actor, supporting actress, sound, art direction and screenplay.* Nearly forty years later, a young audience at a Hollywood film festival gave it a standing ovation. It may be significant that *Dodsworth*, the Goldwyn picture that holds up best, is the one on which its producer had the least influence.

Early in 1936, on the way back from one of his periodic business trips abroad, Goldwyn, now fifty-four and apparently in glowing health, was suddenly stricken with a severe gall bladder attack. When the ship docked in New York, he was rushed to Doctor's Hospital. The physical pain, which was considerable, was aggravated by the psychic shock of confronting his mortality. Sam had never been so ill—or so scared.

* Only art director Richard Day won an Oscar.

In the hospital, he had an unexpected, uninvited visitor: his former mother-in-law, Sarah Lasky. The schism between the Laskys and the Goldwyns had endured for more than twenty years. Sarah's daughter, Blanche, was dead. Ruth, the daughter of Blanche and Sam, had grown up, married an artist and borne a child of her own; but she and her father remained strangers. When Sarah learned that her former son-in-law was lying helpless, possibly dying, in a nearby hospital, she seized upon the opportunity to mend the rift. How she gained entry into Sam's room is a mystery; certainly he would not have welcomed her intrusion. But Sarah was the toughest of all the Laskys, and when the occasion demanded she could be as stubborn as Sam. She appeared at his bedside all in black, and greeted him somberly. "I have come to tell you this," she said commandingly, with the style and authority of a distaff Moses. "If God spares your life, you will take your daughter back into your heart—*and* her husband—*and* their child—and you will take care of them, and you will give them whatever they need!"

Goldwyn, racked with pain and riddled with guilt, would have agreed to anything. Weakly, he gave Sarah his promise. Miraculously, or so it seemed, he recovered. He kept his word. The long years of neglect could never be erased, but Sam, in his fashion, tried to make amends. He gave Ruth's husband, McClure Capps, a job in his art department—a remunerative but awkward position for Capps, who did his best to avoid the "boss's son-in-law" label. Capps' work was more than competent, and Goldwyn saw that he was steadily employed as an assistant art director—but he was never allowed to function as art director in his own right, a position for which many of his colleagues felt he was qualified. Despite Capps' efforts to keep his in-law status a secret, studio scuttlebutt made it common knowledge. Less common, however, was the knowledge that Charlie McLaughlin, Irving Sindler's assistant, was Frances Goldwyn's brother. Even though nepotism was an accepted practice in Hollywood, Goldwyn was particularly sensitive to the charge. He did not want it known that his wife's brother had the menial position of assistant prop man.

Goldwyn was oddly ambivalent about wanting to help his in-laws, his brother Ben and, later, his own son. If the assorted relatives he employed through the years had not carried their weight in their respective jobs, he undoubtedly would have let them go. But when they carried more than their weight, as Mac Capps often did, he did not advance them. Probably he felt he had fulfilled his obligation by hiring them in the first place.

Goldwyn's illness incapacitated him for over a year, during which the studio was in the capable hands of Merritt Hulburd. Hulburd was a charming, erudite, strapping six-foot-four-inch young man from the right side of Philadelphia, where he had been an editor of *The Saturday Evening Post* for seven years. His credentials intrigued and impressed Goldwyn, who hired him as an associate producer.

Hulburd's predecessor had been Arthur Hornblow, Jr., the son of a socially prominent New York editor. Hornblow had made himself extremely valuable to Goldwyn—but not, as he mistakenly came to believe, indispensable. When Hornblow demanded what he considered his rightful share of public recognition—screen credit!—Goldwyn accused him of ingratitude and disloyalty, the most heinous crime of all. Sam could be generous with money, but the idea of sharing the credit for his pictures was unthinkable. He did the financing; he took the risks; he deserved all the credit. That was his reasoning, and all arguments went unheard. Once Hornblow realized the finality of Goldwyn's position, he left to produce pictures on his own.

Thinking he might have been mistaken in giving Hornblow too much authority, Goldwyn replaced him with *two* men—that way, he reasoned, neither would have the leverage to challenge his omnipotence. Freddie Kohlmar, a former publicist and agent, took over Hornblow's production duties, and George Oppenheimer assumed the editorial tasks. This solution worked satisfactorily as long as Sam was on the scene, but when he left town, somebody had to have the authority to make decisions based on an overview of what was going on. Goldwyn's gall bladder made it imperative to find a surrogate Sam, and Merritt Hulburd was cast in that role.

Goldwyn was hospitalized in New York for weeks before he was moved to California, where his recuperation continued at home. At the end of the summer, he was again hospitalized for gall bladder surgery and an appendectomy. Meanwhile,

Dodsworth and *Come and Get It,* the latter an adaptation of an Edna Ferber novel, were in production. Even though Goldwyn was confined to his bed miles away, he demanded frequent briefings on what was going on at the studio.

Marguerite Courtney was story editor at the time. "The reverberations would come down from Goldwyn's house, and everybody started passing the buck. For instance, he would roar, 'How did Paramount get this *story*? I hear it's the *perfect* story for so-and-so!' The secretaries would alert me; they'd say, 'Goldwyn is raising *hell* about this story, do you know anything about it?' I'd rush to my files, get out my card, and by the time they came to me I'd be ready. They'd say, 'Do you know anything about this *Ladies' Home Journal* story?' I'd say, 'Oh, yes, that was no good at all. The girl was a paralytic and the hero was blind. Anything else you'd like to know?'

"They were all like children when Goldwyn was on the rampage. For some strange reason, Goldwyn really rode people that he was fond of. He was very fond of Merritt. At one point, Merritt was on the set and he was under such stress, for some reason, that he just suddenly felt he was breaking, and he just *shot* out of the studio—just *left!* And nobody could find him! Repairing his soul, I suppose. Goldwyn was frantic, calling on the phone. 'Where is he? I need him! He's not at home! Why did he do it?' Finally he got Merritt and he said, 'Merritt, how can you *do* this to me? You are my *wife,* Merritt! You are my *wife!*'"

With Hulburd as a welcome buffer between himself and Goldwyn, Wyler shot *Dodsworth* in the summer of 1936. Goldwyn had passed up a chance to buy the screen rights to the Sinclair Lewis novel in 1932, before it was published. It should be explained that Sam's knowledge of literature was based on oral summaries presented to him by writers and story editors and, increasingly as the years went by, his wife. Employees were given to understand that Mr. Goldwyn was far too busy to do his own reading. In truth, Mr. Goldwyn lacked the education to read, except with painstaking effort. The only book he was ever known to finish was *The Wizard of Oz,* and that took him weeks. And even though an impartial observer would have admired him all the more for having succeeded despite the handicap, Goldwyn was ashamed of his inadequacy and developed skillful ways of hiding it. Occasionally, these maneuverings led to bizarre misunderstandings. In the case of *Dodsworth*, the story of the deterioration of the marriage of a retired industrialist, Goldwyn got it into his head that it was a book about the automobile industry. That subject intrigued him; but he had lost money on Lewis' *Arrowsmith*, or so he claimed, and considered the author to be box-office poison. Only after Sidney Howard adapted *Dodsworth* into a hit play, with Walter Huston in the title role, did Goldwyn buy the property. The price, $165,000, was eight times what he could have had it for originally, but he reasoned that the prestige value of a successful Broadway run justified the extra cost.

Walter Huston recreated his stage role and Ruth Chatterton gave one of the best performances of her career as Dodsworth's silly, snobbish wife. Mary Astor played the Other Woman so sympathetically that audiences cheered her at the end, when she got her man.* As usual, Wyler won no popularity contests among his actors. He got along well enough with Huston, of whom he was somewhat in awe, but Astor found him meticulous, picky, sarcastic and impatient. Novice David Niven played a minor role and became "a gibbering wreck" under Wyler's treatment. While Niven performed in front of the camera, Wyler sat behind a copy of *Variety*, glancing over it only to tell the actor, "Do it again." Ruth Chatterton, who had been a Broadway star in the twenties, had terrible fights with Wyler about the interpretation of her part; on at least one occasion, she slapped his face and locked herself in her dressing room. Wyler says she was neurotic.

In spite of all the behind-the-scenes friction, what emerged on the screen was pure gold. When it was previewed, Goldwyn was still not well enough to attend; but the film was run for him at home and, after insisting on one minor change (in this case Mandell felt he was right), he was satisfied.

While Wyler was driving his actors to distraction on

* When Astor's celebrated custody battle with her husband (who used his wife's diary chronicling her hot affair with George S. Kaufman as evidence) broke during the filming, Goldwyn declined to invoke the morals clause in her contract, saying, "A mother fighting for her child is good publicity."

Dodsworth, Howard Hawks was directing *Come and Get It.* He was also, unbeknownst to Goldwyn, rewriting some scenes. Hawks had previously directed Goldwyn's *Barbary Coast,* a 1935 release that recouped some of the losses incurred by the Anna Sten debacle. *Barbary Coast* was a romantic western with a surefire script by Charles MacArthur and Ben Hecht (who insisted on payment in cash at the close of each working day) and an interesting cast: Miriam Hopkins as a saloonkeeper; Joel McCrea as a poetic prospector; and Edward G. Robinson as a dandy. Hawks doesn't particularly like or remember *Barbary Coast.* He had higher hopes for *Come and Get It,* which turned out to be an even bigger disappointment.

Come and Get It had possibilities that never quite came off. It was yet another romantic melodrama, but it had an original setting: lumberjack country. Edward Arnold played a logging baron who gains an empire but loses the woman he loves. The feminine lead, Frances Farmer, played a dual mother-daughter role, reminiscent of the part played by Vilma Banky in *The Winning of Barbara Worth.*

When Goldwin recovered enough to view *Come and Get It,* he was infuriated that Hawks had dared to tamper with the script. Although his doctors had cautioned him against excitement (advice as useless as telling a politician with laryngitis to keep his mouth shut), Goldwyn summoned Hawks to his beside and demanded that he reshoot the picture as originally written. Hawks maintained that his revisions had improved the script, and refused to change anything. Neither man would back down and after a heated argument, Hawks walked out of the room and his contract.

Goldwyn asked Wyler, who had just completed *Dodsworth,* to do the retakes on *Come and Get It.* Wyler, aware that the salvage job would do his career no good, also refused. Goldwyn went berserk. Wyler says, "He carried on like a madman about me having to do this, that I was legally obligated to do it and that he'd ruin my career if I refused. He got so furious that Frances Goldwyn took a flyswatter and beat it over his legs on the bed and I ran out of the room . . . In the end, I had to do it. I don't think it helped much." * Wyler wound up re-

* Axel Madsen, *William Wyler* (New York, Thomas Y. Crowell Co., 1973).

shooting half of the picture (at a cost of $500,000) and the screen credit wound up reading "Directed by Howard Hawks and William Wyler"; but neither man includes *Come and Get It* in his official list of credits.

Process Shot

I live thirty miles southwest of Hollywood, on a hill near the ocean. On rare days, when rain or wind displaces the smog, I can see, with breathtaking clarity, fifty miles or more: north to Malibu; west to Catalina; east—beyond the collage of little towns, from Westwood to Watts, known as Los Angeles—to the mountains that embrace the "basin."

I can remember when air pollution meant merely the smudge pots warming the orange groves. Jack Benny used to make jokes about it. The view I once took for granted startles and shocks me now with its unexpected beauty. No wonder they called it the city of the angels. Seashore, desert and mountains were a pleasant two-hour drive from Hollywood (now it's one hour, but not pleasant), and the climate was truly utopian. Only the climate remains unspoiled. In December, while avocados ripen on my tree, I can see snow on the mountains.

The smog has steadily drifted inland, climbing the mountains and killing the pine trees at a slightly higher altitude each year. You have to reach the two-thousand-foot level now before the landscape changes from brown to green, the air smells of pine and, instinctively, you breathe deeply. Highway 74 leads to Idyllwild—a rustic, out-of-the-way resort community, five thousand feet above Palm Springs. The town, originally a logging camp, is tiny and picturesque. In the summertime, its artsy-craftsy shops and galleries do a brisk tourist business. Off season, the temperature and the population drop drastically. The handful of year-round locals is a proudly self-sufficient group, undeterred by the town's lack of hospital, high school and other such frills.

Marguerite Courtney, Goldwyn's story editor in 1936 (better known for her best-selling biography of her mother, Laurette Taylor), is one of these hardy individuals. She lives in a comfortable cabin a thousand feet above the town of Idyllwild, with only her dog for company. When heavy snows make the road to her house impassable—sometimes for weeks at a time—she packs her supplies in on foot. Her appearance is youthful, her manner direct and delightful. She seems on the best of terms with her self-imposed solitude. She is writing a novel.

It was a warm summer day, so we sat outside the cabin while she spoke of her "Hollywood period" as though it had happened to somebody else—which, in a sense, it did.

"I'd been working at *Fortune,* and I came out to Hollywood because I needed to make more money. I met Merritt Hulburd through some old friends of my family, and he hired me.

"I was the only woman executive at the studio, which made it pretty tough. But the secretaries were on my side. They would alert me when Goldwyn was on the warpath. He would put the fear of God into people. His methods were just *shriveling* to the soul.

"Thomas Costain had come out to work for him at the time. Costain had been editor of some tremendous magazine like the *Ladies' Home Journal.* He was quite a dignified man, accustomed to receiving very respectful treatment. His viewpoint was purely literary; he didn't have any sense of the drama of motion picture stuff. Every time Costain would go into Goldwyn's office, he'd come out a broken man! Finally he told me, 'I can't understand him! I go in there and I tell him a story, and he sits there and looks at me and *he doesn't say a word!*' Can you imagine? A man who's made a repu*ta*tion—a man who's written some great books, not some beginner!—given that kind of treatment?"

When Ms. Courtney reported for work at the studio, Hulburd told her, "We are just desperate for a story for Gary Cooper. If you can find us one, I'll have your salary tripled."

After some conscientious searching, she found a story called *The Real Glory*. "I thought it was absolutely perfect for what they were looking for. I told Merritt about it and he said, 'Oh, that's just been hanging around in the files. It isn't dramatic.' Well! I thought it was *tremendously* dramatic. I went and got the synopsis of it, and the *reader*, who had *written* the synopsis, had simply missed the whole point of the story. In miraculous fashion, all the drama had been left out! I went back to Merritt and dramatized it for him and he said, 'Can you get a synopsis of that by the time I talk to Goldwyn in the morning?'

"I got a stenographer to type it up, but by the time it was ready, Merritt was already in Goldwyn's office. So I sent it up with George Haight, and as he was passing it to Merritt, Goldwyn said, 'What's that?' and just snatched it out of their hands. When Merritt came back down, he said, 'Maggie, you've just stuck my neck on the block with this story. If it's a lemon, I've given it to Goldwyn!' An hour later, Goldwyn called down and said to buy it. Later, I asked Merritt, "Well? My tripled salary?' He said, 'Oh, we're going to go into B pictures, and that'll be for Joel McCrea.' But they did make it with Gary Cooper, after I left."

Altogether, Ms. Courtney found three stories that Goldwyn bought (the other two were never filmed). "In terms of working for Goldwyn, that was great success. No other story editor had ever sold him one!" But after Merritt Hulburd left, she was ready to move on. She had found the experience "fascinating," but although she lived in Hollywood for over a year, she never felt she belonged there—nor did she wish to. Hollywood parties then (as now) had a vastly overrated reputation. They had little to do with diversion or fun; rather, they were arenas on which were played out minidramas in the ongoing struggle for status. "At those parties, it was so evident who was going up and who was going down hill. Who you were seen talking to. You mustn't be seen talking to that fellow—he hasn't made a picture in two years. As though that's got anything to do with human exchange!

"I was always very surprised to find how quite civilized people I had known in New York became something different in Hollywood. It had something to do with the fearfulness, or the *rank* thing. Of course it was extremely esoteric in terms of Hollywood, 'cause only Hollywood *knows,* or *cares!* But they *know* whether you're making it—if you've got a bad lemon of a picture—whether you're *in* with Goldwyn or you're *out* with Goldwyn. Always that pecking order. I think it's a *loathsome* society."

Ms. Courtney was never a guest at the Goldwyns, but she heard reports of their entertainments from Merritt Hulburd. At Laurel Lane, where propriety was at a premium, spontaneity was rare; but Hulburd was present on one memorable occasion when the unexpected provided genuine cause for hilarity—although the guests found silence the better part of valor. It was Sam's fifty-third birthday, and Frances had arranged a surprise party. She blindfolded Sam and led him into a room in which the guests stood in a large circle. "Now, Sam," she said in a motherly tone, "you stay here. I'm going out. I've got a surprise for you." She went to the door and closed it, but she stayed inside. Sam, standing there waiting with the blindfold on, let out a resounding fart. The guests stared mutely at the floor, not daring to exchance glances. The silence was broken only when Frances opened the door again, as though returning, and, with awesome composure, took Sam by the arm. "Now, Sam," she said, "we're going to go outside"—and tactfully led him around the house before returning him to the assembled guests. The rest of the evening, Merritt told Marguerite, was definitely anticlimatic.

"I wish I could tell you more," said Marguerite Courtney, "but it was so long ago." I snapped off my tape recorder. The only sound was the wind in the treetops, soothing as the surf. Two chipmunks played tag in a pine tree. Hollywood—not just the place, but the state of mind—seemed light-years away. It was impossible to imagine that this eminently sane woman, leading a stripped-down-to-essentials life, could ever have played, even peripherally, the Hollywood game. She had remarked, apropos of her former colleagues, "There's something about working in that atmosphere that spoils you for a calmer one. Like taking dope. You've gotta *have* it!" Was it chemistry or character that had enabled her to get out before she got hooked? Had her mother's alcoholism made her excessively wary of all addictions, including the power/money/fame trip? How had she retained—or regained—that unmistakable sense of self?

To ask would have seemed a kind of invasion, but I have puzzled over the answer to this day. Because of all the people with whom I talked about Sam Goldwyn—many of them hugely successful in Hollywood's terms—only Marguerite Courtney, living on her own terms, seemed secure.

Simi Valley (pronounced see me, accent on the me), northeast of Los Angeles, is a pastoral setting as remote from Hollywood as one can get, and still commute. I drove out there on a sunny June morning. The air was clear and sweet-smelling; clean, green rolling hills stretched to the horizon. In this wholesome atmosphere, Walter Brennan was dying of emphysema.

In both style and personality, Sam Goldwyn and Walter Brennan were at opposite poles. Brennan was warm, approachable, unassuming; he dressed in whatever was handy and comfortable. From his earliest days in Hollywood, he had always lived on an unpretentious ranch outside the city. As the city expanded, Brennan had moved farther out.

He was nearly eighty and just out of the hospital, but when his German shepherd announced my arrival, he stepped outside to meet me looking healthy and rugged, and his handshake was solid. He wore a plaid wool shirt and nondescript slacks, and he seemed taller than he appeared on the screen. He ushered me into what he called "my room"; the paneled walls were covered with photographs and paintings of the actor as himself and as some of the characters he'd portrayed. The display embarrassed him a little—or so he said. "I think I'm an egoist with all these pictures here of myself, but these are all done by artists who have sent them to me. You see this one? You know who this is, don't you?" The artist was Norman Rockwell. "That's life size. I went to sit for him; he says, 'You 'n' I are about the same age. What month in '94 were *you* born? I says, 'July.' He says, 'You're nothin' but a kid. I was born in February!' "

Brennan referred to his illness with casual irritation; he couldn't breathe sitting down, he explained. Leaning against a tall stool, he spoke, in that unmistakable voice, of Sam Goldwyn. Glowingly.

"I was under contract to Goldwyn for ten years, from 1935 to '45. I used to say I was with the country club of the motion picture industry. And I was very proud to be there.

"During those ten years, I made forty pictures. That's really somethin', y'know. Eight of 'em were for Sam, and thirty-two for somebody else. He rented me out a lot; some years, I worked fifty-one weeks! But he protected me. He didn't give me any lousy pictures. He only gave me good pictures. Hence, that's how I got where I got. Which was fair for a guy who used to fall off a horse for a buck-and-a-half." He chuckled. Nervous energy propelled him about the room. "Sam didn't think chicken, y'know. There was nothin' chicken about Sam. He was class. He could be into a picture for a coupla hundred thousand bucks and if he didn't like it, he'd stop and start all over again. Any time you saw a picture that came on the screen that said SAMUEL GOLDWYN PRESENTS, you were seein' the greatest thing in the picture business.

"The first picture I did for Goldwyn was *The Wedding Night*. It was a small character part. I never even met Anna Sten. Then the next year, in July, they called me for *Barbary Coast*. The character was called Old Atrocity.

"That was eleven years after the first World War. I had had a delayed reaction, y'might say. A nervous collapse. I went to war the day war was declared in 1917. Eleven years later, it hit. Guys'd say, 'You crack up yet?' I'd say, 'Don't be silly. Me crack up?' Boy, I cracked up. If it hadn't been for my wife, I'd have jumped off the Pasadena Bridge. I fell away to nothin. I weighed about 140 pounds. Gee, when I got the job in *Barbary Coast*, I was carryin' my ground-up vegetables in a mason jar. They had to build muscles into my clothes.

"Goldwyn wanted to put me under contract, but he offered me so little dough, I was makin' more than that by workin' round by the day. So they finally came up a little, and I coulda gotten a whole lot more, I guess, if I'd held out, but I didn't. I was very happy! As I have often said, when I was with Sam Goldwyn, I was with the country club of the motion picture industry. This, definitely.

"I was gettin' a certain amount for a raise each year, and about the second year, I said, 'Sam, I think I should get twice as much.' He says, 'All right, I'll double your raise, but I want nine more months at the end of your contract.' So I took it. A bird in the hand, see. And the next year, I didn't *get* my raise! I said, 'Sam, I didn't get my raise!' He says, 'You got it last year!' So I ended up in the same spot! It was really funny!

"Now, don't think I'm another name dropper. I called him Mr. Goldwyn for the first four years that I worked for him. Because, after all, he was my employer. Then, because I liked him that well, I said, 'Do you mind if I call you Sam?' He said No."

Brennan was a brilliant mimic, and when he quoted Goldwyn it was Sam's voice you heard. I had been told some wild stories about Brennan's having created havoc at the studio by calling people on the phone—people like Dick Day, Al Newman, even Willy Wyler—and, in Sam's voice, firing them. Then, so the stories went, Brennan had to call them back and rehire them, again as Goldwyn, with nobody the wiser except an hysterical witness or two. Asked for verification, Brennan claimed the tales were exaggerated. "I only fired one guy over the phone that I remember, and that was an accident. It was the makeup guy. Gee, if I could only think of his name . . . Oh, I can't remember. I'm eighty years old in July, so who's kiddin' who? I was in my dressin' room, and I was supposed to go down to makeup and try on a wig. I called this guy on the phone—oh, I almost had his name—and he says, 'Yes, Mr. Goldwyn.' Well, he left me wide open, see. I says, 'You no-good so-and-so, what do you mean by puttin' the makeup like that on Miss Mayo? You're fired!' Well, I'd just wanted to make sure he was down there, so's I could try on the wig. So I went down, and here he is, sittin' on a bench and cryin'! I says, 'What's the matter with you?' STEPHANOFF! *That was his name!* He says, 'The old man just called me up and fired me.' I said, 'That was me!' He says, 'God dammit, I know *you!*' and he wouldn't believe me! So I went back on the phone and hired him again! He told that story on himself till the day he died."

Although Brennan collected three Oscars * during his years under contract to Sam, the Goldwyns' guest list excluded

* For *Come and Get It*, *Kentucky* (for which he was loaned out) and *The Pride of the Yankees.*

actors below superstar status (Cary Grant, Jimmy Stewart, Joan Fontaine), and Brennan was never invited to Laurel Lane. Brennan didn't mind. "I never socialized with any of them Hollywood guys. I'm a loner. But I did like Frances. A remarkable woman. She lifted Sam, too, I think. She was a Follies girl.

"I consider the time I worked for Goldwyn the most constructive years of my whole life. Boy, I have a soft spot in my heart for Sam. I'm a great pray-er, y'know. I kneel down by my bed and I say my prayers every morning and night. And I have Sam on my list of prayers for the repose of his soul. He's just added on to fifty-seven others that are gone. Even the guys I don't *like* I got on my list! Gee, when I think of these guys that I knew that are gone. Jesse Lasky, what a fine guy! He's in my prayers. Coop—he wore like an old boot. They've all passed away. I'm the last of the moccasins around here."

In a profession that offers all the stability of highwire walking without a net, Walter Brennan maintained his balance for forty years. "About one hundred and fourteen feature pictures. Some of them I was only atmosphere. Plus two hundred an' twenty-four *Real McCoys*, thirty-two *Tycoons*, fifty *Guns of Will Sonnet*, twenty-four *To Rome With Love*. I've been blessed in the parts I've had, and also in my domestic life. Been married to the same gal for fifty-three years. Never chased around, happy about it. Isn't that wonderful? Most wonderful person I've ever known."

Politically, he was said to make John Wayne look like a radicalib. But he had lived by the principles he espoused, and age seemed to have softened the edges. He had promised me half an hour, but he warmed to his subject as he spoke; he was "on," where every actor longs to be, and clearly enjoying himself. Ninety minutes passed before he glanced at his watch and said, "Hey, I don't want to dominate your book!" He and the dog walked me to my car, and we shook hands again. "It was real nice talkin' to ya," he said, smiling. "All this nostalgia. I should be very interested to see your book when it comes out. Very interested."

He stood in the sunlight of his driveway waving goodbye, looking as though he'd stepped out of that Rockwell painting. Surely, I thought, reports of his illness had been exaggerated. Driving back into the L.A. smog, I envied the grace with which he had grown old, and would surely grow older. But Brennan barely survived his eightieth birthday. Hearing of his death just weeks after our visit, I wondered, Who prays for the repose of the soul of the last of the moccasins, when the last of the moccasins is gone?

13. "The Great Goldwyn"

As the sole stockholder in his corporation, Goldwyn was under no obligation to make his profit and loss figures public. Box-office receipts could be authenticated, but his expenditures could not. His version of the earnings of any given picture were elastic, stretched to suit the occasion; the actual figures will never be known. Certainly he made, and lost, many millions. Judging by the longevity of his career and the size of his estate when he died, he managed to stay well ahead of the game.

Goldwyn released five pictures in 1936. Two of them—*These Three* and *Dodsworth*—made very little money, he claimed, because they were too classy for the masses. The three moneymakers were *Strike Me Pink*, *Come and Get It* and *Beloved Enemy*. The latter (originally titled *Love Under Fire*) was a Hollywood version of how peace was restored between the British and the Irish in 1921, and took such farfetched liberties with historical fact that one reviewer predicted that "If, when the film is shown in Dublin, a tidal wave engulfs Hollywood, it will bc caused by the Emerald Isle turning somersaults."

1937 began auspiciously for Goldwyn. He had regained his good health, his financial position had never been more secure, and his social position had risen to the point where an invitation to dine at Laurel Lane was equivalent to a command performance. But Sam distrusted prosperity; when he couldn't find a worm in the apple, he invented one. Sam Goldfish was a continuing source of embarrassment, and Goldwyn renewed his efforts to kill him off. But Goldfish was very much at home on Laurel Lane, and frequently behaved as though he owned the place. The deviltry he performed there in private—throwing his clothes and his towels on the floor, hollering "Frances!" at the top of his lungs, treating the servants so crudely that Frances permanently positioned herself as intermediary between her husband and her help—all of that could be tolerated. But Goldwyn was more determined than ever that Goldfish be kept out of public view. This required a new master plan for his public relations staff.

Goldwyn had always made it his policy to hire the hottest PR men in town. He told them, in effect, that he didn't care what they wrote about him as long as they kept it clean and spelled his name *Goldwyn,* not *fish.* Since columnists preferred colorful copy, the flacks zeroed in on what seemed the most natural angle: Sam's language. It was painful to watch Sam try to express himself in English. Even on the rare occasions when he was able to synchronize his mind and his tongue, his command of the language limited him to simple questions and expressions of extreme pleasure or displeasure, with no subtleties in between. When one enterprising flack coined the word "Goldwynism" to describe his mixed metaphors and malaprops ("Include me out" was the most famous), the strategy caught on and the anecdotes spread, as a Goldwynism would have phrased it, like wildflowers. A Goldwynism was easily remembered and passed along. "It rolls off my back like a duck." "Anyone who would go to a psychiatrist ought to have his head examined." "You've got to take the bull by the teeth." "I read part of it all the way through." "We can get all the Indians we need at the reservoir." "A verbal agreement isn't worth the paper it's written on." Apropos of his illness, "I was on the brink of a great abscess." Most of these quotable one- and two-liners originated not in Goldwyn's mouth but in old vaudeville shows and joke books, and at staff meetings and lunches where contests were held to see who could come up with the most inventive phrase. The lines were picked up and printed in nationally syndicated columns, and brought Goldwyn more press coverage than that received by all the other studio heads combined. While Jack Warner,

William Fox and Louis B. Mayer remained nonentities to the general public, moviegoers chuckled and remembered Goldwyn's name. Short of scandal, nothing could have brought Goldwyn more attention.

Sam allowed and abetted the promotion of Goldwynisms for nearly a quarter of a century, but middle age made him more conventional than ever. The fact that his fame was based on stories that made him look like a clown began to gall him; it smelled of the Goldfish touch. New directives were issued. Henceforth, all publicity would be keyed to dignity, taste, perfectionism, class. Goldwyn was to be presented as he now saw himself: a culture *mavin.*

His desire for the new image was magnified by the 1937 publication of *The Great Goldwyn* by Alva Johnston, a frequent contributor to *The New Yorker.* The book, while entertaining, was as lightweight and laminated as Johnston's magazine profiles. For an unauthorized biography, it was unusually laudatory, glossing over Sam's vanity and ignorance and so loaded with anecdotes that reviewer George S. Kaufman suggested the publishers "ought to give away a hammock with each copy."

Critic Edmund Wilson, writing in *The New Republic,* took exception to the flattering tone of the book; it made him, he said, slightly sick. "It has the slave brand of Hollywood upon it." To prove his point, he quoted Johnston's final paragraph:

> Last year was Sam's twenty-third in the movie business; his press department at that time spotted him two years and celebrated the completion of his quarter-century in the business. Next year is Sam's real silver jubilee. It is something for everybody to get patriotic about. The USA leads the world by a wider margin in pictures than anything else, and one of the chief reasons is the Great Goldwyn.

"I for one will be damned," said Wilson, "if I will feel patriotic about Sam Goldwyn's silver jubilee, which his aides have already celebrated two years before it was due. In what sense does the United States lead the world in moving pictures? We make more of them and are more proficient mechanically, but have we ever had any picture that was comparable artistically to the best Russian, French, or German films?" After sweepingly indicting

Goldwyn, Johnston and finally the entire industry, Wilson concluded, "It is quite plain that the producers of today, including the Great Goldwyn and the late lamented Irving Thalberg, are the same megalomaniac skates they always were. You have only to look at their pictures. You have only to look at their slaves. From the servant you may know the master. Mr. Johnston can have had only a brief submergence, but look at the book he has produced!"

When Goldwyn got wind of the book, he threatened Johnston and the publisher with a lawsuit if they printed any inaccuracies. But when he eventually read *The Great Goldwyn* (or perhaps had it read to him), he interpreted it as glowing, unadulterated praise, and gave away hundreds of copies. He did not even object to Johnston's exposure of some of his favorite publicity ploys: padding the reception committee at the train station (whenever Sam returned to Hollywood from his travels) with personal friends carrying cameras; padding his press conferences with extras coached to pose as journalists from mythical publications, asking rehearsed questions. If a turnout for a press conference was less than capacity, the studio shook with Goldwyn's wrath. His press agents, said Johnston, "boast of the terrific punishment they took under Goldwyn. They speak of Sam as they speak of operations . . . When Sam finds a newspaper full of wars, floods and crimes, he is furious with his publicity department for letting digressions and irrelevances leak in."

The publicity-with-dignity campaign was only partially successful. Even though his publicists stopped disseminating Goldwynisms, columnists with space to fill exhumed the old ones, always good for a filler, often with variations. Even Sam's obituaries were sprinkled with the hated phrases. As always, Sam Goldfish had the last word.

Dead End—a hit play with a social message—seemed a surefire way to enhance the new image; besides, Goldwyn liked the play. We think of *Dead End* as camp today, forgetting that, in its time, it was shockingly original. That its characters—Bogart's snarling Baby Face Martin, his henchmen, his whining martyred mother and, most of all, the Dead End kids themselves

—became favorite targets for satirists was not the fault of the author. Sidney Kingsley wrote the play as a sincere outcry against what poverty does to people. It was already a long-running hit on Broadway when Goldwyn bought the rights and asked Lillian Hellman to adapt it for the screen.

Hellman, who had been criticized for the drastic changes she had made for the film version of *The Children's Hour,* now was damned for leaving *Dead End* virtually as it had been on the stage. *Variety's* reviewer found "no inventiveness or imaginative use of the cinema to develop the theme further" (that tenements breed gangsters, and nobody does anything about it). Both play and movie were so naturalistic that the audience could all but smell the garbage in the streets. Wyler had wanted to heighten the realism even more by shooting on location, in a New York slum; but Goldwyn feared losing control of both Wyler and weather, and instructed Dick Day to design a tenement which was constructed inside a sound stage. Day's imaginative set possessed infinite photographic possibilities, which were eagerly explored by Gregg Toland. Projection background photography, as when the tugboat passes by in the opening sequence, added to the realism.

Sam cast his stock hero, Joel McCrea, as the Good Guy (opposite Sylvia Sidney, the Good Girl) and convinced him that he had the best part in the picture; but McCrea's performance merely served as counterpoint for those of Bogart and the six Dead End Kids, who amused themselves between takes by tossing Irving Sindler's props into the tank of water that represented a portion of the East River. The kids also stole the picture.

The elements of sentimentality, sensationalism and "significance" paid off at the box office, and the picture was received by most critics as another "important" Goldwyn film. But that wasn't enough for Sam. He wanted, and expected, the Oscar for Best Picture of the year. He even had an acceptance speech prepared. But the award went to Warner Brothers' *The Life of Emile Zola.*

Goldwyn's next production was a remake of *Stella Dallas.* Like most producers, Goldwyn believed that if once was good, twice would surely be better. Usually, it wasn't. His resurrection of Stella, with Barbara Stanwyck, Joel McCrea and Douglas Fairbanks, Jr., was a good example.

Wyler was loaned to Warners, making *Jezebel*, so Goldwyn engaged King Vidor to direct. Vidor was a philosopher, not a fighter; but after *Stella Dallas*, he put a note in the top drawer of his desk. It said NO MORE GOLDWYN PICTURES.

Midway through the shooting, Sam had stormed onto the set one afternoon in a frenzy. "He said, 'Everyone is terrible in the film! It's awful! Bad performances! We have to change this person and that person!' He wanted to fire me and the cast, and call off the whole project. He seemed quite out of control. One of the leading actresses was in tears; it ruined her makeup. We had to quit work for the day."

Vidor was shocked and hurt; he had thought the work was going swimmingly. He went home in great distress, and got to sleep late, with difficulty. "Around one in the morning, the phone rang. It was Goldwyn. He'd done a complete reversal. He'd just seen the rushes again; they looked wonderful. I should have a good night's sleep, he said! He was always calling people in the middle of the night like that. He used to call Leonard Praskins, the writer, and say, 'Is this Mary Garden?' when he thought Praskins was being temperamental."

Vidor never learned what had prompted Goldwyn's outburst. "It was painful to work for him. And yet, at a party, in the evening, he did a lot of laughing. He could be very pleasant. There was a time when I was socially connected to them. They had more or less formal dinners. I can't remember him talking about anything besides pictures. Maybe money. Maybe Wall Street. He dropped Lord Beaverbrook's name a lot. He was always talking about Beaverbrook.

"There was a big social division in Hollywood at the time. As highly as Goldwyn thought of Gregg Toland, he probably rarely would have a cameraman to dinner. It would have to be a top writer, a top director, a top star. I suppose that began to break down during World War II, when servants were harder to get. I don't know that it *ever* broke down with the Goldwyns, though. I doubt it."

Sam's fondness for Stella Dallas was ironic, for Stella was

a casualty of the class system that dominated Goldwyn's life-style. Her problems began when she tried to rise above her lower class beginnings by marrying a gent. The miseries that ensued shall not be recounted here, but they provoked buckets of tears from grateful audiences who, in the depth of the Depression, eagerly sympathized with someone even worse off than themselves. The story, in all its incarnations, was quintessential soap opera, but Vidor remembers his version kindly. "I've made some pictures I like to forget, but that's not one of 'em. It was nothin' to set the world on fire, but it was entertainment."

14. *Business as Usual*

Goldwyn did not customarily cause disturbances on the set. His emotional pyrotechnics usually took place in his office, for the benefit of agents, distributors, writers and directors who challenged his omnipotence. Some of the most spectacular displays of all were reserved for his story editors.

Of all the departments in the studio, the story department was the scene of the most frenzied activity, the least accomplishment and the highest turnover of personnel. Goldwyn respected writers for their education (always overvalued by the uneducated) and resented them for their intellectual superiority. His ambivalence manifested itself in a capriciousness that kept writers and story editors perpetually off balance. Unpredictable, inconsistent actions, based on an interior logic Goldwyn could not have communicated even had he chosen to, were the order of the day.

The story department was presided over by a succession of extremely able men (Marguerite Courtney was the lone woman) whose job description seemed simple enough: to find properties suitable for motion pictures. Recommendations were to be based on the editor's knowledge of industry cycles (were gangster movies on the way in or out?) and what the competition was up to. The job offered a great deal of money and prestige. The frustration factor was incalculable.

Sam Marx had been Thalberg's story editor at MGM, where he had also produced the first Andy Hardy movie. In 1937, after Thalberg's death, Marx went to work for Goldwyn, who dangled before him the prospect of producing. "He completely disarmed me. He said, 'I want you to work for me, now tell me how much you want to make you happy.' Later on, I found that Sam Goldwyn, when he wanted anybody, could promise them the world. It didn't mean a damn thing to him, because he was always capable of getting rid of anybody. For example: he asked me to get Anita Loos to work on a picture. Anita didn't want to work at that time. He said, 'Offer her $5,000 a week for fifty-two weeks.' I said, 'Mr. Goldwyn, that's an awful lot of money! You're not gonna make that many pictures!' He said, 'Offer it! Offer it! When she finishes the assignment, we'll let her go!"

Goldwyn promised Marx he would make him an associate producer, on the condition that Marx find a story to film. In effect, this made Marx a story editor again. Marx found the stories, but "Everything I brought him, he turned down because of eccentricities or idiosyncrasies. He turned me down when I brought him *For Whom the Bell Tolls*. He turned down Cronin's *The Citadel*, which I wanted him to buy; he said *Arrowsmith* had also been about a doctor, and it had lost money. Goldwyn invariably claimed that every picture he ever made lost money. Every time a story would come up, he would point back to some movie that he'd made that lost money and say, Why should he do another one on the same subject?"

Goldwyn's story editor on the east coast was Beatrice Kaufman, wife of George S. When Goldwyn offered her the job she had hesitated, telling Sam that she felt awkward about her husband's lawsuit against him (for his *Roman Scandals* money). It had been settled a few months before Sam made his offer, and George was not happy with the outcome; although the settlement had been in his favor, legal expenses had taken most of the money. "The thing to do," said Sam Goldwyn to Beatrice Kaufman, "is to pretend it never happened. And then it never happened." To illustrate this technique, he opened his eyes wide, feigning innocence, and asked, "What's this about a fight with your husband? It *never* happened!" *

According to Sam Marx, "Bea did exactly what Goldwyn

* Scott Meredith, *George S. Kaufman and His Friends* (New York, Doubleday, 1974).

wanted. She mixed with the group at Alex Woollcott's island in New Hampshire, she was always talking about George and Moss and Lillian Hellman, Dorothy Parker, Fannie Hurst and Edna Ferber—all names that Goldwyn doted on. We had a marvelous rapport. We both hated our jobs. When Goldwyn would leave Hollywood to go to New York, we would celebrate at the studio like it was Armistice Day. At the New York office, they'd be plunged in gloom. Then it would be in reverse when he started back west.

"One time he was going away on a holiday, to Hawaii. He called us all into his office. Garson Kanin was there; Jock Lawrence, his publicity man; Freddie Kohlmar; Hulburd; George Haight; Dick Day; David Rose, his right-hand financial man. We were the staff. We all stood around his desk while he gave us his pep talk, how he wanted us to work hard while he was away. And then, very gravely, he walked around and shook our hands, each one of us, and said, 'Bon voyage.' As usual, when Goldwyn did things like that, you didn't realize it was funny until afterward. And when we got outside, somebody said, 'Why did *he* say Bon Voyage?' But two or three weeks later, we decided he knew what he was doing—because we were, almost all of us, leaving."

When Bea Kaufman quit in the fall of 1937, Marx hired a bright young man named Julius Evans as her replacement. Marx realized that Evans lacked the cachet Goldwyn found so impressive, and admonished Evans to keep out of Goldwyn's sight, at least until he proved himself in the job. But Evans was brash and ambitious. He knew Goldwyn was looking for a property for Jon Hall, whom he had just starred in *Hurricane;* and Evans, through some elaborate maneuvering, had obtained the inside track on an option of *Golden Boy* before it opened on Broadway.

"Julie" Evans, who later combined a talent for screenwriting with a genius for real estate speculation, thereby acquiring a fortune that would have impressed even Sam Goldwyn, recollects his first meeting with Sam clearly and with some amusement. "I heard that Goldwyn was in New York, so I called his hotel, introduced myself, and asked him for an appointment.

He said Okay, come on over. I went up to his suite. He said, Okay, whaddya wanna see me about? I could see he wasn't very thrilled that a young kid was supposedly representing him.

"I said, Mr. Goldwyn, I have an opportunity to get first crack at this new Clifford Odets play. He said Okay, what's the story? He went into the bathroom and started shaving or something while I was telling him the story. That was usual motion picture producer procedure. They'd either go to the throne or go to the bathroom, and you'd be telling them a story. I got halfway through and he said, What kind of a story is that? A boy who's a prizefighter, his father wants him to be a violinist? Just a minute. I'll show you something!

"He picks up the phone and calls Clare Boothe Luce. The night before, *The Women* had opened. He says, I'll show you what I mean. Well, I have never heard such a line of *shmooz* in my life. 'Clare, I am the *only* one who can produce your play. It'll make a *beautiful* picture. I think you are absolutely *brilliant*. . . .' A real line! He said, 'Clare, don't you *dare* give this property to anyone else! You *know* the *quality* I give my pictures. I *must* produce this picture! Now give me your *word*, Clare, that you will not sell this picture to *anyone* until you've talked to us!" This went on for about fifteen minutes! Finally he turned to me—she's still on the line—and said, 'Okay, see what I mean?' I nodded. He said, 'Good-bye, son. Good-bye. Good-bye.' Two days later, I got my notice."

Previous occupants of Sam Marx's office included George Oppenheimer (twenty months), Edwin Knopf, author of *The Wedding Night* (seven months) and Marguerite Courtney (one year). They all went through the same process of disenchantment, at varying rates of speed. As Marx explains it, "For the first couple of months, working for Goldwyn seemed ideal. You felt like you were in Paradise. He seemed to have his entire group in on *everything;* this was unique for me, coming from MGM, where it was impossible to be in on every picture because there were so many. But I discovered after I'd been there a short time that there was trouble in Paradise. Nobody was really happy there. Because Goldwyn might act like he was your dearest friend for a while, and then he'd somehow get the idea that he hated you! Or that you were robbing him! I don't know what passed through his mind, but *overnight*, where he'd been your best friend before, he *hated* you! Openly! And I became dreadfully unhappy."

Every few weeks, Marx would ask Goldwyn to let him out of his contract. "Each time, I was told No and sent back to work. Dick Day wanted desperately to leave; I guess maybe his contract was up. Goldwyn tried to talk him into staying; but he left, anyway. And about four or five months after I went to work there, Merritt Hulburd suddenly resigned."

Hulburd had contributed significantly (as "associate producer") to *Dodsworth, Come and Get It, Dead End, Hurricane* and *Stella Dallas*. But the pressure of being Goldwyn's "wife" had taken its toll. He developed terrible headaches and hypertension, and began to look back longingly on his relatively serene life in Philadelphia. He returned to his old job at the *Post,* but his health continued to deteriorate and within a year, at the age of thirty-five, Hulburd was dead.

Goldwyn had another associate producer working for him at that time: George Haight, a former vaudeville producer, sometime playwright and amateur magician whose neatest trick was avoiding work whenever possible. A sign over his desk cautioned NEVER LOSE YOUR TASTE FOR CHEAP FOOD, but Haight would have been the last to heed that advice. He loved the prestige of working for Goldwyn so much that he made no complaint when Sam assigned him to *Woman Chases Man,* a comedy so unfunny that Willy Wyler went on suspension rather than direct it. Goldwyn hired John Blystone, a director of westerns and comedies, and cast two of his stock players, Miriam Hopkins and the ubiquitous Joel McCrea. The script, not much to begin with, suffered from so many rewrites that its plot, characters and dialogue were incoherent. The preview audience sat through the picture in bewildered silence. Sam Marx has reason to remember that preview very well; it ended his honeymoon with Goldwyn, along with his friendship with George Haight.

Marx had persuaded Goldwyn, who was looking for a script for Merle Oberon, to buy a book by James Hilton called *We Are Not Alone.* With Goldwyn's authorization, Marx made the deal with Hilton's agent over the phone. That night, *Woman Chases Man* was previewed. Next morning, Goldwyn called Marx into his office and said, "That book—I don't wanna buy it!"

"But Mr. Goldwyn," Marx protested, "on your instructions, I notified the agent yesterday that we were agreeable to buying it!"

"Who's the agent?"

"Bill Dozier."

Goldwyn got Dozier on the phone. "That book that Mr. Marx called you about. He had no authority. I do not buy the book."

Dozier got a better offer the very next day, so neither he nor Hilton had any complaint. But Sam Marx was deeply offended, as well as baffled, by Goldwyn's behavior—until George Haight enlightened him. Following the preview the night before, Goldwyn and Haight had left the theater together, in Goldwyn's limousine. "I realized," Haight admitted to Marx, "that if I didn't throw some dust in his eyes, he'd start talking about *Woman Chases Man,* what a disaster it was. I can't do anything for that movie now. That movie's done. So in order to keep his mind occupied, I ripped the hell out of the Hilton book."

Says Sam Marx, "I lost my taste for George then and there. Haight himself fell into such bad repute with Goldwyn that in the end, to get *him* out of his contract, Goldwyn put him in a little cubbyhole and made him a reader! He became the highest paid reader in Hollywood for a couple of weeks, until he finally quit."

Marx renewed his pleas to be released from his contract, not realizing that in so doing he was pushing Goldwyn's perversity button. The more anybody wanted out, the more determined Goldwyn became to keep them. He would let them go eventually—but at *his* pleasure, not theirs. Sam Marx had a two-year contract. At the end of the first year (during which he maintains he accomplished ten years' worth of work), he resigned himself to making the best of a bad bargain, and settled in for the second year. At that point, Goldwyn called him to his office and inquired, as though he had just noticed that something might be awry, "You're not happy here, are you?"

"No," said Marx, mystified. "I'm not."

"Okay," said Goldwyn, satisfied that he was holding all the aces. "You wanna leave Saturday?"

With Willy Wyler loaned to Warners again, Goldwyn hired John Ford to direct the picture Ford later called the nadir of his career. *Hurricane* is grand camp, memorable chiefly for Dorothy Lamour's first appearance in a sarong. Background footage was shot in the south seas, but the town of Manakoora (as in "The Moon of Manakoora," the picture's theme song) was constructed on the lot, where special effects wizards created the disaster that destroys the town and most of the characters at the end of the picture.

John Ford had Goldwyn completely cowed. During the shooting of *Arrowsmith,* he had informed Sam that his suggestions were unwelcome and his interference in the cutting room would not be tolerated. During the shooting of *Hurricane,* Goldwyn had the rushes screened surreptitiously, to avoid Ford's wrath. The rushes contained fewer close-ups of Lamour and Hall than Goldwyn thought necessary. Now he had a dilemma: how to impress Ford with the need for more close-ups, without letting Ford know that he had been sneaking looks at the rushes?

The next day, Goldwyn asked Sam Marx to accompany him on a visit to the *Hurricane* set. "Maybe he picked me because I was the husky one. We walked to the stage where the *Hurricane* company was shooting. We had hardly opened the door when everything seemed to stop, even though we were far from the set. There was silence. Then Ford said, 'Whaddaya want?'

"Goldwyn didn't move or speak. Ford said, 'You! Mr. Goldwyn! Whaddaya want?'

"We walked toward the set, and Ford got up and came toward us. Goldwyn said, *very* carefully, very *tentatively*—not indicating that we had seen the cut film—that he wondered if Ford was making enough close-ups. Ford said, very pugnaciously, 'Now, I'll tell you, Mr. Goldwyn. *I'm* making this picture the way *I* feel it should go. If I want a close-up this big,' and he hit Goldwyn right in the belly with the flat of his hand, 'I'll make 'em that big. Or if I want 'em *this* big,' and he hit him in the chest, 'they'll be this big.' And then he clinched his fist right in Goldwyn's face and said, 'I might want them even bigger!' "

Speechless and thoroughly intimidated, Goldwyn signaled to Sam Marx and they left the stage together. As they walked back across the lot, Goldwyn felt compelled to have the last word—if not to Ford, at least in his own mind. "Well, anyway," he muttered to Marx, "I put it in his mind."

The first time Gary Cooper worked for Sam Goldwyn (*The Winning of Barbara Worth*), Cooper made seventy-five dollars a week and was grateful to get it. In 1937, Goldwyn made a three-picture deal with Cooper. This time, the price was $100,000 a picture—and *Goldwyn* was grateful. He starred Cooper in two spectacular action flicks—*The Adventures of Marco Polo* and *The Real Glory*—and a comedy only slightly funnier than *Woman Chases Man* called *The Cowboy and the Lady*.

The Cowboy and the Lady (Merle Oberon was the lady) was another example of Goldwyn's inability to know what he wanted until he saw it—or to leave it alone when he did. Leo McCarey originally sold Goldwyn the story for $50,000—only it wasn't really a story, just a thin yarn spun off the top of McCarey's head. By the time shooting began, under Wyler's direction, Goldwyn had exhausted the brains of fifteen additional writers, including Anita Loos, Frederick Lonsdale, Dorothy Parker, Edward Chodorov, Gene Fowler, Robert Riskin, Sonya Levien and S. N. Behrman, the last two of whom shared the screen credit—or blame.

After just a few days of shooting, Goldwyn decided, much to Wyler's relief, that the director was too slow. He replaced him with Hank Potter, who was unfamiliar with the script and unprepared for the technical problems. Potter valiantly did his best to salvage an impossible situation, but the result was predictably horrendous.

Goldwyn next cast Cooper, improbably, as Marco Polo. Goldwyn had bought this script on the strength of the reputation of its writer, Robert Sherwood, who had just won his second Pulitzer Prize (for *Abe Lincoln in Illinois*). Sherwood was a member of the Algonquin crowd (Benchley, Parker, *et al*), and a close friend of Sidney Howard, whom Goldwyn greatly admired. As *Life*'s film critic during the 1920's, Sherwood had been one of the first serious movie reviewers in the country. (Each year, *Life* published Sherwood's list of best films. The only Goldwyn film on any of his lists was the silent version of *Stella Dallas*).

Sherwood had a wry, tongue-in-cheek sense of humor which manifested itself in *Marco Polo* at the expense of the script. When Cooper/Polo discovered spaghetti in China, the audience merely snickered; when he taught the Chinese princess (played by Goldwyn's Flatbush-born "Norwegian" discovery, Sigrid Gurie) how to kiss, they fell out of their seats. The direction caused as many problems as the script. When John Cromwell quit after five days of shooting, Sam tried to talk Wyler into taking over. Wyler turned him down flat, preferring to go on suspension. The director Goldwyn wound up with was Archie Mayo.

Mayo's initial exposure to the industry had been as a shirt salesman, making the rounds of the studios and soliciting orders from actors, directors and executives. Eventually he became a genial director of comedies and musicals. But geniality produced a psychic backlash in Goldwyn, who interpreted it as a sign of weakness and an invitation to inflict indignities. When *Marco Polo* supplanted *The Cowboy and the Lady* as Goldwyn's worst failure since Sten, Sam dumped all the blame on Mayo, and made his life hell, trying to force him to break his contract. Mayo would receive instructions to report for work at nine A.M. He would show up on time, only to find there was nothing for him to do. Everywhere on the lot, he was treated like an office boy. Wyler advised him to walk out, rather than submit to Goldwyn's humiliations. But Mayo had no desire to return to the haberdashery business, and he had bought a new house on the strength of his three-year contract with Goldwyn. Torn between security and self-respect, Mayo chose security.

The Real Glory was another action-adventure spectacle. Coop played an Army doctor who attempted to quell a terrorist uprising in the Philippines just after the Spanish-American War. Henry Hathaway directed in the spirit of C. B. De Mille; the picture cost more money ($2,000,000) and took more time (two hundred working days) than the original campaign in 1906. But none of this could overcome the deficiencies of the script. *Variety's* reviewer wrote: "Moro uprisings, guerrilla warfare, cholera epidemics and fancy exhibitions of inhuman cruelty are the frame against which innocuous melodramatic yarn is told. Cooper plays probably the busiest medical officer the Army ever produced. And he takes all his assignments in his long stride, ranging from individual dashes into the enemy forests, the care of hundreds of dying civilians, and finally the military command of the besieged settlement. En route, romantic interest is established with the daughter of his ailing commanding officer."

Goldwyn had not invested $2,000,000 in *The Real Glory* in order to please the critics. He knew the picture had all the elements needed for commercial success: Cooper in action, Cooper in close-ups, Cooper in love. Bingo.

Process Shot

Niven Busch lives and teaches in San Francisco, but he was in town conferring with Frank Capra about a potential motion picture. Busch suggested we meet at Capra's office. Capra's office is on the Goldwyn lot.

As the guard waved me through the gate (on Niven's authority), I felt dizzily gleeful—behind enemy lines, and without having had to climb the back fence!

The opportunity to reconnoiter the lot was irresistible; the shock of nonrecognition, profound. For openers, the seven acres that had been the back lot—where had stood the castle, the moat, the western street, the Russian village, the New York street, the mining town, the huge tank used for marine effects—were now the site of row upon row of ugly power equipment, property of the Department of Water & Power! The remaining ten acres, to which Sam had gradually acquired sole ownership, were occupied by deserted (on that day, at least) sound stages and some unprepossessing offices in which industry figures, many of them retired or semiretired, endlessly negotiate and discuss properties that have infinitesimal chances of ever reaching the screen. Since 1958, when Goldwyn produced his last picture, the studio has been, essentially, a real estate operation, leasing sound stages, office space and its sound and editing services to independent television and feature film producers, as well as to individuals.

The Goldwyn lot is a familiar place to Niven Busch. A dynamic, attractive writer who could pass for a character in one of his own novels (the best known is *Duel in the Sun*), Busch went to work for Goldwyn in 1938, assigned to the screenplay of *The Westerner.* Busch liked and admired Sam, and understood him better than most of his colleagues. "It was very hard," says Busch, "for Goldwyn to get the finesse of story points from discussion or even from reading. But he would have a sense of when it was good or when it was bad. He'd try out different versions of material on different people. By getting a sort of caucus, he'd arrive at a feeling about a script."

Busch worked for Goldwyn for two years. "I was supposed to have a contract. For two years, my agent asked him, 'What about Busch's contract?' And Goldwyn would say, 'Do I need a contract with this man? I'm like his father! He's like my son! I don't need a contract with my son!' The day he decided he hated me, he said, 'Niven, I got no contract with you.'

"Mrs. Goldwyn at that time was beginning to come around the studio a lot. She'd come in the projection room, sometimes she'd go in the office, and she'd try to steer his taste and keep him from making some sort of gaffe. She selected his clothes. He was by all odds the best dressed man in Hollywood, producer or not. His clothes were made by a very good English tailor, his shirts were all custom-made, his shoes were made in London. Gary Cooper and the other good dressers in Hollywood just looked at Goldwyn and they thought, Wow!

"As a host, he was always very gracious. His house was filled with the greats. Anyone that came through from Washington that was a Democrat would visit him. He used to have actors at his parties, but only those who wouldn't eat their peas off the knife or anything like that. He didn't have a very high regard for actors. To him, they sat below the salt a little bit."

Sam used the same ploy on Busch that he'd used on Sam Marx: come to work as my story editor and executive assistant, and I'll let you produce a picture. When the picture failed to materialize, Busch, with very little to keep him busy, began writing a novel—on Goldwyn's time. "I'd had this understanding with him that he couldn't walk into my office, any more than I could walk into his office. I said, 'I have to have privacy.' And I wouldn't have an intercom on my desk. He had to call me on the phone. That was for my own protection. I'd seen the way he'd beat executives down. If they let him dump his manic tensions into their subconscious, he'd destroy them! Merritt Hulburd died of a heart attack. You could tell he was going to—he was shaking!

"I figured out that the best time for me to work on my novel was when he went to lunch. He had a dressing room over in the office complex, and after lunch he'd lie down there for forty-five minutes. So I could count on him being gone from 12:00 to 2:30. I'd have a sandwich sent up, and that was the time I'd do my writing."

The routine worked smoothly until the afternoon when Niven, after a big night, finished his writing stint and lay down for a nap of his own. His secretary awakened him with a summons from Goldwyn, which Busch promptly obeyed. Sam stared at the writer for a long moment before saying, his voice dripping with ersatz concern, "Niven, you're a young man. You're not living right."

"What's the matter, Mr. Goldwyn?"

"In the middle of the day, when you should be at your best, you are lying on your couch snoring!"

The guilt-stricken Busch sputtered and stammered. "Niven!" Goldwyn went on. "Please! Don't lie to me! I was in your office just now. I went in on tiptoe. You were snoring. Niven, I could have had your watch! I could have taken your wallet! I tiptoed out. But that is no good. ON MY TIME!!!"

Squirming with embarrassment, Busch apologized profusely, promised never to repeat the offense, and returned to his office where he berated his flabbergasted secretary. "Goddammit, Elsie, what the hell did you let Mr. Goldwyn in my office for?"

"I didn't!" she protested.

"He walked in the office! He saw me asleep! You had to let him in, there was no other way he could have gotten in!"

"As God is my judge," said the poor woman, on the verge of tears, "I didn't let him in!"

At that moment, Busch caught a glimpse of himself in the mirror and instantly grasped what had happened. "I saw that from lying down on the couch, the back of my hair was standing up *just a little bit*, the way it will if you're snoozing and you don't comb your hair. He had jumped on that one little clue and put things together. Just to have muscle on me! To have a momentary advantage! 'I could've had your watch!'

"You never knew whether his rages were phony. Nat Deveridge told me a story that illustrates that. Nat was an agent who used to play cards with Goldwyn and a couple of other fellows. One day, Goldwyn became dissatisfied with him because of a contract. Goldwyn wanted a revision, and Deveridge stood on the terms. So Goldwyn threw one of his fits. He told Deveridge, 'I want you out of my sight! Don't ever doity up my office as long as you live, and I don't want you to put *foot* on the lot!' Then he picked up the phone and called the gate and said, 'This is Mr. Goldwyn. Do not never let Mr. Nat Deveridge on this lot for his lifetime! Thank you! Good-bye!' And he said to Deveridge, 'And if you see me on the street or in a restaurant, turn your face the other way because I will not speak to you, Deveridge! This is the last time, and I am showing you the door! There is the door! Go through the door!'

"So Deveridge came out pale. He was really shocked, convinced that a terrible thing had happened. He and Goldwyn had been friends for years. He was really sick about it. He went home feeling ill, and went to bed. About ten o'clock that night, the phone rang. It was Goldwyn. He told Mrs. Deveridge he wanted to speak to Nat. Nat had gone to bed, she said. Was there any message? Goldwyn says, 'Well, yes! I'm here at the house and we're waiting for Nat for bridge!' "

Niven glimpsed a seldom-seen side of Goldwyn one afternoon. "We were having a conference and he was visibly upset. He kept getting these phone calls and asking me to leave his office—which was unusual. Finally I asked his secretary what was going on. She told me young Sammy had run away—he must have been about eleven at the time—and they didn't know where he was. Then Goldwyn called me back into his office and got *another* call, which he took this time with me sitting there. He was crying—very much the concerned father. 'Sammy, where are you? Can't we come and get you?' You ought to ask Sammy what that was all about!"

Looking past Niven's shoulder through the window, I could see a sign on the opposite building that designated the office of Sam Goldwyn, Jr. I told Niven that Mr. Goldwyn had expressed some reluctance to see me, but Niven encouraged me to circumvent channels and simply approach him straightforwardly. Why not, I thought. At least I can *meet* the man. Without thinking beyond that impulse, I crossed the street and reached for the doorknob. It didn't turn. The place was locked up. For minutes? For lunch? For ever? I knocked. No response. So much for impulsiveness.

Continuing my surreptitious tour of the lot, I came upon the jerrybuilt elevator that was installed when Sam could no longer negotiate the stairs to his office. Just beyond was the exterior iron staircase Sam used to call his fire escape. Expecting that at any moment I would be placed under arrest—or shot—I ascended the stairs and peeked through the window of Sam's office. Years after his retirement, months after his death, it remained exactly as it had been described to me by secretaries, directors, actors and reporters who had not seen it for decades. The furniture was expensively austere. The room was dominated by Sam's red-leather-topped desk. "I always think of him as a batter at the plate," a onetime publicist told me. "The people he conferred with—or bawled out, as was more often the case—sat in chairs at the corners of the room. It was one of his ways of reminding you who was in charge."

I crept back down the stairs and went looking for the commissary, which I remembered but could not find. A friendly janitor enlightened me. "Commissary burned down three years ago. Never did rebuild it. Catering truck comes by around noon."

Further exploration seemed pointless. The atmosphere seemed oppressive, and I was eager to leave. Within weeks, a friend telephoned one afternoon, greatly excited. "Turn on Channel 5! The Goldwyn Studio is on fire!"

It was not the first serious fire on the lot, nor was it the most costly (in 1958, the *Porgy and Bess* set burned, to the tune of $5,000,000). It was, however, the most spectacular. Local television coverage, aerial and ground level, was extensive. For one bad hour, it appeared that the entire studio and the surrounding neighborhood might be reduced to rubble. On the television screen, the scene had overtones of the surreal Burning of Hollywood in *The Day of the Locust*.

When the ashes settled, it was determined that a defective

spotlight had showered sparks on a flammable set for a television series and within forty-five seconds, according to one witness, the wall of the stage collapsed. Three sound stages were razed, and two office buildings sustained extensive smoke and water damage.

Watching the holocaust on television, Sam was much on my mind. His reaction would, I believed—on the basis of previous catastrophes—have been perfectly predictable. First, was anyone hurt? One crew member. Second, will the insurance cover the loss? Yes. Finally, how much space will the newspapers give us? Plenty. The next morning, the *Los Angeles Times* headlined, on its front page, $10 MILLION BLAZE DESTROYS 3 GOLDWYN STUDIO SOUND STAGES. (The estimate was later revised to two million. But as Sam would have pointed out, ten million made a hell of a lot better headline.)

15. The Goldwyn Follies

Ever since Sam had introduced his Goldwyn Girls to the screen in 1932, he had talked of out-Ziegfelding the Great Showman (who died in '32) with a musical extravaganza that would begin where Ziegfeld's *Follies* left off. *The Goldwyn Follies* (1937) had everything but the Goldwyn Girls, and they were absent only for lack of room! It had George and Ira Gershwin to write music and lyrics, and tenor Kenny Baker to warble their songs; George Balanchine to direct the dances, and The American Ballet Company of the Metropolitan Opera (with soloist ballerina Vera Zorina, said to be one of the most exquisite women in the world) to perform them; soprano Helen Jepson to sing arias from *La Traviata;* Edgar Bergen, Charlie McCarthy and The Ritz Brothers to do comedy; Gregg Toland to guide the camera; Richard Day to design the sets; George Marshall, a veteran of the silent days, to direct; and more writers than anyone could keep track of to put together a script that would encompass all these disparate talents.

Goldwyn had borrowed George Marshall from Fox, where he was under contract. Marshall felt fine about it—at first. "It started off beautifully. Good cast, good writers, wonderful art director. Our sets were excellent. I was quite happy—we *all* were quite enthusiastic—until Sam started changing things. He changed the whole story! The whole concept! I came in one morning and found out from George Haight that I was working on the wrong script!

"Our original setup was a pretty straight line, without the contrivance of 'Here we do a number' and then do the number. That's what made it so nice. There was a flow to it, so that our *story* really kept the numbers together. For example: Adolphe Menjou tricks the millionaire, Bobby Clark, into backing a show. The millionaire says he'll give Menjou the money if he can get Helen Jepson in the show. Menjou says, 'I know Helen like that, no problem!' The millionaire goes out, and Menjou says, "Who the hell is Helen Jepson?' That kind of flow. Light comedy. So somebody says, 'Well, she's singing down at the Opera House right now!' So we went from that right onto the stage, with Jepson singing the song! Then after the song, we picked up Menjou coming backstage and meeting Helen. That's the flow we had.

"Dorothy Parker and Alan Campbell were working on the script. Not a bad combination. All it needed, actually, was sort of a climactic finish—nothing too difficult, like in all musicals, there's one big thing at the end, everybody's happy and together, on stage. No problem. It was just a matter of working it out with a little fresh approach, with all the cast on, and that would've been it. But it didn't work out that way. Because Ben Hecht talked Goldwyn out of it!"

Ben Hecht spent from two to twelve weeks in Hollywood each year, during which he earned enough money (his record was $100,000 in one month, for two screenplays) to live on for the rest of the year in New York, where he did what he considered his serious writing. Hecht contributed to sixty screenplays, many of them for Goldwyn. Hecht considered producers to be "the trusted loyalists of cliché. Writers and directors can be carried away by a 'strange' characterization of a new point of view; a producer, never." He conceded that some producers were brighter than others, however, and considered Goldwyn one of the brightest. "Inarticulate but stimulating. He filled the room with a wonderful panic and beat at your mind like a man in front of a slot machine, shaking it for a jackpot." *

One of Hecht's favorite pastimes was a game called Getting the Best of Goldwyn. Its first round was played in 1931, when Hecht (with his partner, Charlie MacArthur) knocked out

* Ben Hecht, *A Child of the Century* (New York, Simon & Schuster, 1954).

an abomination called *The Unholy Garden* in twelve hours. Hecht subsequently received a fan letter from Arthur Hornblow, Jr.: "After reading your magnificent script, Mr. Goldwyn and I both wish to go on record with the statement that if *The Unholy Garden* isn't the finest motion picture Samuel Goldwyn has ever produced, the fault will be entirely ours. You have done your part superbly." *

The Unholy Garden was produced exactly as written, and was one of the biggest (and, unintentionally, funniest) bombs ever made by *any* studio.

Hecht and Goldwyn, both shrewd egomaniacs, were alike in many ways. On balmy days, when windows were open, their shouting matches could be heard halfway across the lot. On one occasion, Hecht played hard to get until Goldwyn agreed to his demand for $5,000 in cash at the end of every week, *and* the provision that if Goldwyn spoke so much as one word to him, the deal was off. Hecht, knowing exactly what would happen, reported to the studio every day for two weeks but never turned in any pages. Finally, the phone in his office rang. "Ben," said Sam, "this is purely a social call." "That cancels the deal," said Hecht, who hung up and walked out the gate with his $10,000.

So when Hecht talked Goldwyn out of the Parker-Campbell script and into a new one by Hecht, it was just another variation on the game. Hecht's script was written in two weeks, and showed it. George Marshall calls it "a hodgepodge of 'Now we do a number.' A different story entirely! What we had before didn't fit any more!"

Marshall went back to Fox to see if there was any way he could get out of doing the picture. Shooting hadn't begun. "But they told me I had to stay with it. So I tried to make it as good as possible. Sam always liked me; it wasn't any personal thing. It was just his method of making pictures! I've made over four hundred pictures, and I never ran into anyone else who operated that way consistently. Still . . . it was his money!

"I understand that Sam liked to have people come to his house for dinner, and then he would show the dailies—which I feel was wrong. For example, Fred Astaire and Sam

* Ben Hecht, *Charlie* (New York, Harper & Bros., 1957).

were good friends. I don't know who else he had up there, quite possibly Doug and Mary. Sam would ask what they thought, and they would try to be nice, but not having a knowledge of the whole piece of wax put together, I'm sure at times he got opinions that were not good. I can understand his wanting to get a lot of reactions, but it might've been better if he'd had someone who had read the story first! Just looking at one segment, it's hard to have an intelligent, informed reaction. *The Goldwyn Follies* could've been such a really good picture, and it became just . . . average. I could really have shot Ben Hecht."

George Gershwin was given an office on the lot, and his piano playing became a familiar sound to Sam Marx, whose office was just upstairs. Goldwyn frequently interrupted Gershwin to check on his progress and to assure the composer that if he worked hard, he could write hits like Irving Berlin's (Goldwyn's favorite composer). Gershwin vowed that when he completed the assignment, he would return to New York and do some serious work—perhaps another opera, or a symphony.

Gershwin wrote five songs for *The Goldwyn Follies,* including "Love Walked In" and "Our Love Is Here To Stay." They were the last songs he ever wrote. Before he could begin the ballet music, severe headaches forced him away from his piano. The headaches were a symptom of the brain tumor that killed him, with shocking speed, at the age of thirty-eight. Days before his death, S. N. Behrman visited him at his home. Behrman was alarmed to find his friend feeble and despondent. "I had to live for this," Gershwin said bitterly. "That Sam Goldwyn should say to me, 'Why don't you write hits like Irving Berlin?' " *

George Balanchine, the brilliant young (thirty-three) choreographer, was hired on the strength of his international reputation and his rave notices for the Broadway musical, *On Your Toes.* Balanchine, who had never worked in Hollywood, was thrilled when Goldwyn offered him more money than he had ever made in his life—$1200 a week—and agreed to hire twenty-five members of Balanchine's ballet company.

* S. N. Behrman, *People in a Diary* (Boston, Little, Brown & Co., 1972).

When Balanchine arrived at Union Station, he was greeted by the same frenzied press reception (only the faces were different) that had greeted Maeterlinck, Mary Roberts Rinehart, Coco Chanel, all the celebrities Goldwyn had introduced to Hollywood. Balanchine, a man of enormous ego but simple tastes, was not impressed. "I am myself," he told photographers, and refused to pose in accordance with their ideas of what a Russian choreographer should be. At the studio, he informed Goldwyn that the sound stages, with their battered floors and drafty spaces, were not suitable for his company to rehearse in. Goldwyn agreeably had his studio workmen construct, in one miraculous day, a dance studio complete with mirrored walls, hardwood floors, dressing rooms, showers and everything else required for a first-rate ballet studio. Now, Balanchine was impressed. His biographer reports that "In the grandeur of such gestures, Goldwyn reminded Balanchine of a Russian nobleman of the days before the serfs were emancipated." *

In addition to his twenty-five dancers, Balanchine's entourage included his pianist, wardrobe attendants, makeup artists and assistants. He moved his company into its new quarters and he locked the doors. His security was impenetrable even to Goldwyn's spies. Sam himself was not allowed in the building.

For three weeks, the company rehearsed the big ballet number in secret. Lacking original ballet music by Gershwin, Balanchine and Ira Gershwin had decided to adapt the existing *An American in Paris* music and, together, had prepared a scenario. Balanchine was eager to try out some revolutionary ideas about the use of ballet in motion pictures. He conceived the *American in Paris* ballet as a fantasy quest (similar in many ways to the version later filmed with Gene Kelly and Leslie Caron); as innovative in its way as Busby Berkeley's routines had been in theirs.

After three weeks of rehearsals, Goldwyn was invited to attend a runthrough. Balanchine had arranged crude props—stepladders, chairs, swings—to suggest the various settings. When the pianist began to play, and the dancers to dance, the choreographer enthusiastically piloted the producer around the

* Bernard Taper, *Balanchine* (New York, Harper & Row, 1960).

sets, in order that he might see the dancers from the camera's angles. He insisted that Goldwyn crouch and squat in one area, then another, all the while explaining, in English as convoluted as Sam's, where the camera would be.

Until now, Goldwyn had fawned on Balanchine. But whenever Sam became confused, he instinctively said no. After a few minutes, he told the choreographer, "I've seen enough!" and walked out. When Balanchine followed him back to his office and demanded an explanation, Goldwyn readily confessed his confusion and his unwillingness to risk $100,000 of his money on an experiment too highbrow, as he put it, for the miners in Harrisburg to understand.

"Mr. Goldwyn," said Balanchine haughtily, "I am not President Roosevelt, and I am not interested in what the miners of Harrisburg think. Besides," he remembered, "there are no miners in Harrisburg. I've been there!" *

Goldwyn was adamant; no *American in Paris* ballet. Balanchine, equally adamant, quit. Only the intercession of Dick Day, Balanchine's friend, persuaded the choreographer that for the sake of his company, he should work out a compromise with Goldwyn, who promised Balanchine that if he would take the conservative route on this, his first time out in motion pictures, he could have complete freedom on his next assignment.

It was six years before Goldwyn made another musical, and there was no next assignment for Balanchine. The ballet he ultimately conceived for *The Goldwyn Follies* was the highlight of the picture, but by no means revolutionary. It was a sort of modern version of *Swan Lake* (a Goldwyn favorite), danced to music written by Vernon Duke. In it, Vera Zorina emerges as a water nymph from a pool at a garden party, and dances a *pas de deux* with one of the guests. At the end, of course, she descends into the water, leaving her lover high and dry.

Goldwyn adored the water nymph ballet. For years afterward, he delighted in showing it to dinner guests, introducing it as the greatest example of dance on film. In fact, he told George Marshall that he was very happy with everything about the picture, and assured the director, "It's gonna do great things for you, George!" He announced his intention to produce an

* *Ibid.*

annual version of the *Follies*, as had Ziegfeld—but the reviews ended all talk of that. One of the most charitable was written by Frank S. Nugent for *The New York Times:*

> Sam Goldwyn has been dreaming about a *Goldwyn Follies* for so many years, it was inevitable that its realization on the Rivoli screen should have a certain nightmarish quality . . . I stayed awake, sometimes with an effort, and found his *Follies* a hodge-podge. Since it bears the Goldwyn trademark, it goes without saying that it is a superior hodge-podge. . . . But none of it, good or bad, has been brought into a semblance of continuity. We are always hearing about faces on the cutting room floor; this is one time when the script wound up there. On the evidence, it appears that Mr. Goldwyn tossed the story out to make room for the cast.

16. Wuthering Heights

Wuthering Heights was Goldwyn's favorite of all his pictures. Long after the picture's 1939 release, Frances Goldwyn gave a *Los Angeles Times* reporter her version of how it came about:

> Emily Brontë's *Wuthering Heights* was in public domain when Walter Wanger engaged Ben Hecht and Charlie MacArthur to turn it into a screenplay. Wanger thought it was too sad; no comedy. Ben and Charlie had their office here on the lot, and Ben swept up the backstairs and handed the script to Sam. Sam took it home, read it and phoned Ben back the same evening: "Let's do it!"

The first sentence is accurate; the rest, fodder for the myth.* The fact is that Wanger had commissioned the Hecht-MacArthur script with two of his contract players, Sylvia Sidney and Charles Boyer, in mind for Cathy and Heathcliff; but both actors declined to play the parts, on the grounds that they would have been grievously miscast. Sylvia Sidney showed the script to Willy Wyler; it was he who took it to Goldwyn, and it was Sam, not Wanger, who rejected it because it was too sad. Wyler

* Richard Griffith, writing in *Samuel Goldwyn, The Producer and His Films,* contributed more fodder. According to Griffith, Wanger took the script to Goldwyn "for advice. The story was powerful and grim. How could it be lightened? After reading it Mr. Goldwyn, outraged at the suggestion of any change in what he considered to be the best film script ever brought to his attention, insisted on buying the story from Wanger and producing it himself."

insisted it was a great love story; Goldwyn, that he didn't like stories with people dying in the end. Stalemate.

Some months later, when Wyler was working at Warners, he discussed with Jack Warner the possibility of a production of *Wuthering Heights* with Bette Davis as Cathy. While Warner was thinking it over, Wyler went to Goldwyn with what he knew was irresistible bait: the news that Jack Warner, one of his fiercest competitors, was planning to buy the script. No more was needed to convince Sam of the desirability of the property, and he quickly bought it, with Wyler's assurance that the part of Cathy was made to order for Merle Oberon, whom *Goldwyn* had under contract.

Wyler wanted an all-British cast, and Sam agreed. Wyler had seen the young, relatively unknown-in-America Laurence Olivier in a New York play, and had come away impressed. He sold the idea of casting Olivier as Heathcliff to Goldwyn, who tried to sell it to Olivier, who turned him down flat.

Olivier's only previous experience in Hollywood had been a humiliating one. Garbo had chosen him as her leading man in *Queen Christina,* but after shooting began, the director had replaced him with another actor. The incident had reinforced his conviction that the stage was the only place for a serious actor. In the summer of 1938, when his agent cabled Goldwyn's offer, Olivier was living blissfully on the coast of France with Vivien Leigh (both were obtaining divorces from their respective spouses). Although both had achieved success in the theater, their audience was an elitist one; and while neither of them could have known it, this would be their last summer of anonymous privacy.

Goldwyn ignored Olivier's negative reaction and sent him a copy of the script, which the actor found surprisingly good. When Olivier returned to England in August, Wyler paid him a series of visits. Realizing, shrewdly, that money would not be an inducement, he concentrated on the challenge the part offered to an actor's skill. Olivier was intrigued, but one drawback remained. He did not want to be separated from Vivien Leigh; but in the end, it was she who persuaded Olivier to take the part, arguing that their relationship would suffer if either of them sacrificed roles that might help their careers. Early in November, Olivier sailed for America—alone.

When Wyler returned to Hollywood, he learned that David Niven was not "set," as he had thought, for the second lead. Niven, who considered himself something of a ladykiller, had balked at the prospect of playing Edgar, the cuckolded husband. He told Goldwyn it was the worst part ever written, and chose to go on suspension without pay rather than play it. Wyler took him to dinner at Chasen's and charmed him with flattery that Niven, whose experience was rather limited, found irresistible. "You're one of the few people in the business who can make something out of this part," Wyler told him. When Niven reminded him how badly the director had treated him on *Dodsworth,* Wyler laughed and said, "I've changed. Come and play the part. It's a wonderful cast. . . . It'll be a great picture and I'll make you great in it." * Niven reported for costume fittings the very next day.

Goldwyn went to great lengths to achieve technical authenticity, and wrung every possible drop of publicity out of the expense. As art director he hired James Basevi, who had been raised in Yorkshire, where the story was set. Basevi even imported a thousand heather plants, with which he recreated the moors on the plains of the San Fernando Valley.

The contrast between the romanticism of the story and the battle of egos that raged throughout the filming would have been wildly funny to an objective observer—but in the production of a movie, nobody is objective. Olivier was shocked when the charming, civilized Wyler with whom he had felt such rapport in England became a ruthless, uncommunicative tyrant on the set. Olivier felt insecure and in dire need of support and empathy, neither of which was forthcoming from Wyler. It seemed to Olivier that the director was excessively preoccupied with Merle Oberon's performance. Oberon's point of view was just the opposite; she felt that Wyler virtually ignored her!

The mutual resentment of the two stars peaked during the shooting of the first love scene. A consistent hazard in any love scene is the necessity of uttering lines audibly without

* David Niven, *The Moon's a Balloon* (New York, G. P. Putnam's Sons, 1972).

spraying saliva into the face of the "beloved" whose lips, to accommodate the camera, are an inch from one's own. When Olivier delivered his lines in the runthrough, Oberon responded with a frigid, "Please don't spit at me!" The scene was repeated, and so was Oberon's response. Olivier's biographer reports that he "suddenly lost his temper and said a number of things which he afterwards regretted. His rudeness magnified a trivial incident into ridiculous proportions, and they both marched off the set really angry. Wyler remained apparently unconcerned, and after a suitable pause asked them to come back . . . [and] informed Olivier and Merle Oberon that he wanted them to play the scene again. The same scene. Still inwardly raging, the lovers returned to the conversation which had to suggest great depths of mutual passion. The camera searched their faces in vain for expressions of anything but love." *

While Olivier suffered, miserably convinced that his acting career was being destroyed, David Niven was realizing that he'd been snookered. On the very first day of shooting, Wyler made Niven repeat a simple scene over forty times, then wound up printing the first take. Niven, the veil of flattery lifted from his eyes, caustically told the director, "You really are a son of a bitch, aren't you?"

"Yes," said Wyler, "and I'm going to be one for fourteen weeks!" †

The best story (both anecdotally and metaphorically) about the making of *Wuthering Heights* is Niven's. At the end of the picture, when Edgar arrives at Cathy's deathbed, the script required that he break down in sobs. When the reserved Englishman had difficulty, Wyler called for the prop man, Irving Sindler. "Through a handkerchief," writes Niven, "Sindler puffed menthol into my open eyes. 'Bend over the corpse . . . Heave your shoulders . . . Make a crying face . . . Blink your eyes . . . Squeeze a little.'

"A terrible thing happened. Instead of tears coming out of my eyes, green slime came out of my nose.

" 'Ooh!!! How *horrid!*' shrieked the corpse, who shot out

* Felix Barker, *The Oliviers* (New York, Lippincott, 1953).
† David Niven, *The Moon's a Balloon.*

of bed and disappeared at high speed into her dressing room." *

Goldwyn's contribution to these troubled waters was more waves. He was as insecure about his investment as Olivier was about his reputation. Watching the rushes of Heathcliff as a grubby stable boy in the picture's early scenes, Sam began to feel he wasn't getting his money's worth, and complained to Wyler, "His face isn't even clean!" Wyler, who had heard similar complaints about the dirtiness of the *Dead End* set—crucial to the central theme of the picture—paid no attention. Goldwyn then appeared on the set, where he marched up to Wyler and told him, in tones deliberately loud enough for Olivier (and most of the cast and crew) to overhear: "If this actor goes on like this, I'll close the picture!"

To add injury to insult, Olivier had contracted a severe case of athlete's foot which forced him to hobble around on crutches when not on camera. A lesser actor could easily, at this point, have said to hell with it and given a perfunctory performance—or simply walked out. But Olivier persevered, and out of his physical and psychic pain created a fine and memorable performance, acquired a new perspective on his craft, and a new respect (for which he gave Wyler full credit) for the potential of film.

The promotion of *Wuthering Heights* was masterful. The ads promised "The Strangest Love Story Ever Told," and featured a gruesome, greenish close-up of Olivier's tortured face under the caption, THE MARK OF HELL WAS IN HIS EYES. Before the heavily hoopla'd Hollywood premiere, the Goldwyns threw a celebratory dinner party. The guests included Eleanor Roosevelt, Irving Berlin, Norma Shearer, Merle Oberon. The William Wylers were not invited.

Goldwyn loved everything about the picture: the romanticism, the sentimentality and, especially, Wyler's little human touches, such as Merle Oberon lifting her skirts to warm herself in front of the fire. But Sam had a genius for seeing the trees and not the forest. Absorbed in minutiae, he was unaware that Emily Brontë's story had, in translation, lost its subtlety and, with it, its soul.

Reviewers obediently paid homage to the authenticity of

* *Ibid.*

detail, but they also pointed out lapses. Goldwyn's idiosyncrasies included an abhorrence of the bustle and an admiration for Merle Oberon's bare shoulders. He advanced the period of the story by forty years, to 1841, so that Oberon could wear the flattering gowns of the Victorian era. He had a bathtub scene inserted—more shoulders. And the much-publicized heather turned out to be of hothouse origin, noticeably taller and more luxuriant than the real thing. But these were petty criticisms. The extent to which the story's integrity was violated is exemplified by the ending he tacked on. "I don't want to look at a corpse at the fadeout," he told Wyler, who refused to direct the scene (another director shot it) showing the ghosts of the lovers walking through clouds toward Penniston Crag, to the strains of Alfred Newman's violins.

Like most of Goldwyn's productions, *Wuthering Heights* was a slick, expensively mounted entertainment, with pretensions that left critics brainwashed and goggle-eyed. Just as Frank Nugent was unable to call *The Goldwyn Follies* a hodgepodge without qualifying the term with "superior," so *Variety*'s critic felt impelled to praise Goldwyn for his "courage" in filming a story with "less than sympathetic" leading characters and an "uncompromising finale which utterly disregards all popular theories of screen entertainment"—*i.e.*, the obligatory happily-ever-after ending. No mention was made of the fact that despite Toland's artistic photography and lighting, Wyler's sensitive direction, Basevi's authentic (more or less) sets and Olivier's moving performance, the atmosphere and the plot of the novel were lost in a haze of cheap sentiment and schmaltz—green slime disguised as real tears. *Wuthering Heights* was, in fact, the *Love Story* of its day, with this important distinction: *Love Story* didn't pretend to be art.

The European promotion of *Wuthering Heights* was a brilliant variation on the sales strategy Sam had conceived for his Eminent Authors: snob appeal. Instead of exporting the picture through customary channels of sales and distribution, a print was personally delivered to the King and Queen of England by the new vice-president of Samuel Goldwyn Productions: James Roosevelt, eldest son of FDR.

At thirty-one, Roosevelt was tall (six feet three inches), gaunt, balding. His prior business experience consisted of representing an insurance firm and engaging in some marginal political activities. He knew nothing whatever about the film business when Goldwyn hired him at $25,000 a year. "I fell in love with Jimmy the minute I met him," he told a fan magazine writer. "Great mind! Great mind! He knows everybody! Knows all the world leaders!"

To Sam Goldwyn, being the boss of the President's son represented the ultimate proof of his power—his entree to the center of the innermost circle! In Hollywood, he and Roosevelt were social equals; they called each other Jimmy and Sam, and strolled down Sunset Boulevard together. Jimmy's mother, the First Lady, dined at Laurel Lane. Goldwyn made Roosevelt a sort of prize exhibit; he would guide reporters and other visitors (what Danny Mandell called The Entertainment Committee) into Roosevelt's office for a glimpse, perhaps even a chat with the aristocratic scion.

And what occupied Roosevelt's time, when he was not on display? "I go over contracts," he told a reporter, "keep track of renewals of options, go over financial reports, check progress on productions, discuss contracts with agents and actors and directors, go over stories in preparation with the story editor and with Goldwyn. I act as liaison between our New York and Hollywood offices." He did a lot of gladhanding with exhibitors, film salesmen, bookers and circuit heads in the United States and abroad. He scrupulously avoided any activities that might be construed as political, and never publicly expressed a political opinion. He said he intended to make motion pictures his life's work.

The culmination of the Goldwyn-Roosevelt association (their five-year contract was terminated after one year, "by mutual agreement") was the whirlwind promotion in England and on the Continent of *Wuthering Heights*. During the course of this trip, FDR asked his son to visit the King and Queen ("While you're in London, Jimmy, would you mind just dropping in . . . ?") to discuss the details of their forthcoming visit to the United States. Ambassador Kennedy made arrangements for Roosevelt to spend a weekend at Windsor Castle. Seizing upon this golden opportunity, Sam instructed his vice president to arrange a screening of the picture for the King, the Queen and the Ambassador. When Roosevelt got to Paris, another screening was arranged for the United States Ambassador there, along with the Duke and Duchess of Windsor. These events generated such a flood of publicity about the film that European distributors were fighting for distribution rights, and the public, in America as well as abroad, couldn't wait to see this phenomenal film.

Wuthering Heights was sandwiched between two more modest productions, both released in 1939. The first, *They Shall Have Music,* was a musical with a *Dead End* setting; it starred Joel McCrea (in his last picture for Goldwyn) and featured none other than Jascha Heifetz (Goldwyn *loved* violin music!) as the hero who rescues a music school for underprivileged kids from being shut down. The hapless Archie Mayo directed. The second was *Raffles,* a remake of the Ronald Colman starrer that had been such a success in 1930. This time out, David Niven played the gentleman thief.

Goldwyn had given the unknown Niven a seven-year contract in 1935 because he had heard that Thalberg was interested in the actor. If Thalberg wanted him, Goldwyn had to have him. Four years elapsed, during which Goldwyn got his money's worth. When Niven wasn't working for Sam, he was loaned out—always at a profit to Goldwyn. His performance in *Dawn Patrol* (at Warners) won him star billing; but he was still contracted to Goldwyn at a minuscule salary.

Niven, realizing that his value to Goldwyn had skyrocketed, tried to renegotiate his contract. Sam paid no attention, and cast him in a part Niven considered so awful that he turned it down and went on suspension. Goldwyn then offered him the part of Raffles, which the actor was dying to play. But on the advice of his agent, who assured Niven he could get him a more equitable deal, he stalled. While the agent wrestled with Goldwyn's lawyers, Niven was called to the studio one day for some unrelated purpose. Wherever he went on the lot, he noticed—could not help but notice, since it was staged for his benefit—another actor, wearing the unmistakable white tie and tails of the Raffles character and prominently displaying the prop revolver and diamonds that were Raffles' trademark, posing for stills for the studio photographer. Sam hoped that if Niven saw another actor apparently being groomed for the part, it would panic him into signing—on Goldwyn's terms.

Eventually, a compromise agreement was reached and Niven made the picture, with Olivia de Havilland costarring and Sam Wood, a superior director of comedy (*A Day at the Races, A Night at the Opera*) borrowed from MGM to direct. The script was by John Van Druten and Sidney Howard, with a rewrite by F. Scott Fitzgerald (who claimed that he liked Goldwyn because "You always knew where you stood with him: nowhere.") The film editor was Sherman Todd, who found himself in the uncomfortable position of mediator and translator.

"I would go into the projection room with Mr. Wood and Mr. Goldwyn. Mr. Goldwyn would have his say, and Sam Wood would answer him. Both of them were very emphatic about what they said, and neither one of 'em could understand each other! They'd both talk at the same time, and I was in the middle. Finally Mr. Goldwyn would say, 'Do you understand what he's talking about?' and I'd say, 'Yes, I do.' He'd say, 'Can you do it?' and I'd say, 'Yes, I think so.' 'Well, all right.' We'd leave, and on the way back to the cutting room, Mr. Wood would ask me what Mr. Goldwyn was hollering about and what his complaint was, and I'd tell him. Then five minutes later, the phone in the cutting room would ring; they'd tell me to go up to Goldwyn's office. Then *Goldwyn* would ask me what Sam *Wood* had been hollering about, and I'd explain what *he'd* said.

"You might say Mr. Goldwyn had a communication problem."

Process Shot

Celebrities were never a big deal to me; they were what my father sold for a living. I met them frequently, and was not impressed. Dana Andrews, however, was the exception that proved the rule. At fifteen, I would have died for Dana Andrews. At forty, I found myself knocking on his door. Dana Andrews, as it happens, is the actor who holds the longevity record for staying under contract to Sam Goldwyn.

Meeting one's idol is asking for trouble—especially when the meeting comes twenty-five years after the fact. For one thing, he is bound to be twenty-five years older. And life-size. As this crossed my mind, the door opened and the object of my adolescent adoration invited me into his comfortable, though far from luxurious, North Hollywood home.

A few facts about Dana Andrews. He is sixty-five, and looks fifty. The son of a Baptist minister (who forbade him to engage in the sin of moviegoing), he saw his first movie at the rebellious age of fifteen. At twenty, he gave up a promising future in the business community of Austin, Texas, and moved to Los Angeles, where an agent pointed him toward an acting career. In 1938, after nine years of apprenticeship at little theaters and the Pasadena Playhouse, his agent arranged a screen test at Goldwyn's studio.

"Goldwyn was out of town; his vice president, Reeves Espy, set it up. Gregg Toland made the test. It was what they called a stool test. They sat you on a stool and a property man turned it around—kind of a silly thing to do. But when Goldwyn saw the test, he signed the contract. He gave me a few lines in *The Westerner,* but he wasn't planning to make any more pictures until he settled his lawsuit with United Artists.

"I had met Mary, my wife, at the Pasadena Playhouse, and I told Mr. Espy that I wanted to get married. He said, 'Dana, we have this hiatus coming up, we have you under contract and we won't be able to put you in any pictures. And nobody *else* is gonna put you in a picture until *we* do. Would you be agreeable to dating some starlets to get your name in the papers?' He said, 'We can't tell you whether you can get married or not, that's up to you. But I think this would be wise, for your career!' "

Andrews agreed, reluctantly, to go along with the idea, but after six months he told Espy that it was putting a real strain on his relationship with his intended. Espy suggested he talk to Goldwyn about it. "I'll make him feel good that you want his advice. It'll help you establish a relationship with him."

Andrews made an appointment to see Goldwyn. "In the meantime, he was having an argument with David Niven. They were photographing me as if I were to play Raffles! They always had the camera setups where Niven could see them. I was not fooled; I knew what they were doing." Just before the time for his appointment, a fire flared up in a projection room. "Jimmy Roosevelt was in there. Firemen were rushing by, the alarm bells were ringing. I looked across this ring of people and there was Mr. Goldwyn. He motioned that I should come over to him. The racket was terrible. He shouted in my ear, 'I UNDERSTAND YOU VANT TO TALK TO ME. VAT DO YOU VANT TO TALK TO ME ABOUT?' I had a speech all made up that I was really gonna try to sell him. This was the most important thing in my life! So I shouted back, in *his* ear, 'Sam, I've got a speech all made up for you. I want to beard the lion in his den!' He took me by the arm and led me two steps back, as if this was gonna quiet the noise, and shouted in my ear, 'Beard me now!'

"I laughed. I said, 'Sam, I wanna get married and I wanna know what you think about it!' He said, 'I'll think about it. I'll let you know.'

"Two weeks later, nothing had happened. No word. I was in talking to him about something else. The marriage was very much on my mind. As I was leaving, I turned, trying to be very nonchalant about the whole thing, and I said, 'Oh, by the way, Mr. Goldwyn, you were gonna tell me what you thought about my getting married.' He said, 'Oh, I forgot all about it. Sure, go ahead.' "

With his production schedule in abeyance, Goldwyn attempted to recoup his investment in Andrews by selling half of his contract to Fox—a practice not uncommon with boxers or racehorses, but unprecedented, at the time, with actors. This arrangement lasted for eleven years, during which Andrews made his best pictures, including *Laura,* for Fox. "When I worked for Goldwyn, *he* paid me. When I worked for Fox, *they* paid me. And when I was on salary and not workin', they divided the bill. Goldwyn, however, had the ability to loan me out—and Fox didn't. So a lotta times he would preempt Fox by loaning me out to somebody. He got more money than he paid me, of course."

During the war, Andrews, over draft age and with two children, had all the work he could handle at Fox; their roster of leading men was decimated by the draft. By 1943, he was becoming so well known that Goldwyn promised that when the wartime freeze on wages was lifted, he would renegotiate Andrews' contract at an additional $500 a week—not out of generosity, but, as Andrews explains it, "to keep me from being unhappy. Because when you're unhappy, you get sick a lot."

Two years passed before the war ended; by then, thanks to pictures like *The Oxbow Incident* and *Laura,* Andrews was a star. His agent demanded that Goldwyn pay him a star's salary—considerably more than the $500-a-week raise Sam had promised. It took seven months to negotiate a new seven-year contract. During one round, which took place in Goldwyn's office, Sam, furious that Andrews did not feel bound by their oral agreement, accused the actor of breaking his word.

"Sam," said Dana, "I studied business law in college, and I know that an oral contract is no good after a year. You've forgotten what you said. I may have forgotten what *I* said. Neither one of us would have a case in court."

Goldwyn turned purple. "I feel entitled to slap you in the face!" he shouted.

"Okay, Sam," said Dana, acting much more cocky than he felt. "You go ahead and slap me in the face. I promise you I won't slap you back."

"GET OUTA MY OFFICE! I'LL NEVER SPEAK TO YOU AGAIN! I WON'T TALK TO YOUR AGENT! DON'T WRITE ME LETTERS! DON'T CALL ME ON THE TELEPHONE! I'M THROUGH WITH YOU! AND WHEN I'M THROUGH WITH YOU, YOU'RE *THROUGH!*"

Somehow, a contract was finally negotiated. It included a payment of retroactive salary amounting to something like $178,000, and Andrews was satisfied. Socially, the Andrewses and the Goldwyns never mixed. So Dana was surprised when he heard, through his agent, that Goldwyn was hurt that Dana hadn't invited him to a big tenth-anniversary party. "It's very simple," Andrews explained to his agent. "I've been under contract to Sam for ten years. He's had a lotta parties, and he never invited us. So I don't invite him to mine!"

The next next day, Andrews was walking down a hall in the studio and heard someone call his name. "It was Frances Goldwyn! She came running towards me. She said, 'Oh, we're having a few friends for dinner. I wonder if you and Mary could come over. Benjamin Fairless, the President of United States Steel, and his wife are coming.'

"We went. There were only ten people. The Firestones, Hedda Hopper, Anatole Litvak, Mr. and Mrs. Fairless and Mary and me and the Goldwyns. Then I realized that Frances thought she was gonna give me and Mary a great treat by having us meet the Benjamin Fairlesses. Well, when I walked in the room, he got up and walked over to me and said, 'Well, Dana! It's been a long time!' Frances was absolutely stunned! I've known Ben for years! Leonard Firestone said, 'Mr. Andrews, my name is Firestone. I'm in rubber.' As though you didn't know a god damned thing! Then Goldwyn was telling Ben what a model husband and father I'd been, kept my skirts clean and all, and I said, 'Sam, what about the time I got picked up for drunk?' He said, 'Vell, you know, ve all make mistakes.' We were never invited back again."

Although technically a senior citizen, Andrews is hardly ready for Sun City. Our meeting was postponed for months while he toured the "dinner theater" circuit ($10 buys dinner and the show; the house makes its money on the drinks), appearing in light comedies in El Paso, Omaha, Dallas, Minneapolis, Chicago. "It's fun," he says, "and *very* lucrative. I make more money doing this than I did for *Laura*, or for *Best Years*. Up to $4,000 a week!" During one of his infrequent visits home, he agreed to see me, then had to cancel out because of (1) work on *Airport, '75;* (2) a quick trip to the Philippines to judge the Miss Universe contest; (3) a visit from his grandchildren. When we finally met, however, he could not have been more gracious—or loquacious. His comments about Goldwyn were interspersed with his views on religion, philosophy, nature, life after death, politics.

An actor, if he is any good, *must* be self-absorbed; his instrument, which is himself, requires constant attention, and leaves no time for probing the motivations of other people. But Andrews' *observations* of Goldwyn's behavior were thoughtful and right on.

"He was indomitable, as far as giving up. He would spend loads of money trying to prove an unprovable point. Like trying to prove that Virginia Mayo was a great actress. Everybody talks about the "Goldwyn touch," but Mr. Goldwyn made a lotta bad pictures. I was in a couple of 'em. People say Sam Goldwyn had immaculate taste. I don't think so. He *tried* to find out what *was* good taste. He asked a lotta people. A lotta times he'd ask the wrong person, and he'd *believe* them! Because he was *not able to discriminate!*

"I always called him Sam. But when he would say, 'Dana, I love you like my own son!'—look out! Like the time he came to me in my dressing room, when I was making *The North Star*. There was this girl that he wanted to put in a musical he was going to make—but he wasn't happy with her test. He told me that this girl was crazy about me, and if I would be nice to her—that is, have an affair with her—it would make her a lot more confident. I laughed! He said, 'She's in love with you! She told me so!' I said I'd heard about producers doing these things, but I'd never believed it. He said, 'If you tell this, it's a lie and I never said it!' He turned around and walked out."

I shook Dana Andrews' hand, thanked him for his time, wished him luck and walked out into the sunlight feeling grateful, disoriented and depressed. He *was* life-size. He *was* twenty-five years older. And so was I.

17. Disunited Artists

In 1925, only three years after vowing never again to involve himself in a partnership, Goldwyn became a member of United Artists, the company formed in 1919 by Mary Pickford, Douglas Fairbanks, Sr., D. W. Griffith and Charlie Chaplin. According to the company's Articles of Incorporation, its purpose was "to improve the photoplay industry and its artistic standards and the methods of marketing photoplays" and "to market photoplays in the interests of the artists who create them." In other words, the artists wanted a bigger piece of the action.

United Artists produced no pictures itself, but assisted in obtaining financing for its member producers (who used their pictures as collateral). The corporation was essentially a distributing agency, its function limited to selling the pictures of its members. It was a convenient go-between, connecting producer with exhibitor. Its salesmen offered UA films to exhibitors on a percentage basis (up to 70 percent for UA) instead of the conventional flat rental fee. The average UA picture played about ten thousand theaters and grossed, domestically, about a million dollars. Between 1919 and 1939, the company released more than three hundred pictures, most of them at a profit. Forty-six of these were Goldwyn's.

The association started out with great optimism on all sides, but as the years passed, Goldwyn, inevitably, wanted more control. The more insistent he became, the more his partners resisted; after all, they *had* founded the company. Finally, in 1937, Goldwyn and Alexander Korda tried to buy out the other three members (Griffith had already departed) for a reported $6,000,000. Goldwyn claimed that the company's policy of releasing "cheap" pictures of outside producers was defeating its purpose, undercutting its reputation for quality pictures. He described Pickford, Fairbanks and Chaplin as "parasites" and said they were "drinking his blood." The parasites were willing enough to sell, but Goldwyn then changed his mind. (According to Korda, the cost of borrowing the money would have been prohibitive.)

The other partners repeatedly invited Goldwyn to withdraw from the corporation on the condition that he relinquish his stock in the company—for which, like the founders, he had paid nothing, and which was now worth between $500,000 and a million dollars. Board meetings gradually degenerated into name-calling sessions, with Chaplin and Board Chairman A. H. Giannini (of the Bank of America) having forcibly to restrain Fairbanks from doing violence to Sam. ("I apologize," Sam later told Fairbanks, "for calling you a crook. I can't prove it.")

Goldwyn's contract with UA gave them exclusive distribution rights to his pictures through September, 1945. Goldwyn maneuvered around this by simply stopping all production (after *Raffles*). In March of 1939, he filed suit against UA for breach of contract. His complaint, including exhibits, ran more than 150 pages. As *The New York Times* reported it, "Goldwyn charged that his studio was carrying the production burden while all owner-members shared equally in the profits. The producer claimed he was making picture after picture, but that in recent years other members had virtually retired from active production or curtailed it to the extent that the Samuel Goldwyn studio was the corporation's breadwinner. He pointed out that Chaplin had produced only *Modern Times, City Lights* and *The Great Dictator* in the past ten years."

The December, 1940, issue of *Fortune* contained a lucid, in-depth account of the dispute, pointing out that Goldwyn had made himself one of the most valuable men UA ever had. "In 15 years he produced over 40 big, generally profitable pictures against only 5 Chaplins, 7 Pickfords and 8 Fairbanks. *Hurricane* rolled up one of the heaviest UA grosses in recent years and while he naturally has turned out a few turkeys, his pictures have the rather mystical quality known as *The Goldwyn Touch* and they bring top percentages. . . . Without Goldwyn, UA, on a good many occasions, wouldn't have made money." Fairbanks, Chaplin and Pickford, however, felt that since they had started the company and kept it going, they were entitled to the fruits of ownership. They argued that Sam had also benefited hugely from certain bonus deals UA had adopted.

The suit dragged on until February, 1941, when Pickford, Chaplin and the Fairbanks estate bought Sam's interest for $300,000—half of what Goldwyn claimed it was worth. The amount of the legal expenses incurred in the two-year court battle was not made public. Thereafter, Goldwyn's pictures (all but his last two) were released through RKO.

In the early thirties, Goldwyn had released an average of five films a year; but after 1939 (partly because of his dispute with UA, partly because of other, industry-wide factors) he never released more than two. With his output so drastically curtailed, his margin of profit depended more than ever on how long exhibitors were willing to run his pictures. The policy of double features became his favorite target; he maintained that double features antagonized the moviegoing public—the picture they wanted to see wasn't on until ten-thirty, and bad pictures drove them from the theaters—and encouraged the production of cheap pictures (with which his expensive pictures had to compete) to meet the exhibitors' insatiable demands. He became practically rabid on the subject. In a *Saturday Evening Post* article under his byline, he even announced that he had persuaded Dr. George Gallup to conduct a nationwide poll on the double feature as a public service!

In 1940, the whole industry bit the bullet. The war in Europe had once again eliminated that important market, and the Far Eastern market shriveled as well. Taxes increased, while trade unions proliferated and made unprecedented demands on management. Budgets and salaries were pared, and pared again. In September of that year, Goldwyn released *The Westerner*, a better-than-average western directed by Wyler, photographed by Toland, and highlighted by Walter Brennan's characterization of Judge Roy Bean, on whose life the story was (just barely) based.

The Westerner caused Goldwyn much anxiety. Because of the weather (half of the picture was shot on location) and other unforeseeable delays, the picture far exceeded its budget. When the picture was released, Goldwyn was dismayed to learn that UA's salesmen had distributed it to Loew's theater chain for what he, Goldwyn, considered a ridiculously low price. He called his onetime publicist, Howard Dietz, who was then working for Nick Schenck, the owner of Loew's. "Do me a favor. I've got a great picture, *The Westerner.* It's better than *Gone With the Wind,* but not as long. Loew's paid 70 percent of the gross for *Gone With the Wind.* All I want for my *Westerner* is 50 percent of the gross." The deal that had already been made with Loew's was for 25 percent. "For old times' sake," Goldwyn wanted Dietz to persuade Schenck to tear up the perfectly valid contract so that Goldwyn could sell him a new one, at double the price.

"Sam," said the amused Dietz, "that is an impossible request. I'm afraid Schenck might ask me who I'm working for!"

"I guess you don't stand in so good with him!" said Goldwyn.*

* Howard Dietz, *Dancing in the Dark* (New York, Quadrangle, 1974).

Process Shot

Collier Young's office is pure Raymond Chandler. The neighborhood (borderline Burbank), the building (stucco) and the tiny, viewless room in which Young negotiates six-figure deals are tacky and anachronistic. The unmatched furniture is vintage Salvation Army, or Swap Meet; the decor—some crooked paintings and a couple of huge plastic daisies—Woolworth's, or worse. Aside from a few scripts on the beat-up coffee table, the only reading matter in sight is a book commemorating the fortieth anniversary of Young's 1930 graduation from Dartmouth. A layer of dust covers everything, except Collier Young. His face is familiar; two of his four marriages were to Ida Lupino and Joan Fontaine, and fan magazines frequently published pictures of him with his glamorous wives. Even in his salad days, Young was not a handsome man; now, nearing seventy, his slightly simian face has an abused, three-o'clock-in-the-morning look, orchestrated by an alarming cigarette cough. But in spite of his unprepossessing looks, in spite of the eccentric ambience of his office, it is easy to see why, thirty-five years ago, Sam Goldwyn hired him as his story editor. At thirty-three, Young had already been successful as a copywriter for Young & Rubicam, a literary agent for Myron Selznick, and a story editor for RKO. Goldwyn recognized a young man in a hurry when he saw one.

He installed Young in the office that had been Jimmy Roosevelt's. "It even had a private lavatory. I thought I was really doing well!" One of Young's first assignments was to fire some writers. "I was the butcher, and not always for a good reason. Sometimes it just reflected his nervousness before he started a picture. One indication was his consumption of water. He kept a pitcher of spring water on his desk. When he was really nervous, he drank *gallons* of it.

"The picture I was closest to, which was the best experience of my life—being a baseball fan—was *Pride of the Yankees.* I was nursemaid to Babe Ruth. Ruth drank inordinate amounts of beer, *cases* of beer—and I ordered cases of beer to be put in his dressing room. Better than his drinking anything else. Goldwyn took some exception to that. He thought I was coddling him. Of course, I drank quite a lot of beer *with* him."

What was a story conference with Goldwyn like? "Long. A lot of 'em were held on the weekend. He didn't do anything for the institution of marriage. You were really on call, like the White House calling the advisers, wherever they are. A lot of weekends at the house. As if that weren't enough, if he felt that an artist was unhappy, we'd have the meeting and then he'd say, 'Go over to Hope's house'—Saturday night!—and I'd say, 'Why not phone him?'

" '*Go over and see him! Tell him what we're going to do!*' Preparing for a production, it was always a seven-day week.

"Later, I became his equerry—traveled with him. Back and forth to New York, a couple of times a year. Those endless rides on the Super Chief. We had adjoining drawing rooms. He taught me to play gin rummy, at considerable expense." Was Goldwyn restless on the train? "Oh, my God! The Super Chief'd stop in Kansas City around nine-thirty and he'd say, 'Let's take a walk.' I'd say, 'But I've got my pajamas on! My dressing gown!' He'd say, 'That doesn't make any difference. Let's take a walk!' And he'd lope up and down the platform in his dressing gown—and of course, one night, goddamn nearly got left.

"In New York, we'd stay in the tower apartment at the Waldorf. He was a visting celebrity there—big dinner parties with important people with important names. He loved success, successful people around him. He'd go to the theater, talk to the actors—one trip was to see Danny Kaye in *Let's Face It.* He rather enjoyed the theater, and never fell asleep. And he'd spend time with Jim Mulvey, who ran his distribution offices back there."

Young was frequently interrupted by his telephone, which he answered himself; there was no secretary. All his callers seemed to be old friends, whose conversation Young prodded along, polite but impatient, with a nearly continual, encouraging, questioning "Mmm-hmmm, mmm-hmmm?" After each interruption, he resumed his thought without breaking stride.

"I had just gotten married. Goldwyn liked my wife very much. He liked pretty women, and she was very pretty. He'd occasionally invite us to dinner—often on hardly any notice at all. He called me into his office one day and said, 'I want you and Valerie to come to dinner tonight.' I said, 'But we have another engagement.' He said, 'Oh, the hell with that. I *need* you for dinner tonight.' And he named some people who were coming. His star guest, he said, was Buddy Manchester. I said, 'Buddy Manchester?' He said, '*Yes, Buddy Manchester!*' The mystery guest, Buddy Manchester, turned out to be Manchester Body, the publisher of the *Daily News!* I thought he was talking about a musician!

"He was exciting—and maddening. When he got into one of his spasms, I laughed a good deal—which was probably a dangerous thing to do. But in many cases, it worked. A couple of times he said, 'Get the hell out of my office. Get that grin off your face!' I never take anything that seriously."

Had Young always dealt directly with Goldwyn, or was there sometimes an intermediary? "Only Frances. She came to the studio quite often." For what purpose? "I don't know exactly! I do think she had a great influence on his life-style. She was a good hostess—she always had the right place cards for the right people. She had good taste in his clothes, food, wines, which he knew nothing about and didn't like anyway. She really did shape his life." Had she a sense of humor? "She had a very delayed fuse in that regard. Once in a while I'd say something I thought was devilishly funny. Nothing. But she was always kind to me. And she *adored* Sam. I think. God knows she was the Patient Griselda. And Sam was always very discreet about his extracurricular love life. There was a little dressing room stuff—that private dressing room next door to his office. . . ."

Whatever basis there may be to this and other hints that Sam at times strayed from Frances' fold, a central truth about Goldwyn was that work, not women, was his passion. During all those long, late hours alone with Young on the Super Chief, work dominated all conversation. "He never once referred to anything to do with the period before he met Lasky. *That's when his life started.* He blotted everything before that out. For a long time, I didn't know he'd been married before. He *never* referred to his first wife, and *very* seldom to his daughter." Had Young, who had worked with Mac Capps, known that the assistant art director was the boss's son-in-law? "I'll be damned! No! I never knew that until this very moment!"

Young left Goldwyn at the end of 1942, to join the Navy. "H. N. Swanson—I'm sure you know that name [I didn't]—said, 'Leaving Goldwyn to go to war is the greatest single act of cowardice in World War II.' " After the war, Young worked for Jack Warner, then for Harry Cohn, and finally produced some pictures on his own. More recently, he conceived the *One Step Beyond* and *Ironside* series, and when I saw him he was juggling a half-dozen potential new projects. His vitality is awesome; his warmth, contagious; his recall, apparently total; his mood, on the morning I saw him, mellow. He wished me luck with my project. I wished him luck with his. As I left, he said, without a trace of nostalgia, simply stating a fact, "I sure miss seeing him walking up Sunset Boulevard, in those beautifully cut clothes."

18. The Midas Touch

Goldwyn followed *The Westerner* with *The Little Foxes.* Lillian Hellman's screenplay (based on her Broadway hit) dealt with a mendacious, manipulative Southern family at the turn of the century.

Much to the amusement of Willy Wyler, Goldwyn missed the picture's heavy social message (the exploitation of cheap labor) entirely; he thought it was a kind of nasty love story. "If Goldwyn only knew what I'm doing with *Little Foxes!*" Wyler confided to friends. "He doesn't know it's an indictment of a part of industrial society that he belongs to. He is very much a part of that same family!"

Bette Davis, whom Wyler had directed at Warners in *Jezebel* and *The Letter,* was his first choice for the heartless Regina, who looks on unmoving as her husband suffers a heart attack and dies. But Davis was under contract at Warners, and Jack Warner was not inclined to do Sam Goldwyn any favors. However, Warner wanted Gary Cooper, still under contract to Goldwyn, to play Sergeant York. A trade was arranged.

The Little Foxes put such a strain on the Davis-Wyler relationship that they never worked together again. Davis insisted that although she did not want to copy Tallulah Bankhead's one-dimensional stage interpretation of Regina, the part, as written, could be played no other way. Wyler argued that a more subtle interpretation would give the character more credibility. Both were strongminded perfectionists. Irresistible force met immovable object. More than once, Davis walked off the set and Goldwyn was called down to reason with her in her dressing room—which happened to be adjacent to the glass-enclosed booth which, in those days, housed the sound boom. While Davis unloaded her complaints about Wyler's stubbornness, his inadequacy, his stupidity, to Goldwyn, the director would listen in on the sound boom. To Goldwyn's credit, he backed his director up all the way; but Davis' performance wound up satisfying neither actress nor director. Davis considered it one of the worst performances of her career.

The actress also complained about the unprecedented intensity of light on the set; she felt it made her face look pale and washed-out. The light had neither that purpose nor that effect, but was required to implement the breakthrough in cinematography that culminated Gregg Toland's years of experimentation. Toland had figured out a method of using a wide angle lens in such a way that both foreground and background could be in focus at the same time. The technique, called "deep focus," was the biggest technical advancement since Technicolor. It meant that instead of cutting from close-up to close-up in order to show one actor's action and another's *re*action, the director could work, as it were, in three dimensions. He could compose long, complicated scenes involving numbers of people, uninterrupted by cuts. Close-ups, used more sparingly, became that much more effective. The technique was also a boon to actors, who were able to build fuller, richer characterizations in long scenes than in a series of short, choppy ones.

During the hiatus that followed *The Westerner,* Goldwyn had loaned Toland to RKO, where he did his first deep-focus work on *Citizen Kane*. The effects he achieved for Orson Welles were so outstanding that Toland could have named his price at any studio in town, had he wanted to buy his way out of his contract with Goldwyn. But money wasn't what Toland was after. He told Goldwyn that he wanted to direct. When Sam, realizing that Toland was infinitely more valuable as a cameraman than he could ever be as a director, put him off with promises and maybes, Toland was disappointed—but glad to be working with Wyler again, and with Danny Mandell.

Most of the supporting players had appeared in the stage production (Teresa Wright, making her movie debut as Regina's daughter, was an exception), and the acting was uniformly good. But the tension between director and star infected the atmosphere, and everyone was relieved when shooting was completed.

The picture was one of Goldwyn's greatest critical successes, and the performance that Bette Davis considered one of her worst was praised by reviewers as one of her finest. Movie historian David Shipman calls the film "the classic example of its kind (passions in Southern mansions) and type (photographed plays)." *The Little Foxes* was one of the top grossers of 1941.

Goldwyn's other 1941 release, also a moneymaker, was *Ball of Fire*. The original story, by Billy Wilder and Thomas Monroe, was brought to Goldwyn's attention as a vehicle for Gary Cooper. Sam liked the idea, but he wanted Billy Wilder and his frequent collaborator, Charlie Brackett, to write the screenplay. Brackett and Wilder were under contract to Paramount, where William Dozier was then story editor. Goldwyn called Dozier on the phone, saying, "Bill, you and I should start doing each other favors."

"Fine," said Dozier. "I'd like that very much."

"Let's start by you doing me one. I want to borrow Brackett and Wilder."

Brackett and Wilder were like gold nuggets at Paramount, but Goldwyn had set his mind on getting them. To that end, he put pressure on Dozier, on Dozier's boss and on Dozier's boss's boss, until he wore them down and Brackett and Wilder wound up working for Goldwyn for more than three months.

Ball of Fire was a comedy based on character (the best kind). The humor stemmed from the unlikely juxtaposition of a square, scholarly professor (Cooper) with a burlesque queen. He is compiling a dictionary of American slang, and tries to enlist her as a research assistant. Goldwyn wanted Ginger

Rogers to play the stripper (Sugarbush O'Shea), but Rogers, who had just won an Academy Award for her performance in *Kitty Foyle,* sent word to Goldwyn that henceforth she would play only ladies. Sam's high-decibel response, delivered to Rogers' agent, was, "You tell Ginger Rogers for me that ladies stink up the place!" Sugarbush was played by Barbara Stanwyck. *Life* commended Goldwyn for *Ball of Fire,* calling it "a surefire holiday delight." It was December, 1941.

It was easy to rationalize the prosperity of the war years as a reward for patriotism. In a time of crisis, it was the industry's *duty* to keep the populace entertained! It was easy, too, to ignore the implications of the government's antitrust suit against the block-booking practiced by the major studios. Years of legal delays would ensue before the action revolutionized the basic structure of the industry.

Another government action did come to a head in 1941: Joe Schenck, head of Twentieth Century-Fox and one of Goldwyn's oldest friends, was convicted of income tax evasion and perjury (he had bribed some union racketeers) and went to jail. Goldwyn, who always had a torrent of crocodile tears on tap, shed real tears when he got the news about Schenck. One of his executives walked into his office that morning and found Sam with his head down on the desk, sobbing, "It's terrible. It'll ruin him. It'll kill him." The embarrassed executive excused himself, feeling that "Whether Schenck was guilty or innocent, I think Goldwyn was deeply humiliated for the early Hollywood." The Schenck case foreshadowed Hollywood's long-postponed confrontation with reality. But that showdown was still years away—and nobody was thinking very far ahead.

Goldwyn was preoccupied with his only release of 1942, *The Pride of the Yankees.* The project had begun as a token of Niven Busch's affection for Teresa Wright, whom he was dating (and later married). Busch saw the picture as a perfect vehicle for Teresa and Gary Cooper, and told Goldwyn, "You ought to make a picture about the life of Lou Gehrig."

"Who is Lou Gehrig?"

Busch explained that Gehrig was a famous ballplayer who had recently died. "I'm not gonna make any pictures about ballplayers," said Sam, who had never attended a ball game in his life. "If people want to see ball playing, they go to the ball park!"

"But Sam," Busch protested, "he wasn't just any ballplayer! He was a hero to the young generation of kids today. At the top of his career he got an incurable disease and he died of it, and he died very bravely. His life was sort of an inspiration to people!"

"Well," said Goldwyn with finality, "he was a ballplayer. I don't make pictures about ballplayers."

Busch adopted another strategy. "I got the newsreels of Gehrig Day—the day the ball fans and the Yankees said farewell to him at Yankee Stadium. He still had several months to live, but he'd lost a lot of weight, and he was on his way out. Gehrig made this strange, touching speech, where he said, 'I think I'm the luckiest guy on the face of the earth.' It was a very moving scene.

"We had the newsreels of the members of the team lined up, and the fans—it was absolute capacity—and Lou Gehrig saying good-bye. We ran the film, and when we turned the lights on, Sam was crying. He said, 'Run 'em again.' So we ran 'em again. Then he said, 'Let's go back to the office.' He called his New York representative, James Mulvey, and he said, 'Get the rights to the Gehrig story!' "

Goldwyn's publicists had a field day with *Pride of the Yankees.* One release had it that Cooper was cast only after an exhaustive talent search, and that four baseball fanatics—Eddie Albert, William Gargan, Dennis Morgan and George Tobias—had offered to play in the film just for the glory. The truth was that Cooper was the only actor ever considered for the role—despite the fact that Coop, who had played rugby and cricket during his school days in England, had never played baseball and knew almost as little about the game as Goldwyn.

With Wyler in the Air Force and Toland in the Navy, Goldwyn hired cameraman Rudolph Maté and director Sam Wood. The two Sams got along no better on *Yankees* than they had on *Raffles;* if anything, the communication gap between them had widened. Wood was a competent but autocratic director—gruff and alternately opinionated and ambiguous. No compensating qualities instilled loyalty, or even liking, among the crew. The Gehrig Day sequence—the climax of the picture—was salvaged by Danny Mandell in the cutting room. "Sam Wood tried to add things that never happened, to make it more dramatic. How could you make a thing like that more dramatic? I got all the newsreels that I could on Gehrig Day, and I cut the whole thing just the way it was in the newsreel, with the exception that they never showed the mother and father. I had establishing shots of the band marching around, the lineup of the players and all that, which I used. And I inserted closeups of Cooper making the speech, just as it was in the newsreel. There couldn't be anything more dramatic than that."

Mandell deserves much of the credit for the authenticity of the baseball scenes. The script called for a montage, covering a three-year period, showing Gehrig's development from a rookie into a polished player. Mandell was given some film showing "a couple of old baseball players down in the old Washington Park, and one was just batting a ball to another guy, who was supposed to be Lou Gehrig. He'd field the ball and throw it back again, and that was it! So I took the film up to the projection room, and I asked Mr. Goldwyn to come and look at it. I said, 'I'm supposed to make out of this Lou Gehrig learning to be a polished ball player!?'

"Goldwyn called Sam Wood and the production designer, Bill Menzies, and raised hell about it. They admitted there wasn't enough there, but they said, 'What can you do with the guy?" meaning Cooper. 'He's not a ballplayer! Besides, he's right handed!' Gehrig was a southpaw.

"I said, 'Well, put the letters on his shirt backwards, and the number backwards, and when he stands up at the plate right-handed, we reverse all the film. We'll have him run to third base instead of first base.' Then we covered it by showing a double running like hell and sliding into a base, and cut to a closeup of Cooper getting up. I don't remember all the things I told 'em to do, but it turned out very well.

"Remember the scene during the ball game where Gehrig tells the manager, 'I can't make it, you'd better put somebody in for me'? We've already seen the scene where he's wrestling around with his wife. We saw the scene in the training camp, where a ball is thrown at him too close and in trying to get away, he almost falls down. And somebody says, 'What's the matter with Lou?' There was also the scene where he comes home with the garland of flowers and he says, 'They were great to me. I struck out every time.' But Wood went overboard, making the point. He put in a montage of people saying, 'What's the matter with Gehrig?'—even a dentist saying, 'There must be something wrong with his teeth!' If you overdo that stuff, the end of the scene is very anticlimactic. So I took it out. Sam Wood was very angry, but Goldwyn backed me up.

"I didn't tell you all that to show you how clever I was," adds Danny Mandell—a genuinely modest man.

The Pride of the Yankees was mawkish, sentimental, juvenile and just plain corny; it even included a syrupy arrangement (lots of violins) of Sam's favorite song, "Always." It was perfect, in other words, for the mentality of its day—a mentality we now find it fashionable to ridicule for its naïveté. We've come a long way since then, we say, as we line up for *Death Wish . . . Love Story . . . Deep Throat.*

Process Shot

The Malibu Colony was formed in the late twenties by a handful of picture people seeking a weekend retreat at the seashore. In contrast to the elaborate Santa Monica beach homes like Goldwyn's, built for elegant entertaining, the Malibu scene was—well, tacky. The mile-long stretch of private beach contained around sixty small, ramshackle bungalows no more than six feet apart. The crowding, the thin walls and the inescapable smell of mildew made it the world's most exclusive slum. But if one had no privacy from one's neighbors, one was securely protected from the prying public by walls, alarm systems and a twenty-four-hour guard at the gate.

There was a great sense of camaraderie and community among the original residents of the Colony. Nobody lived there all year round, but every Sunday was one big open house; every door was open, and the booze flowed as freely as the tide. These Colony pioneers included Warner Baxter, John Gilbert, Clara Bow, Barbara Stanwyck, Ronald Colman, Dolores del Rio, Constance Bennett, Corinne Griffith and director David Butler, who still lives in the same Colony cottage—now worth *one hundred times* its original purchase price of $2,000.

Butler is a large, heavy man who carries his weight and his years with good grace. He directed his first picture, a silent called *High School Hero,* at Fox, in 1928. In the thirties, he directed Shirley Temple and Will Rogers and the Hope-Crosby-Lamour *Road* pictures—so when Goldwyn borrowed Hope from

Paramount in 1943 for two comedies (*They Got Me Covered* and *The Princess and the Pirate*), Dave Butler was a natural choice to direct.

The Goldwyn-Butler relationship was strictly business. "We never got close. Hope used to kid him, and he used to *roar* at everything Hope said. He'd say, 'Isn't this a pretty sky?' and Goldwyn would laugh sincerely! Hope would say to me, 'What the hell is he laughing at?' Every time he'd *see* Hope, he'd start to laugh. 'Isn't he a funny man!' he'd say to me.

"The thing about Goldwyn, especially with Hope—he'd have three different teams writing a story. But he'd tell them, 'Don't say! Nobody knows!' Then he'd pick out this and pick out that, he'd get it together like crazy quilt! He would bring a writer in and say, 'See what you can do with this story.' Well, naturally, the writer would fix something—whether it needed it or not. He would never say it was all right!

"He had his foot in everything. You knew you were working for Goldwyn when you worked for him. He came down every morning and looked around, talked to me, saw every set. When we were working on the story preparing *The Princess and the Pirate,* Goldwyn called me in. He wanted to add a gag at the end of a picture Danny Kaye had just finished. He said, 'You're gonna do the next picture with Hope anyway, so I'll just send you down a script, it'll probably take you half an hour to do it. Just one gag.' Well, it turned out to be five days work! The toughest days you ever saw in your life! I had every stunt man in Los Angeles, and a double for Danny Kaye. The whole thing musta run a reel! Goldwyn never said thank you, never said he liked the stuff. That's the way he was. No pay, nothing! When you do that *now,* you *have* to get paid for those days. Not even a thank you. I don't think he thought he *had* to thank you. As long as I was working for Sam Goldwyn, he thought that if he told me to clean out that grate over there, I should do it! Warner, he would tell you sometimes, 'That was great! I liked it!' Never Goldwyn. Just, 'Hello, Butler.'

"On the other hand, if he wanted something, he didn't care what it cost. In *They Got Me Covered,* we had a café scene with about one hundred fifty extras. Dorothy Lamour and Hope were supposed to go into the café and sit down at a table, and the maitre d' came up to them, seated them, and they ordered drinks. We worked about two days in the café. Halfway through the second day, I got a call to go up and see Mr. Goldwyn. He says, 'You'll have to shoot all that stuff over.'

" 'Why? What happened? Didn't you like it?'

" 'Oh, yes. The scenes were fine. But I *hate* that maitre d'!'

"He was the fella that was the maitre d' at Santa Anita at the time. A real maitre d'! He was in every scene, in the back! I said, 'But we'll have to shoot it all over again, with all those people!'

" 'I don't care what it costs—shoot it over! I can't stand to look at that man!' Goldwyn never said *why* he hated him. He just didn't like his face! It cost him about fifteen thousand dollars. That's the way he was.

"I never had any real trouble with him. He was very nice. They say he raved like hell, didn't he? I've been very fortunate. I never had any trouble with any producer. *Because I made pictures that made money.* I didn't make great big artistic triumphs, but they all made money. I made some good ones—*San Antonio, Calamity Jane*—but the rest of 'em were like *Tea for Two* or *Walking Down Main Street.* They bought a whole list of songs, and then they made pictures about 'em. *On Moonlight Bay. By the Light of the Silvery Moon.* My pictures never ran overtime, the cost was all right, and they made money. That's why I worked for so many years. When it was my time to retire, I had to retire. But I may produce a picture in England, if they can raise the financing."

A widower, Butler lives alone; a cleaning woman comes in once a week to dust the 1930 rattan furniture, the well-stocked bar, the books and the scripts that cover every horizontal surface. What cards were to Goldwyn, horseracing is to Butler; he can be found at Hollywood Park, hanging out with retired and semiretired cronies (Mervyn LeRoy is President of the Turf Club) almost any day of the season.

The changes the Colony has gone through since Butler moved there parallel those of the industry. First came the innocent pleasure-seekers, then the status-seeking parvenus and, finally, the present generation of (primarily) Establishment wealth, for whom Colony property is more investment than home. The last lot of damp Colony sand sold in 1973 for $161,000. Rentals go these days for $2500 a month. Privately, residents express concern that liberalized public access laws may soon make academic the signs reading NO TRESPASSING ABOVE THE MEAN HIGH TIDE LINE.

Thanks to the Santa Monica Freeway and the widening of Pacific Coast Highway, the Colony, once considered remote, is now just a forty-five minute drive from town. Dave Butler commutes—but not to the studios. He hangs out at the race tracks, the prizefights, the ballpark. If the transition from the center of the action to spectator status causes him pain, he hides it well; he projects an unflappable image of ingenuous good will. With obvious pride, he showed me the plaque designating him a "Champion of Champions Director (All Time)". "That means I've made the greatest number of moneymaking pictures," he explained. "I'm still number one." And added, more to himself than to me, "Wish I'd die number one."

It's unlikely that Goldwyn knew, when he signed Ernest Fegte to a two-year contract, that the art director had dated Frances Howard practically up to the eve of her wedding. In 1943, Fegte had just won an Oscar for *Frenchman's Creek*, which had something to do with pirates, so Goldwyn assigned him to *The Princess and the Pirate.*

In the purple-and-gold living room of his apartment, adjacent to the Hollywood Freeway (exhaust fumes obscure the view), Fegte speaks with the authority of fifty-five years in the business.

"I knew Goldwyn had a reputation for being tough, but I always wanted a tough producer. It was a challenge for me. He offered me almost exactly double what I had been getting at Paramount. Naturally, I took the job."

Fegte is an open, casual man who laughs a lot. His informality apparently made Goldwyn uneasy and, very quickly, things began to go sour. "I read the script and broke it down, did the things than an art director does before a movie starts. I saw Goldwyn several times to ask questions, to find out what was in his mind, and I kept calling him Sam all the time. I believe in being on a first name basis with people. I get along much better that way than with that Mister stuff.

"The studio business manager was a man who was formerly an accountant. Marvin Ezell. A very pompous guy, and a typical accountant, believe me. Didn't know anything about art. Money was his middle name. That was Marvin. And Marvin always used to tug at his lapels, very nervous like, and adjust his glasses. Maybe he had a twitch, I don't remember, but that's the type. So after one of these meetings with Goldwyn—I'd been there two or three weeks by then—Marvin called me into his office and he said to me, 'You know, you mustn't call Mr. Goldwyn Sam. He likes to be called Mr. Goldwyn.' And that was the rupture of my intimate association with Goldwyn. Now I had to call the man Mr. Goldwyn. And I want to tell you something, it is like an obstacle in the road that shouldn't be there. This Mister stuff."

And what had Goldwyn called Fegte? "Faggoty. He called me Faggoty. If he wanted me in his office, he'd tell his secretary, 'Get me that Faggoty!'

"He was really a peculiar guy. Very irascible. On *The Princess and the Pirate,* there was a scene with Walter Brennan, on the pirate ship. The day after they shot it, I get a call to my office—please come up to see Mr. Goldwyn. *That was always horrible,* because you knew something was wrong and you were in for some kind of a battle, Lord knows what. I went up and he said, 'Faggoty, let's go see the film. Something is wrong. I think the set is wrong.'

"We looked at the film, and I didn't see anything wrong with it. I said, "It looks pretty good to me, Mr. Goldwyn.'

" 'Well, it's not right.' He called the photographer, Vic Milner, into the projection room, showed him the same film and said, 'Something's wrong. I think it must be the photography.' *He could never pinpoint what was bothering him!* He would call the head of every department into his office—separately, not together!—and give 'em the same spiel and say It's not right. He was very positive that something was wrong. It turned out that he didn't like Walter Brennan's work in the scene. I think Dave Butler did a couple extra close-ups, and he was happy.

"If I had kept calling him Sam, I woulda got along with him swell. It so happened, I *didn't* get along well with Sam. This is typical: When *Princess and the Pirate* was in preparation, he called this old friend of his from New York, a muralist. Unbeknownst to me, he called him in and commissioned some drawings for the picture. He did that all the time! He would change with the wind—you never knew what would happen next! That's why, when you got a message to go see Mr. Goldwyn, you always knew it was trouble. *Always* trouble. Never anything nice. But I wanted a tough producer. Well, I got one. But it was so typical of Goldwyn to get outside help in the middle of the production of a movie.

"Mac Capps, Goldwyn's son-in-law, was my assistant. You would call him almost Mister Milquetoast, but he's a very nice man. Mac wasn't a designer, but he was a great help to me. Because when you move into a new studio, you don't know the people, you don't know what to expect. You have to play it by ear for awhile. When the picture was finished, I wanted to give Mac special screen credit. Goldwyn couldn't figure that out at all. 'Why give Mac Capps the credit! *You* did the sets!' I said, 'Because he deserves it! He was my right-hand man, he helped get things together, and I think it's worth a mention on the screen.' He finally did give him credit. But their relationship was nil. There was no relationship, none whatever. He worked for him, but he never saw him.

"One day Mr. Goldwyn hurt his finger, he had a little scratch or something, and I saw him walking down the steps from his balcony. He says, 'Say, Faggoty, do you know where the First Aid place is?' Imagine! Here's the man who owns the studio, and he doesn't know where the First Aid place is! I had to take him by the hand, so to speak. That's typical. He never knew what stage was where, what the number of the stages were, where the company was shooting. For a man who had owned the studio quite a long time, he really didn't know his way around!"

Fegte's second assignment for Goldwyn was *Wonder Man,* a Danny Kaye comedy directed by Lucky Humberstone. One of the key sets was a cabaret where Danny Kaye performed. Fegte designed a set "painted all titty pink, with white

Anna Sten

William Wyler and Greg Toland, *c.* 1938

King Vidor
when he directed *Dead End,* 1936

Walter Brennan, *c.* 1940

Dana Andrews, *c.* 1943

Farley Granger

1940 farewell party for Reeves Espy, during shooting of *Ball of Fire*. In Sam's private dining room. L to R: Publicist Bill Hebert, Niven Busch, Greg Toland, Gary Cooper, Espy, Goldwyn, Marvin Ezell, Howard Hawks, Sam Goldwyn Jr., Irving Sindler

Danny Kaye and Sylvia Fine

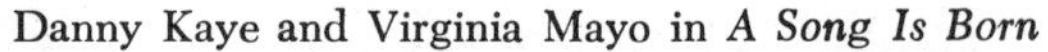

Danny Kaye and Virginia Mayo in *A Song Is Born*

Producer Samuel Goldwyn, with Thalberg Award and Best Picture Award (1947).
The Best Moment of The Best Years.

Sam and Frances on their twenty-fifth anniversary, 1950
International News Photo

railings and white accoutrements, white tablecloths—a simple, plain set. Now, when you design a set, there must be some accent somewhere. Otherwise, you haven't got anything. In this case, I got in touch with Tony Duquette. He was in the Army, down at Fort MacArthur. He had worked for me before. He would dip cloth, laces, fabrics into plaster and drape them. The plaster would harden and it became a piece of statuary.

"In spite of being in the Army, he made sketches. I took the sketches to Mr. Goldwyn. I said, 'This Tony Duquette is a fabulous character. A creator of the first order. You would be very proud of his work.' I had six statues, seven feet high, on pedestals, to be placed along the dance floor at intervals, three on each side. And the only thing against this titty pink background were the white rococo figures.

"Goldwyn put his John Hancock under the sketches, okayed them, was willing to pay six hundred dollars each for 'em. Came the day of delivery. It was lunchtime. They put them on Stage 5, on the floor, and left them there uncovered.

"As the company drifted in from lunch, they couldn't help but pass by and see these figures lying on the floor. Like fifteen minutes later, I get a call from Mr. Goldwyn. 'Vat's dis, Faggoty, with dose figgers? Meet me on Stage 5!'

"Now I knew there was gonna be trouble. I met him on Stage 5, the figures still lying on the floor, not even in an upright position. Goldwyn threw his arms in the direction of the figures and he says, 'I can't use dat!'

" 'Why, Mr. Goldwyn? You okayed the sketches. Let me put them in the set, you can look at 'em, and if you don't like 'em, we'll take 'em out. But you okayed the sketches, don't forget! This man is very much wanted—he's a protégé of Mary Pickford!' I thought I'd throw some names around. And Duquette *was* a protégé of Pickford at the time, but that didn't make any impression. He says, 'No, I don't vant 'em.'

"I said, 'But the whole set is based on these things!'

" 'No,' he says. 'I don't vant em!'

He never did see the figures in an upright position. What had happened is, a little troublemaker, a scriptgirl of Humberstone's, had seen them there and had told Humberstone, 'You better tell Goldwyn about this because I don't think this is the kind of thing we should have in the movie' What does she know? A lousy little scriptgirl, and a troublemaker to boot.

"Goldwyn says, 'See, Faggoty? Dot is de vaste in Hollyvood. Dot is de vaste!' I said, 'Mr. Goldwyn, it's *you* who's doing the waste!' He says, 'Dot is de vaste! I can't use dem! Just throwing money out of de vindow!' He was mad!

"We were supposed to shoot the next morning. You have no idea what a poor art director goes through to make the schedule be realized for the next morning's shoot. Impossible! The whole set was built around these magnificent stylized figures. I went through some very bad hours. The whole set built, ready to go, dressed—but with the figures missing. What do you do? How do you make it possible for them to shoot?

"I had a brilliant idea, which I grabbed at in desperation. I went to Irving Sindler, the prop man, and I said, 'Go out and get me those big white flowers with the long stems that bloom early in the spring.' He came back with a whole flock of those things. We found six vases that matched, and that took care of the shoot for the next morning. It was *nothing* like what I had planned, but in a pinch, it did the trick."

Fegte's story has an epilogue. "I knew that Goldwyn was stuck for thirty-six hundred dollars—not a small amount. That's like seven thousand today. I called up an old friend of mine, Cedric Gibbons at MGM, and I told him, 'Tony Duquette made these figures for me, which would be fabulous for one of your musical numbers. Goldwyn paid for these magnificent figures—seven feet high, on pedestals, *magnifique,* fabulous, unusual, unique, all those adjectives—thirty-six hundred dollars. Do you think you can use them? Can I sell them to you for $3200?'

" 'Sold!" Gibbons said.

"Elated, I went to Marvin Ezell, the money man. The CPA. I said, 'Marvin, I think I did a good job for you and for Mr. Goldwyn. I sold the figures to Gibbons at MGM.' No reaction whatever. Blank face. I expected 'Thank you so much! What a relief!' *Some* sort of reaction from Marvin. But nothing. Never a thank you for anything. Never a bonus. Never a party, or gifts for the crew. In Hollywood, that's very unusual."

Thirty years after *Wonder Man,* Fegte still steams up

when he recalls Goldwyn's tactics. The picture ended with a big musical number, for which Fegte did a number of sketches. "But I couldn't sell a one of 'em to Goldwyn. Not a one. I had practically given up. I didn't know what I could do to please the old man. So what did he do? Unbeknownst to me, he engaged a man, Lionel Banks, who happened at the time to be between movies. Lionel Banks moved in, and one morning I came to the studio and saw a completely different set! He had done it overnight! He'd done a clever job, I must say. But this is how Goldwyn worked. It didn't faze him in the least to hire somebody else, out of the blue. He didn't care how I felt about it!"

After *Wonder Man,* Goldwyn loaned Fegte to René Clair for *And Then There Were None.* "I found out later that Goldwyn got twice my salary from René Clair. It was not unusual, when you loaned out *stars,* or *directors,* to charge what the traffic would bear. But it *was* unusual for a producer to go all the way down to an *art director,* and make money on *him.* But Goldwyn would. Not that I blame him. After that, he loaned me to Wes Ruggles, who had to pay *three* times my salary. And after that, I said, 'You know, Sam—Mr. Goldwyn—I don't care if we terminate our contract right now.' He said Okay, fine. I was so happy when he relieved me of that contract!

"With Goldwyn, you never felt safe. Always the sword of Damocles hanging over your head. I spent at least two years there. I was very glad to leave. I was always in an uproar inside, like I'm on a teeter-totter, gonna fall down. But that damn Mr. Goldwyn stuff—that is what killed my whole association with him!"

19. The North Star

When a Goldwyn production turned out well, it was always because the director—usually Willy Wyler—seized artistic control of the picture and hung on like a bulldog. *The North Star* was a classic example of what happened in the absence of that authority. Everyone involved was at cross purposes, and the picture reflected the chaos from which it came.

The North Star was one of a half-dozen wartime films celebrating the courage and loveable character of our Russian allies. Lillian Hellman, author of the original screenplay, meticulously researched the manners and customs of the Russian peasantry in peace and in war; she even tried, in the dialogue, to approximate their idiom. But the idiom died in translation, and so did the characters. Her story of the heroic villagers reacting to the invading Nazis (they practically defeated them with their bare hands) was heavy-handed, one-dimensional propaganda. The saving grace of the screenplay was its simplicity, but even that was lost in the process of filming.

Hellman calls the picture a sentimental mess, and blames the producer, the actors and the director, Lewis Milestone. But it was Hellman who persuaded Milestone to take the assignment. "I never wanted to get involved with Goldwyn," Milestone told me. "I'd known him for a long time, and I knew everybody who worked for him. I had plenty of warning. But Lillian is a very good writer, and the background they selected was a Russian thing (Milestone is Russian); the combination intrigued me and I said Yes. That was one time I shoulda said No. As it turned out, Lillian knew *nothing* about Russia—especially the villages!"

Milestone has directed some distinguished war movies, including *All Quiet on the Western Front,* but *The North Star* resisted his best efforts to assume control. "Goldwyn's reputation was that he ate directors for breakfast. When you went in the gate, you were searched to see if there was a written word on you. Directors direct, actors act; the roles were too rigidly defined. What if you have an idea? You tell it to the writer! But Lillian was *very* difficult to work with, and Goldwyn was too dictatorial. You had to do it his way! He was like a seasoned politician. He didn't take anything seriously. When it's finished, the whole thing is forgotten. If you feel bruised or wounded, that's up to you. *He* never feels bruised or wounded. With him, it's all in a day's work. *Nobody* could work with him, except Willy."

That was true. Only Wyler could—or would, for the sake of getting what he wanted on the screen—put up with games such as the one Goldwyn played with Milestone one afternoon. A favorite, and brutally effective, tactic of Sam's was to humiliate one employee in front of another. This time, he called Danny Mandell, saying, "I'm gonna have Milestone come into my office after he finishes shooting today, and I want you to *be* there." When Milestone arrived, a few minutes after Mandell, Goldwyn started yelling about the director's having changed a line in the script. When Milestone tried to reply, Goldwyn yelled louder, pounded the desk and turned purple.

Milestone controlled himself as long as he could, but was finally driven to ask, "If my work is so terrible, why don't you fire me?"

"No!" shouted Goldwyn. "I won't fire you!"

"Go ahead! Fire me! I'm sick and tired of this!"

"NO! I WON'T, AND THAT'S FINAL!"

Shaking with rage, Milestone turned and walked out. As the thoroughly uncomfortable Mandell got up to follow him, he noticed Goldwyn's complexion rapidly returning to its normal color. "I told him, didn't I?" he said, grinning broadly. And laughed.

Milestone saw the picture as a fairy tale about "a never-never land, where the people work very hard but seem to be happy with their lives. Then an intruder comes in and tries to take their never-never land away from them. They fight like mad, and they won't let him do it." For a fairy tale, it was extraordinarily grim. The most shocking scene showed the Nazis taking blood from Russian children for transfusion to wounded soldiers. The film ends with Anne Baxter * delivering these improbable lines: "Wars do not leave people the same. All people will learn that and come to see that wars do not have to be. They will make this the last one, a free world for all men. The earth belongs to us, the people, if we fight for it. And we will fight for it."

That the simple story of simple villagers became a sprawling, sentimental spectacle was due in large part to the production designer, William Cameron Menzies. Menzies was one of the most prestigious art directors in the business; he had worked for Goldwyn in the Colman days, and had won an Oscar for *Gone With the Wind.* A self-proclaimed genius, Menzies set out to make *The North Star* a Russian *Gone With the Wind,* with the climactic burning of the village eclipsing the burning of Atlanta in the Selznick film. He designed a magnificent village that covered the entire ten-acre back lot of the studio, previously the site of the English village in *Wuthering Heights,* the tropical village in *Hurricane,* the Philippine village in *The Real Glory.* Despite the government's wartime ceiling of $5,000 for building materials for any movie, the cost of the labor—including the transplantation of hundreds of trees—brought the cost of the village to $260,000. The village, which was *called* North Star, was complete with thatched-roof cottages, hospital, school, radio station, railroad station, farm administration buildings—everything that might have been found in a real Russian village, including the livestock. Irving Sindler even secured authentic props from Los Angeles' Russian colony.

At the climax of the picture, when the Germans invade

* Baxter was an eleventh-hour replacement for Teresa Wright, who learned, after her costumes had been made, that she was pregnant and could not play the part. This cost Goldwyn money, and caused him to tell Niven Busch, then married to Teresa, "Niven! When you were screwing Teresa, you were also screwing me!"

in force, the peasant population scorches the earth before fleeing. The entire set was leveled by fires so fierce that fifty of the extras riding in the wagons that careened through the flames suffered minor injuries, and one of the booby trap explosions accidentally burned out the roof of a sound stage.

The picture was hyped as the first major attempt by a major United States producer to deal with the invasion of Russia, but the critics did not come in on cue. After the lavish New York premiere, Goldwyn was shocked by a frontal attack by the violently anti-Soviet Hearst press. The New York *Mirror* headlined its review, "Unadulterated Soviet Propaganda"; its anonymous reviewer called the picture "Pure bolshevist propaganda, as raw as Warner Brothers' *Mission to Moscow,* and even more insidious. Had Stalin paid for the making of this film, it could not have been more offensive to American audiences, which are willing to listen to all sides of all controversies, but have revealed a sharp distaste for deliberate attempts to poison their free minds with inspired pressure, presented in the guise of entertainment." Lillian Hellman was called "a partisan pleader for Communist causes." The Hearst *Journal* went the *Mirror* one better by suggesting that the film was not only Red, but also *Nazi* propaganda.

In Hearst's *Los Angeles Examiner,* Neil Rau wrote: "It is hard for this reviewer to understand why Mr. Goldwyn squandered a cold $2,000,000 in the making of *North Star.* It is a picture that should never have been made—especially by an American presumably as patriotic as Samuel Goldwyn." Rau predicted that the picture "should get more Communist converts among unthinking, sophomoric minds than the late Emma Goldman tried to snare before her deportation," and warned against the danger that "someone may take the picture's musical comedy version of life in the Soviet Union before the Nazi invasion as the real thing." Rau concluded by asking, "Why not American propaganda?"

On November 8, *Variety* published this story, headlined "Mr. Goldwyn Comments":

> In discussing his current production, "The North Star," Samuel Goldwyn draws a parallel between the Russian and the American people and declares that Americans sold Russia

> short because the Hollywood screen had never presented, in entertainment form, a true picture of contemporary Russia, while Soviet films had only a limited audience because they were dismissed as "arty" or "propaganda." Thus, he avows, the American masses were ignorant of the true life of the people of that country.
>
> "The more we delved into research for the picture, the more amazing it became that Americans had never previously been educated to their kinship with the Russian people," he says. "Russia and America and the peoples of the two countries are alike in many ways. Both are peace-loving; both love their land. The pioneering in Russia, as its vast resources were opened to development by the people, resembles the development of our own West. In telling the story of the Russian people we can't help but feel that we are telling the story of a people who think and act as do Americans.
>
> "Walter Brennan, who plays the homespun, earthy philosopher, has his counterpart in every American town. Sometimes he's the barber, sometimes the station agent, perhaps the town tinker. Walter Huston, the village scientist, is the country doctor known to every American. Anne Baxter and Farley Granger, the romantic leads, represent the ambitious boy and girl who embody the future of every free nation. Jane Withers, Ann Harding, Dana Andrews, Esther Dale, wearing Russian costumes, appear in scenes representing Russia, but their American counterparts are readily recognized."
>
> As in the several other pictures currently being produced in Hollywood of Russia at war, politics is not involved in this film.

The controversy did Goldwyn no harm at the box office, but the picture never did earn back its cost, and it was one of the first films Goldwyn sold to television. For that purpose, the title was changed to *Armored Attack* and the optimistic ending was scrapped in favor of a shot of a military parade in Red Square, with a voice ponderously explaining that although the Russians were once our allies, "They have not kept their promise!"

20. *Enter Danny Kaye*

While *The North Star* was falling, Danny Kaye's star was rising. When Goldwyn first saw him (on Broadway, starring in *Lady in the Dark*), the comedian had already paid eleven hard years' worth of dues on the Borscht circuit, in nightclubs, wherever he could scrounge a job. His name meant nothing to the moviegoing public—but neither, Goldwyn reasoned, had Eddie Cantor's, until *Whoopee* was filmed. Hoping for another golden harvest such as Cantor had provided, Goldwyn brought Danny Kaye and his wife, Sylvia Fine, who wrote his special material, to Hollywood in 1943. He agreed to pay the unknown comic nearly half a million dollars for four pictures. It was his biggest gamble since Anna Sten.

He already had the property for the first picture: *Up in Arms,* a comedy about the adventures of a hypochondriacal elevator operator who is drafted. The insubstantial story was a springboard from which Danny launched two of his most famous routines: "Melody in 4F," an expanded version of a number about a draftee (with which he'd stopped a Broadway revue), and "The Lobby Song," written for the picture by Sylvia Fine and Max Liebman (who later wrote Sid Caesar's best material). "The Lobby Song" told the story, in rapidly increasing tempo, of an imaginary motion picture; to this day, it probably remains the number with which Danny Kaye is most closely associated. Both "The Lobby Song" and "Melody in 4F" gave Danny the opportunity to display his unique "riddle-de-biddle-de-reep" scat-singing and his brilliantly pantomimed, zany delivery. In addition, his warmth and vulnerability, qualities missing in the slicker style of a Cantor or a Hope, came across strongly on the screen. Although Dinah Shore and Dana Andrews appeared in supporting roles, there was no question but that Danny, with the help of director Elliott Nugent, carried the weight of the picture and made it work.

Danny Kaye was as warm, lovable and entertaining offstage as on. Everybody at the studio was crazy about him—while his wife, Sylvia, drove everybody crazy. Their roles were clearly defined. He was the hero. She was the heavy, and took the heat. When Danny was unhappy with a line of dialogue or a costume or a fellow actor or the way a scene was lit, it was Sylvia who protested, finagled and fought until the changes Danny wanted were made. She had an infallible sense of what made him look good and what made him look bad, and she was as vigilant as any stage mother in looking out for his interests. Her methods were often tactless and won her few friends, but her efforts contributed immeasurably to the rise of her husband's career.

Lucky Humberstone directed Danny's second picture: *Wonder Man,* costarring Vera-Ellen, in *her* first film, and Virginia Mayo, in her third. Virginia Mayo was another manifestation of Goldwyn's Sten syndrome. Like Anna, Mayo was blonde with a long, graceful neck, and somewhat resembled the young Frances Howard. Goldwyn had spotted her in a vaudeville act at Billy Rose's Diamond Horseshoe. The act had consisted of two men in a horse costume, dancing and doing tricks. Virginia's brother-in-law was the back end and Virginia (who was known as the horse's ass's sister-in-law) played the trainer and cracked the whip. She had no lines at all, but terrific legs. On that basis, Goldwyn determined to make her a star.

Virginia Mayo was Goldwyn's first choice for the Dinah Shore part in *Up In Arms.* Although the idea was violently opposed by nearly everybody on the lot, Goldwyn engaged a top acting coach to work with her, and commissioned Adrian to design costumes especially for her, at a cost of several thousand dollars apiece. He made screen test after screen test of her, at a cost of at least $35,000 apiece. Finally, he was persuaded that casting *two* unknowns in the picture would be too risky. Instead, Mayo played a Goldwyn Girl, after which Sam cast her in the undemanding role of the princess in Bob Hope's *The Princess and the Pirate.* Then came *Wonder Man,* another thin story and another showcase for Danny Kaye who, this time, played twins. If one Danny Kaye had been good, Goldwyn figured, two Danny Kayes would be better. As was customary with dual parts, the two Kaye characters were diametrically different. One was an introverted bookworm, the other an extroverted entertainer. The highlight of the picture was, again, Sylvia Fine's special material: a burlesqued operatic aria called "Ochi Chornya."

On the first day of rehearsal, Danny was to run up a ramp and jump into a drum. Although the drum was padded, he landed wrong and broke his leg, thus setting the picture's starting date back fifteen weeks—during which Goldwyn threw out $100,000 worth of sets and replaced the art director with Ernest Fegte. Goldwyn was famous for this sort of flamboyant gesture, which was invariably cited as proof of his desire for perfection. What it really indicated was his inability to visualize anything until he saw it. When Humberstone decided, for example, that a nightclub set was unusable ("I thought I was getting an intimate, compact set. Instead, I got the Coliseum!"), he got his point across to Goldwyn by hiring four hundred dress extras and positioning them on the set. Sam had seen and approved the sketches, but without grasping what they represented. When he saw the constructed set, he said, "They lied to me!" meaning, presumably, his art department.

Lucky Humberstone was jealous of Sylvia's influence on Danny, and barred her from the set—only to realize, belatedly, how dependent Danny was on her judgment and moral support. He declared a temporary truce and invited her to help with the "Ochi Chornya" number, but their relationship remained strained. Goldwyn was not available to mediate; he was in Reno, up in arms over *Up in Arms.*

When *Up in Arms* was released, in the summer of 1944, Goldwyn had offered it to the theater chain that owned all five of Reno's movie theaters. It was a percentage-of-the-gross deal, which would have been highly profitable to Goldwyn. When the syndicate countered with an arrangement that would have been more favorable to its interests, Goldwyn launched a barrage of press releases pleading the case of the independent producer who, he claimed, was being throttled by monopolistic major producing companies and theater chains which, between them, controlled most of the theaters in the country.

To dramatize his grievance, Goldwyn sent his representatives to Reno. They rented a ballroom adjacent to the railroad tracks and announced that the film would be shown there; but fire department officials informed them that their portable projection booth violated the fire laws. Their next strategy was to rent a parking lot, which they planned to surround with a ten-foot canvas fence. This, they were regretfully informed, would violate the building laws.

Undeterred, the Goldwyn forces built a platform outside the ballroom, intending to get around the fire laws by projecting the movie through the window. *Time* magazine reported that the theater syndicate "threatened to bring suit because the platform blocked the sidewalk, and took splashy newspaper ads to point out that Reno moviegoers must now suffer the indignity of 'uncarpeted floors . . . the whistle of freight trains . . . static in the sound system.'

"The wily Goldwyn then executed a dazzling maneuver. He announced that the first night's receipts would be handed to the Red Cross. Official Reno opposition vanished. Then Goldwyn had only to import a non-inflammable film (cost: $1,000) and build a false wooden floor in the dance hall so that 400 borrowed chairs could be nailed down to conform to building laws."

In September, Goldwyn arrived in Reno, trailing publicity men and photographers and accompanied by as unassailable an ally as he could find: Mary Pickford. Goldwyn himself drove the nail that fastened the last chair to the floor, and then made a speech that ended on a patriotic note. "Because of the monopolies existing throughout the country," he said, "the boys when they return from the war are practically prohibited from entering the exhibition of motion pictures. They cannot build or acquire theaters in opposition to the circuits without the consent of the existing owners, or operators, as no product of consequence will be available to them."

In what seemed a scene from a Goldwyn (or Frank Capra) movie, Mary Pickford made an impassioned speech of her own. "Mr. Goldwyn spent a whole year of intensive work and $2,000,000 of his own money. . . . But to what avail? Only to be told . . . that he shall not be permitted to show his picture except as dictated by monopoly

"I would prefer to sit on a wooden chair, bench or even on the floor," she continued, with questionable logic, "than to rest upon plush-covered opera chairs and be forced to witness a dull, stupid and boring film in the finest movie palace in the country. We are making history here tonight—you, Mr. Goldwyn and I—for we are taking our stand for the inalienable rights for free enterprise and as free Americans, to see to it that no one man, group, combine or monopoly shall dictate how and when.

"So I say it is not merely the question as to whether this one or dozens of Goldwyn's pictures do or do not play in Reno or the entire state of Nevada. It's rather the question of whether he or I, or other Americans, are to be given opportunity to carry on our lives and businesses openly and honestly!"

Goldwyn and Pickford may have overstated their case, but in spite of the overblown rhethoric, their cause was just. Two years later, a federal court found the big distributors in violation of antitrust laws, and ordered them to sell their theaters—thus giving independent producers the leverage Goldwyn had sought and, ultimately, revolutionizing the very foundation of the industry.

Process Shot

When Sam Goldwyn left home every morning, he walked briskly (weather permitting) down Laurel Lane to Sunset Boulevard, then east to the borderline between Beverly Hills and West Hollywood—a distance of about three miles. At that point he got into his limousine, which had trailed behind him, and his chauffeur drove him through plebeian Hollywood to the studio. At the end of the day, he reversed the procedure. He performed the ritual religiously, claiming that it kept him fit. "It's wonderful!" he'd exclaim to men half his age, who were hard-pressed to keep up with him. "You can just feel that oxygen going into your system!"

The route he walked changed little, if at all, during Sam's four decades of walking. Huge estates, situated on rises above the level of the broad streets, are visible only from a distance; close up, most are hidden by ten-foot walls, or dense, meticulously manicured shrubbery. Except for an occasional gardener, the wide expanses of lawn are deserted; walking on the grass may be a capital offense. The air is thick with smog and the certainty of the rich. There is a sense of inviolability and, to use the phrase popularized by Forest Lawn, perpetual care. No sign of living inhabitants reaches the street from the elegant houses. The only noise is the traffic, perhaps the most exclusive in the world, reflecting the population's mean income of $34,000. North of Sunset, that figure doubles, triples, quadruples. In that pocket of plutocracy, a stone's throw from Laurel Lane, is situated the imposing home of Mr. and Mrs. Danny Kaye.

Surrounded by opulence and a staff of servants that includes a cook, a housekeeper, a houseboy, a maid, a secretary and a gardener, Mrs. Danny Kaye appears to be exquisitely bored.

As Sylvia Fine, she was never bored. From the time that Danny went to work as a delivery boy for her father, a Bronx dentist, through all his years of struggling for recognition as a performer, Sylvia devoted herself to his career. At various times, and sometimes all at the same time, she was his manager, his lyricist, his coach, his confessor, his booker, his bookkeeper, his audience, his artistic conscience, his critic, his wife. But once he *arrived,* Danny began to resent his dependence on Sylvia. It was a standard B movie plot: successful husband tells loyal wife to shut up and butt out. It was far more complicated than that, of course, but the upshot was that Sylvia gradually withdrew into the background and, pleading laziness, stopped working at anything more exhausting than the role of wealthy woman of leisure.

My appointment with Mrs. Kaye was at two P.M.; she rarely rises before noon. The maid ushered me up thickly carpeted stairs into a bedroom as large and luxurious as any movie set (the whole *world* was beginning to look like a movie set!) Mrs. Kaye was in bed, between pink satin sheets, wearing a silk negligee and looking wan. Although we had discussed my project over the phone, she greeted me by asking, in a curiously flat, world-weary voice, "Now, Miss Easton, what is it you want to see me about?"

When Goldwyn brought Danny and Sylvia to Hollywood in 1943, the young, unsophisticated couple was bowled over by the life-style of the millionaire producer. Frances Goldwyn's example was a powerful influence on the younger woman's developing tastes and also, less directly, on her relationship with her husband.

"Frances Goldwyn," said Sylvia Kaye, "was very bright and *totally* dedicated to Sam. I called her the State Department. Her function was to explain Sam to people—things about him that bothered them. Sometimes she overdid it. She would call and go through some long, drawn-out thing before I'd realize that what she wanted was for Danny to apologize to Sam for something. She'd say, 'You know, Sam is not totally right, but if you want this thing to move, Danny will have to say the first word.' I used to do the same thing for Danny.

"Frances used to talk about Sam the way I sometimes talk about Danny. If I say, 'He's impossible!' all that means is that I'm exasperated at the moment—that he's going to do something I don't think he should, or he's too slow about something. When Sam was so sick, before he died, I'd stop by to see Frances from time to time, and she'd say, 'You know, Sam was awfully good to me. About many things. In his own way, he was really wonderful to me.' So that made up for the times she had to sleep in the upper berth, because the lower was his by divine right—or sleeping in the maid's room in the hotel suite, because he got the master bedroom."

How had Sylvia felt about Sam? "I was crazy about him. He could be maddening, God knows. He had a burning drive to do only very fine things, and he was interested only in very fine people. Sam knew, on intimate terms, most of the great people of the world. This was as big an industry with Sam as the motion pictures. He used to talk to me about his friend Winnie in England; Churchill was his buddy. At his house, you met *the* people of accomplishment of the world—people like Albert Lasker, Bill Paley. If there was a visiting celebrity in town, he would be at Goldwyn's. Sam repeated the story *with pride*—not as a funny story—*many* times, about how Bernard Shaw said to him, 'It's a pity that you're an artist and I'm a businessman.' He was proud of the fact that Shaw thought he was artistic!

"He *never* referred to his first marriage, or his daughter. It was as though he had shed a skin. I'm sure he considered marrying Frances a step forward; she was the *kind* of wife he wanted. She was blonde, she was Aryan. I think that, *in his own way*, he was in love with her. But the passion of his life was pictures. Other people *said* it was, but with Goldwyn, it *really* was."

The subject, and my quite genuine interest, brought about a subtle transformation in Sylvia Kaye. She became more animated, more vital, less remote. She offered me coffee and rang for the maid, asking what kind of coffee I preferred. I said I didn't care. "We have several kinds," she pressed. "What would you like? Real coffee?" I said that would be fine. "Bring Miss Easton some real coffee," she said, "and I'll have my tea."

The maid turned out to be very young, very eager to please and very Mexican, with little English. She carried in an elaborate tray: tea, boiling water, cups, cookies—and, alas, Sanka. Over my protests that Sanka was perfectly okay, she was sent back to the kitchen for real coffee. Mrs. Kaye sighed. There was an awkward silence. "Where were we?" she asked.

The Kid From Brooklyn, I prompted. Danny's third picture. She and Goldwyn had disagreed strongly about the score. "At one point Sam threw up his hands and made Danny a long speech about how his career couldn't depend on one woman, and there were any number of people he could hire who could write the kind of songs the picture should have. I said to Danny, 'By all means. It wouldn't be bad to have Ira Gershwin or Frank Loesser writing for you. It's all right with me!'

"I figured I'd better pick up and go to New York, because this was gonna be too much of a strain on me. I was there five or six weeks. Next thing I know, Frances called me. She said, 'You know, Sam will never admit that he was wrong, but he needs you very badly. Would you come back and write something for the picture?' I said Sure, but there wasn't much time. She said, 'Come down and have lunch with Sam, and don't refer to it until he does.' When I got back, there was a big thing of flowers from Frances. It was signed *Frances and Sam,* but it was written in Frances' handwriting. She had made a date for me and Sam at the commissary for the next day.

"Sam didn't quite know what to say to me. I guess he was embarrassed. He didn't say Hello, how've you been, I'm glad you've come back. He pointed at me and said, 'Say, I ran into a friend of yours last night. Moss Hart! He was having dinner at my house!' I almost collapsed, but I just said, 'Oh, isn't that nice, Sam.' He then proceeded to ask me to write something for the picture.

"Irving Berlin, a close friend of ours, told me, 'You charge him $25,000 for that number. That's what he paid me for one use of "Always" in *Pride of the Yankees.*' My agent told Sam that was my price—and Sam paid it! Which never ceased to astonish me. He could be wildly extravagant and generous, or he could be the most penny-pinching—"

The phone rang. It was Danny Kaye, calling from somewhere on the Benefit circuit. "Hi, Pussy," said his wife, reverting to that oddly flat voice. "Oh, I forgot all about it. Are the Jourdans here? I'd be delighted. Who would you like me to ask? Anybody you want. Are you leaving for New York soon? You're nutty. As a fruitcake. You'll have to sit up all night. No wonder you're tired when you travel. . . ."

Danny and Sam got along better professionally than socially. "They had a sharp difference of opinion about behavior at parties. We invited them to dinner one night with some of their close friends: Jules and Doris Stein, Harpo and Susan Marx, and Harold Arlen. Immediately after dinner, Sam said to Jules, 'Where can we play gin?' And they went into the library and played gin all evening. And Danny said to me, 'You are never to invite the Goldwyns to this house again, and I won't go there!' This went on for years!"

Sam's tactics with Sylvia, when he wanted something, never varied. "He would call me on the phone, and instead of saying Hello, he'd say, 'You're a beautiful woman, and I'm very *found* of you.' He never said fond, always *found.* I knew then either he wanted something, or else I was in trouble. I was anything but a beautiful woman. I was a young girl. And not his type. He'd say, 'You're a beautiful woman, and I've never had so much trouble with anybody in my life!'

"When Sam was *pretending* to be angry, he'd get red in the face. When Sam was *really* angry, he'd get white around the nose. Sometimes you'd be talking to Sam and he'd be looking at you, but he'd get a vacant look in his eyes, and you could just tell that he'd tuned you out."

Most interviews have a predictable pattern: a beginning, in which rapport is established; a middle, in which factual information is obtained; and an ending, in which some conclusions are drawn. Sylvia Kaye, however, trailed off somewhere in the middle—as though she hadn't the energy, or the desire, to form any conclusions.

Leaving that luxurious cocoon of a house, where mistress and servants spoke in hushed voices, I felt the guilty relief with which one leaves a sickroom. Clearly, Mrs. Danny Kaye had subdued her alter ego—the Sylvia Fine who had arrived in Hollywood blazing with curiosity, talent and ambition—with a thoroughness Sam Goldwyn would have envied.

21. The Best Years

When Colonel William Wyler was discharged from the Army in 1945, he still owed Goldwyn one picture. Goldwyn gave him several properties from which to choose, and Wyler selected a short novel, written in blank verse and dealing with the problems encountered by three veterans when they returned to civilian life. It was called *Glory for Me.*

History—press agent history—has it that Goldwyn commissioned MacKinlay Kantor to write the story after Frances had directed his attention to an item on the subject in *Time* magazine. Kantor, a respected journalist and novelist, asked his friend Dana Andrews to read the first draft. Andrews looked at the onionskin pages and asked, "Mac, why did you write this in blank verse?"

"Dana," said Kantor with a wry smile, "I can't *afford* to write in blank verse, because nobody *buys* anything written in blank verse. But when Sam asked me to write this story, he didn't tell me *not* to write it in blank verse!"

Goldwyn decided that Bob Sherwood was the man to write the screenplay; but Sherwood was not interested. He was working on a new play; besides, his sinuses always suffered in the California climate. Sherwood was a slow-speaking, soft-voiced man with a bone-dry wit and a temperament as tranquil as Goldwyn's was volatile. He had worked for Sam before, on *The Adventures of Marco Polo,* and had developed a philosophical attitude toward the producer. "You can't really resent Sam's vulgarity," he once told Anita Loos, "when he himself has never learned the meaning of the word. I find I can live with Sam just as one lives with high blood pressure." * Sherwood declined to do *Glory for Me,* but Sam was determined to have him. He kept after him, offering him living quarters in the Goldwyn house, minimal working hours (four hours a day) and buckets of money, until the writer's resistance caved in.

Goldwyn's awe of Sherwood, a four-time Pulitzer prize-winner, kept his interference in the script to a minimum.

Glory for Me was the story of two couples and a triangle. Harold Russell, a veteran with no acting experience who had lost both hands during the war, played a character much like himself, torn by doubts about whether his prewar fiancee's feeling for him is love or pity. The second couple is a middle-aged banker, played by Fredric March, and his Understanding Wife, Myrna Loy, who provides moral support while he struggles with his newly acquired social conscience. The triangle consists of Dana Andrews, a bombardier captain unable to adjust to his old job as a soda jerk; Virginia Mayo, the wife he hurriedly and mistakenly married before going overseas; and the banker's daughter, Teresa Wright, with whom Andrews falls in love.

Wyler empathized strongly with the trauma of adjusting to civilian life. He had lost most of his hearing during the war, while shooting documentary footage for the Air Force from the waist of a B-25, where the engine noise was, literally, deafening. He feared for a time that the disability might end his career; then he devised an ingenious way to compensate by plugging his hearing aid into soundman Gordon Sawyer's microphone on the set. Wyler felt a personal obligation to transfer the story to the screen as honestly as he could.

With the cast he wanted and Gregg Toland on camera, Wyler had a nearly ideal setup—but he still had Goldwyn to contend with. Years of painful experience had made him the town's leading expert, however, on handling Sam. Niven Busch witnessed a scene that illustrated Wyler's finesse in a critical clash: "The confrontation had a background that I don't think Wyler ever knew. For a long time, Goldwyn had a controller named Reeves Espy. Reeves kept the books. Sometimes he would advise Goldwyn on deals.

* Anita Loos, *Kiss Hollywood Goodbye* (New York, The Viking Press, 1974).

"One day the three of us were in Goldwyn's office and Reeves, the budget man, said, 'Mr. Goldwyn, do you want a really candid recommendation? Get rid of Willy Wyler.'

"Goldwyn said, 'Willy has made some of my biggest hits!'

"Reeves said, 'That's true, but he's also cost you money. Look at Willy's record through the years, and you'll see he's in the red.'

"Well, they brought in the books, they checked all of Willy's pictures to that date. Willy had never made a picture that hadn't had artistic acclaim, but overall, on the box-office records, Willy was in the red. So Goldwyn, who was irritated with Willy at that time anyway, said, 'I'm gonna fire him.' Reeves said, 'Remember, he has a contract.' Goldwyn said, 'Never mind. I'm gonna fire Willy Wyler.'

"They called Wyler in, and they asked me to stay. They wanted me there as a witness. When Willy came in, Goldwyn began to assail him in terms that became increasingly vulgar and aggressive and hard to tolerate. He called Willy an artistic fraud. He said he made pictures that looked good, and that he had an in with the critics, but that his pictures were really flops. He said Willy had made more bombs than anyone in Hollywood, and that he was actually a man of very little or no talent, and that he was stubborn, slow, inartistic and deceitful.

"While he was belaboring Willy in these terms, Willy's face turned purple. Willy had a passionate temper. And then some sixth sense said to him, 'What's happening?' And he looked around and Reeves was sitting there, and I'm sitting there, and Goldwyn is throwing these insults at him—and Willy's whole manner cooled down. He said, 'Oh, Mr. Goldwyn, I'm sorry you feel that way. No, I don't agree with you. Of course, I may be stupid. You may have something there. I'm sorry that one lost money—yes, perhaps it was my fault.' So the desired effect, which was for Willy to lose his temper and say You can take your contract and shove it, never took place. Willy left, the contract stayed in force, and two days later they were the best of friends."

George Jenkins, a young New York stage designer whose sets for *I Remember Mama* had caught the attention of one of

Goldwyn's east coast representatives, was hired as art director. After Jenkins' first meeting with Goldwyn, he was taken to the art department and introduced to Perry Ferguson, Dick Day's successor as in-house art director. "You know," said Jenkins innocently to Ferguson, "I found Mr. Goldwyn very charming!"

"Yes," said the older man. "Like a cobra."

Jenkins learned later that until that moment, Ferguson had been under the impression that *Glory for Me* was *his* assignment. "It was quite a shock to him," says Jenkins, "and Perry could have been terrible to me—but he wasn't. He gave me a lot of advice, although he certainly wasn't my assistant. Mac Capps was my assistant—although I could never understand why. He had *much* more experience than I had!

Jenkins liked Goldwyn "very much. He was very charming. After a little while, when I got to know him, he put his arm around me and said, 'Call me Uncle Sam.' "

Goldwyn hired Irene Sharaff, one of Hollywood's top designers, to do the costumes. Sharaff's reputation was based on her exotic, theatrical costumes; she was totally unsuited (and unwilling) to design the kind of simple everyday clothes worn by the middle-class characters of *Glory for Me*. Asked to produce a simple blouse for Teresa Wright, Sharaff came up with a creation of raw silk with elaborate tucks, darts and embroidery. Wyler went into a rage and sent the wardrobe woman to a local five-and-ten to buy a dress he considered suitably unstylish. He called Sharaff That Woman, and barred her from the set. (He would have barred Goldwyn, as well, if he could have; instead, he did the next best thing. Whenever Sam came strutting onto the set, Wyler would quietly walk off.)

It took nearly four months to shoot the picture. By the time Danny Mandell finished editing 400,000 feet of film down to 16,000—two-and-a-half hours of running time—it had been decided that *Glory for Me* was a bad title. Goldwyn hired the Audience Research Institute to conduct a pool, asking interview subjects to choose their favorites out of ten possible titles. The last title on the list, added offhandedly to make up the required ten, was *The Best Years of Our Lives*. It was chosen by 65 percent of the people polled.

It was customary to have two or three "sneak previews"

in different areas, to get a cross-section of audience reaction. After the first sneak preview, in Santa Barbara, everyone knew the picture would be a hit. At the second, in Long Beach, reaction was even more positive. Goldwyn decided to move the January opening, already booked, up a month, in order to qualify for that year's Academy Awards. *The Best Years of Our Lives* opened at the Astor in New York on November 22, 1946.

Dana Andrews, who saw the picture for the first time that night, was astounded. "That scene where Fred Derry [played by Andrews] is looking at all those old planes—I thought that was a waste of film, just Wyler indulging himself in nostalgia for the 8th Air Force. I thought it would wind up on the cutting room floor. It turned out to be one of the most impressive scenes in the picture! Here's this guy, he's leaving town, and here are the remnants of what were the best years of his life—a graveyard of planes. A very, very strong point in the picture." Andrews walked up to Goldwyn after the picture and said, with genuine enthusiasm, "Sam, that was really wonderful!"

"I'm glad to do it for you," said Goldwyn.

The picture had many memorable scenes, thanks largely to Toland's and Wyler's masterful use of deep focus. The technique allowed Wyler to direct many scenes as though for the stage, shifting the focus of attention through direction, rather than by camera movement. Close-ups, used economically, had more impact, and the photography was, in the trade, the most talked-about, most praised element of the picture.

On his own initiative, Gregg Toland personally ran and checked forty-one prints of the picture. As it opened at theaters in Los Angeles, he went to each theater to examine the projection equipment. He ordered new lenses for the projectors, had them coated, reduced the size of some screens and, in each instance, improved the quality of projection.

Most reviewers were worshipful. Richard Griffith, Goldwyn's most devoted advocate, called *The Best Years* "as near perfection as popular art contrives to be." * A few dissenters, however, including the respected James Agee, found it banal.

* Richard Griffith and Arthur Mayer, *The Movies* (New York, Simon & Schuster, 1957).

It would be unfair to carp, from this distance, about a picture that was so very much a part of its time. If the characters were simplistic, so were we all—clinging desperately to simplistic perceptions of ourselves and our country.

The picture cost (depending on whose publicity you read) between $2,000,000 and $3,000,000. In its initial release, it earned over $10,000,000. In Great Britain, it outgrossed *Gone With the Wind.* Sam's continuing defiance of exhibitors had a lot to do with the huge earnings. "I decided," he told a reporter, "that it was time to get away from the old habit of treating all films alike. I was sure the American public would be willing to pay a fair admission [$1.40] to see a genuinely fine picture, even if the price was higher than that being charged for run-of-the-mill films." He expressed mock surprise that exhibitors, who naturally were looking out for their own interests, "resented this departure from the conventional method. As a result, it was necessary for us to show *The Best Years of Our Lives* in theaters off the beaten path, to guarantee running expenses, to bear the burden of the exploitation campaign." For once, Sam wasn't exaggerating. In one instance, "off the beaten path" meant a run-down, third-rate Chicago porno house, refurbished and staffed by Goldwyn, to the tune of a half-million dollars, just for the showing of his picture. Dana Andrews overheard him on the phone with a theater owner in Georgia, saying, "This is Sam Goldwyn! You're surprised to hear from me, aren't you?" and offering to make up any losses the man incurred by charging the $1.40 admission price. When receipts broke records everywhere, Sam proclaimed loudly that he had proved his point. "If exhibitors insist on charging uniform prices," he warned, "they will get uniform pictures" which, he implied, would drive people away from the theaters.

Nobody could call *Best Years* a uniform picture. It won seven Academy Awards: Best Picture, Best Direction, Best Screenplay, Best Actor (Fredric March), Best Supporting Actor (Harold Russell), Best Editing and Best Musical Score (Hugo Friedhofer). Publicist David Parry wrote most of the acceptance speeches. "Of course there was a great deal of excitement," he recalls, "but it sort of telegraphed its punch. When we first saw the rough cut, everybody knew it was a great movie. Goldwyn was just *standing* there, waiting for us to get out of the screening room and wanting to know, like a benign father, what we thought. And everyone said, of course, as they said about *everything,* It was just wonderful."

On March 24, 1947, *Time* reported: "The presentation of Oscars—Hollywood's annual pat on the back to itself—has to be seen to be believed." *Time*'s correspondent fought his way through "acres of diamonds, mink and glossy black limousines" to describe the proceedings:

> Everything about this year's Academy Awards show was the biggest. There were more jewels, more big names, more hoopla . . . there were 35 Oscars, 16 search lights (criss-crossing in shades of white, blue, red and orange), a 66-piece orchestra, 250 policemen, 90 ushers, 50 stagehands, 6 parking lots and 125 parking attendants. There were three hours of coast-to-coast broadcast * and 6,000 popped flashbulbs.
>
> The whole shebang cost $65,000. The $10,000 stage set was a pylon backed by 6 Greek columns, and topped with a five-foot gilt plaster replica of Oscar. . . . Sam Goldwyn managed, as usual, to get foot in mouth once: Taking pains to commend Hoagy Carmichael (who appeared in *Best Years*), he referred to the singer-composer as Hugo.
>
> When the evening ended, Hollywood . . . had proved that the Academy vote is now reasonably free from political pressure. There was a time when it was possible for two majors to gang up on one independent (like Sam Goldwyn) and deal him right out the back door.

The industry's supreme accolade, the much-coveted Thalberg Award, was presented to a weeping Goldwyn "in recognition of a creative producer who has been responsible for a constant high quality of motion picture production." *Life* reported that after the ceremony he said, "It's not good enough to be good . . . Suppose the next time I make a stinker? I'm worrying about that."

William Wyler never worked for Goldwyn again. As the director's confidence reached new heights, so did his resentment of the indignities to which Sam had subjected him over the

* The proceedings would not be televised until 1953.

years. "*I* made *Wuthering Heights,*" was one of Sam's standard lines. "Willy Wyler only directed it." During the filming of *Best Years,* Wyler's bitterness deepened. "One morning," recalls Dana Andrews, "Wyler came down to the set around eleven. We'd been waiting for him all morning, while he was up in the office talking to Sam. He was *fuming.* 'That son of a bitch! He would like the credits to read SAM GOLDWYN PRESENTS SAM GOLDWYN IN A PICTURE CALLED SAM GOLDWYN PRODUCED BY SAM GOLDWYN DIRECTED BY SAM GOLDWYN WRITTEN BY SAM GOLDWYN . . . !' We didn't work at all that day. He sent us all home."

But Wyler knew he had gone as far as he could go with Sam. He had come out of the Army broke; but a clause in his contract entitled him to a 20 percent share of the profits from *Best Years.** With that as a stake, he became a cofounder of a new independent production company, Liberty Films.

Goldwyn was stunned. He could not believe that Wyler would leave him. How could he be so ungrateful? Hadn't he given Willy the best years of his life?

* In 1958, Wyler announced his intent to file suit against Goldwyn for over $400,000, charging that Goldwyn had understated the profits of the picture by nearly $2,000,000, and that he had given Robert Sherwood 5 percent of the profits which, said Wyler, were improperly deducted as production costs. Goldwyn told a reporter, "Wyler received over $1,400,000 for directing *Best Years.* This suit seems to indicate he thinks he is entitled to more. This is a free country. If Willy feels he has been mistreated by being paid such a paltry sum, he is entitled to the great American privilege of going to court." (*Los Angeles Times,* 7/1/58). The suit was eventually settled out of court for an undisclosed amount.

22. Losing "The Goldwyn Touch"

Goldwyn's acceptance of the Thalberg Award was a rare moment of triumph; Frances likened him to "a child who'd gotten everything he wanted for Christmas." It was a moment Sam Goldfish wouldn't have missed for the world. Even while Sam was taking his bows, he could hear the voice of that *schnorrer* taunting, louder even than the applause. *MACHER!* THIS MISTAKE WILL BE RECTIFIED! YOUR NEXT PICTURE WILL BE SUCH A FLOP, IT'LL MAKE *NANA* LOOK LIKE A HIT! I SHOULD HAVE A NICKEL FOR EVERYBODY WHO STAYS AWAY. FROM HERE ON, *K'NOCKER,* IT'S DOWNHILL. Sam had heard that refrain for years. But this time, Goldfish was right.

Riding high on the crest of his success, Goldwyn did a curious thing. He took his wife to Gloversville. He showed her the glove factory, and the Kingsborough Hotel, where his idols, the prosperous drummers, used to hang out. An invitation to address a group of businessmen (including his old boss) so jangled his nerves that he changed his mind three times about whether or not to allow Frances to wear her mink (was it too showy? should she wear her "old" nutria? All right, wear the mink—but *no jewelry*!). At the meeting, he delivered himself of a concatenation of platitudes, paying homage to the greatness of Gloversville, the important lessons he had learned there, the glories of America, where a poor immigrant could rise to such heights. It could not have been more corney. He could not have been more sincere.

Goldwyn was sixty-five that year, but it would never have occurred to him to retire. In the next twelve years he would produce twelve pictures, among them some of the worst of his entire career. But even if he could somehow have foreseen the decline, he could not have changed course. He was still vigorous. He had no other interests. He was programmed to make movies. It was all he knew.

In each of the first three postwar years, Goldwyn released a Danny Kaye picture. The first two, both directed by Norman McLeod, were *The Kid From Brooklyn,* in which Danny played a milkman turned boxer (and sang Sylvia's $25,000 song) and *The Secret World of Walter Mitty,* adapted from James Thurber's classic short story about the timid Mr. Milquetoast who daydreams of heroism and romance.

Goldwyn assigned writers Ken Englund and Everett Freeman to expand the four-thousand-word story into a feature-length film. They lopped twenty years off Mitty's age, replaced his wife with a girl friend (Virginia Mayo) and a nagging mother, and padded the story with a corny plot. When Thurber objected to the excessive melodrama, Englund went to New York for ten days of rewriting with Thurber himself. They added three new daydreams to the original five, and Thurber was satisfied; but a conflict was already shaping up that would continue right up to the picture's release. The pro-Thurber contingent—Englund, McLeod and Max Wilkinson, Goldwyn's story editor—knew that the story cried out for a light touch, and warned that tampering with the dream sequences would destroy the heart of the picture. The antidream forces, consisting of everybody else, saw the dreams as no more than a springboard from which Danny Kaye, surrounded by Goldwyn girls and flamboyant sets, could perform his proven nightclub routines!

When Englund returned to California, he began receiving regular communiqués from the apprehensive Thurber, urging him to protect the dreams and even proposing some new ones, as some of his favorites hit the cutting room floor. The more dreams that came under consideration, the more people Goldwyn—*who had never read the original story, but had bought the property on the basis of a synopsis!*—consulted and the more confused he became about what to keep, what to discard and what to reshoot.

Art director George Jenkins related a variation on a

familiar theme. "On *Walter Mitty,* I saw a side of Goldwyn I had never seen before. One day he asked me to come up to his office right away. He didn't say why. I went up and I sat down, and a minute later the director came in, Norman McLeod. And he bawled McLeod out for something he didn't like. Right in front of me! Very, very badly! He made a little speech, kind of as though he'd made it before. 'I'm the captain of the ship.' After McLeod left, Goldwyn said, 'Thank you very much for coming up, George.' I didn't ask him what he wanted me for. I knew he just wanted to have McLeod humiliated by having somebody else there to see him bawled out. Not a very nice side of a person."

What was McLeod's offense? "He had used some valuable shooting time for *testing* a hairdresser to play a part in the picture. And that actually is unheard of. Everybody stood around while he made a screen test, in the middle of production. It was real nutty, and I don't blame Goldwyn. But McLeod had gotten the impression somehow that Mr. Goldwyn *wanted* it to be done. He told me that, afterwards. Obviously that had *not* been Goldwyn's desire—but quite possibly he had mentioned, offhandedly, 'Jesus, I wish I had a screen test on that guy!' And then got upset because it was done."

When Goldwyn bought the screen rights to *Mitty,* he also bought *The Catbird Seat,* another Thurber favorite. Thurber agreed to write the screenplay for the latter property himself, and accepted a $10,000 advance, with an additional $40,000 to be paid when he turned in his scenario. But when Thurber saw what Goldwyn had done to *Mitty,* he returned the $10,000 and destroyed his *Catbird Seat* script. Life reported that "James Thurber, a mild man, grows almost profane when he thinks of how his story has been corrupted. He calls the result *The Public Life of Danny Kaye,* and is appalled by the star's songs in gibberish, the Dick Tracy plot and the traditional Goldwyn opulence of production. 'It began to be bad with the first git-gat-gittle,' he says. 'If they'd spent one-tenth the money, it would have been ten times as good.' "

But Goldwyn was well-pleased with the picture. Danny Kaye as Walter Mitty, he said, was as funny as Harold Lloyd!

* * *

A Song Is Born was Goldwyn's last attempt to make a Star out of Virginia Mayo. It was a remake of *Ball of Fire,* with Mayo and Danny Kaye playing the roles originated by Stanwyck and Cooper. Through no fault of Danny's, it was the worst picture he ever made. Goldwyn wanted Sylvia to write three songs for the picture. Sylvia, whose marriage was very shaky at the time, had never liked Virginia Mayo. She told Sam that three songs would cost him $60,000. The outcome was that Danny sang no songs in the picture, and it lost money. Howard Hawks, who had directed *Ball of Fire,* directed the remake as well. Like his earlier Goldwyn film *Come and Get It, A Song Is Born* is not listed in Hawks' official list of credits.

In between *Walter Mitty* and *A Song Is Born,* Goldwyn produced *The Bishop's Wife,* a comedy based on a novel by Robert Nathan. When that unfortunate production got under way, it was already over half a million dollars in the red. The reason, according to writer Nathan, was, "He was so busy getting awards and being congratulated for *Best Years* that he didn't get around to looking at the rushes until after weeks of shooting!"

Robert Sherwood wrote the screenplay and Goldwyn had already cast Cary Grant, Jean Arthur and David Niven in the leads when Charlie Feldman, an agent with the reputation of being able to sell Goldwyn anything, sold him William Seiter, a "quickie" director of Abbott and Costello comedies, for $125,000 —at a time when top directors were getting $50,000!

Seiter was no compulsive worker; a clause in his contract freed him from any obligation to work past five P.M. He affected puttees and a cane, and wore a rosebud in his lapel. Coworkers called it "the old D. W. Griffith bit." Seiter knew from the start that he was in over his head. "I don't know what I'm doing here!" he told George Jenkins. "I'm not a Goldwyn man. But I'm here! And I sure like the money!"

The Bishop's Wife was a light comedy (the bishop's marriage is jeopardized, then saved by an angel), but Seiter's inadequate direction turned it into an unfunny farce. When Sam finally got around to seeing the rushes, he was horrified. Following Goldwyn's instructions, Leon Fromkess, head of production, told Seiter, "We'll say you're sick and we'll settle your contract for fifty cents on the dollar. $62,000. If you won't settle, I'll have to tell the trades we weren't satisfied, and you'll have to come in and sit here every day and do nothing."

Seiter settled.

Production was suspended for six weeks, while Goldwyn regrouped. He got Robert Nathan up to his office and asked him to use his influence to get Robert Sherwood to rewrite the script. While Nathan hesitated, Goldwyn was getting Sherwood on the phone. "Here," he said, handing Nathan the receiver. "Tell him what a great writer he is! Tell him how great the script is! Tell him I'm crazy about it!" As a favor to Nathan, Sherwood—who surely realized precisely what was going on—acquiesced.

Now Goldwyn needed a director. Frances, perhaps on Sam's instructions but probably on her own initiative, asked Leon Fromkess to approach Willy Wyler. "The old man's in trouble, Willy," said Fromkess. "You've gotta help him out." Wyler declined.

Goldwyn invited Henry Koster, director of Deanna Durbin's biggest hits, to the studio and showed him the rough cut of Seiter's work. "I want to throw it all in the ashcan," he told Koster. "I want to start from scratch. And I want to change the two parts around. Niven should play the bishop. Cary Grant should play the angel."

Koster thought that an inspired bit of offbeat casting. Cary Grant, however, disagreed. The funny part was the bishop! He was proven wrong when he got an Academy Award nomination for playing the angel—but during shooting, he sulked, making Koster's life "a little miserable."

During the six-week delay, Jean Arthur, either because of other commitments or simple disgust, left the cast. When Goldwyn hired Koster, he asked, "Would you like to work with Laurette Taylor?"

"I'd love to," said Koster. "She's a great actress. But she's dead."

"She's not dead!" said Goldwyn indignantly. "Two hours ago she was sitting where you are sitting now, and I talked to her!" He pressed the intercom on his desk and asked his secretary, "What was that lady's name who was just sitting here two hours ago? The actress?"

"Loretta Young."

"See!" said Sam triumphantly, "What did I tell you? She's not dead!"

Eventually, Goldwyn got it straight that his leading lady was not Laurette Taylor. After that, he called her "Miss Yeng." Koster he always referred to as "Mr. Kester," but the director took it with good humor. "He couldn't talk as fast as he could think; but he was the greatest producer ever, after Thalberg, because he was *only* interested in quality—even if he had to throw away weeks of work. I truly think that Goldwyn was a great man. Nobody could help but respect him."

The only real difficulty Koster encountered had to do with Loretta Young's belief that her right profile was her "bad side" and should not be photographed. Unfortunately, Cary Grant felt the same way about *his* right profile. When the script called for a love scene, with dialogue that required them to face each other, Koster came up with what seemed an ingenious solution. "I had her step up to the window and look out while she talked about how beautiful the stars were. And he stepped up behind her, put his hands on her shoulders. They were both facing the same way."

When Goldwyn saw the next morning's rushes, he called Koster to his office and asked, "What the hell did you do with that love scene? What are they looking out the window for?"

"Sam," said the director, "I'm facing a difficult problem. Neither one wants their left side photographed! Cary didn't object in the first place, but since Loretta insists, he insists too!"

Goldwyn stormed down his "fire escape" to the set. "Miss Yeng," he said, "is this true, what he tells me? That you don't want the right side of your face on the screen?"

"But I don't look good from that side," she explained.

"All right. From now on, if I only get half your face, you only get half your salary!"

Thanks to an inventive promotion campaign that included a Command Performance for the King and Queen of England, *The Bishop's Wife* broke even, but the industry was sliding into the worst crisis in its history. In 1946, 80,000,000 Americans had gone to the movies every week, seeking not quality, but escape. During the war, it had been virtually impossible for a picture *not* to make money. But as the booming wartime economy began to stall, Hollywood was hit simultaneously by higher studio overhead and production costs, heavier union demands, and a loss of much of its foreign market. In 1947, Great Britain imposed a staggering 75 percent tax on American film earnings, and other countries followed suit. Money was tight everywhere. Over all this hovered the spectre of the television tube. Making his standard plea for fewer, better pictures, Goldwyn asked the rhetorical question: "Who wants to go out and see a bad movie when they can stay at home and see a bad one free on television?"

Another factor that contributed to the tailspin in which the industry found itself—and from which it never really recovered—was foreshadowed in 1940 when Congressman Martin Dies had demanded an investigation of Communist influence in the motion picture industry. The threatened witch hunt was held in abeyance during the war; but when hostilities ended overseas, they broke out in Hollywood.

In 1946, a group of producers met secretly at Hillcrest Country Club to discuss whether Communism *was* a threat in the industry and, if so, what action they should take. As the meeting degenerated into a frightened exchange of rumors and accusations, a few clearheaded individuals demanded facts, dates, names. When one of the speakers named the son of a well-known producer as "a very influential Communist," Goldwyn got to his feet. Along with everyone else in the room, he was familiar with the son's reputation—not as a subversive, but as a total incompetent. "If this snot-nosed baby is the Red boss in Hollywood," said Sam, "we've got nothing to fear. Let's go home." Amid laughter, the meeting broke up.*

That was the last laugh that was heard on the subject. In October, 1947, HUAC hearings began in Hollywood. Within days, the committee's guilt-by-association approach created a panic of epidemic proportions. The producers, under heavy pressure from Wall Street to cooperate with the Committee if they wanted to continue getting financing for their films, were most vulnerable. In November, the producers met again, this

* Paul Mayersberg, *Hollywood, the Haunted House* (New York, Stein & Day, 1968).

time officially, and issued what came to be known as the Waldorf Declaration. In it, they promised (as proof of their patriotism) not to "knowingly employ a Communist" or any suspected subversive. Thus began the saddest, sickest chapter in Hollywood's history.

Goldwyn, who financed his pictures with his own money and was therefore independent of Wall Street, protested the policy, saying, "We have no right to fire these people!"—but to no avail. In 1948, when a member of the Committee claimed that he had detected Communist ideology in *The Best Years of Our Lives*, Willy Wyler declared, "I wouldn't be allowed to make *Best Years* in Hollywood today."

Producers had always engaged in a kind of word-of-mouth blacklisting, but the basis was spite ("I'll see to it that you never work in this town again!"), not politics. Now, panic and paranoia suddenly made hundreds of actors, writers and directors unemployable; many never worked in the industry again. Caution—financial and artistic—prevailed.

Process Shot

I grew up surrounded by actors who didn't. ("Actors are children" is a truism frequently quoted by Goldwyn.) They had some immensely appealing qualities. What great playmates they made!

Farley Granger, one of those professional Peter Pans, sipped coffee at an outdoor café on the Redondo Beach pier. "I was very young," he said, looking not a lot older than he had thirty years ago. He was just seventeen when Goldwyn's casting director, Bob McIntyre, spotted him in a showcase production. (At that time, Hollywood was glutted with little theaters, called "talent showcases," where aspiring actors worked for nothing in order to be "seen" by agents and casting directors.) McIntyre thought Farley looked right for the juvenile lead in *The North Star,* and set up an audition.

Sam signed the boy to a seven-year contract, and set his publicity machine in motion. The first thing they wanted to do was change Farley's name. "They said, 'You have a terrible name.' I said, 'It's my father's name! It's my grandfather's name!' They said, 'It's too long for the marquee. And it's funny. Nobody has a name like that.'

"I said, 'That's why it's good!' No. So they gave me long lists of names—like Gordon Gregory, and Gregory Gordon. They were all interchangeable names like that. Thank God there weren't any Rocks and Tabs and things like that yet. But I just stalled and stalled, and finally they gave up.

After *The North Star,* Farley went into the Navy. His service time was simply added onto the end of his contract. But when he was discharged, "Goldwyn didn't know what to do with me. I was getting paid very little money, like one hundred and fifty dollars a week, and for a bonus they gave me a secondhand Ford. About a year went by, and I was getting desperate. I thought, as many actors do when they're out of work, I'm never gonna work again!" Finally, Goldwyn loaned him to RKO, for *They Live by Night,* and then to Hitchcock, for *Rope.*

In 1947, Goldwyn cast him opposite Cathy O'Donnell, another contract player, in *Enchantment.* But Farley was beginning to feel some resentment. "I was getting to be known, and popular, and Goldwyn was taking all the credit—where it had been Nick Ray [director of *They Live by Night*] and Hitchcock who had created any kind of demand for me." With *Enchantment,* his disenchantment deepened. "During rehearsal, Cathy showed up about an hour late one morning, completely hysterical, weeping and sobbing. She said she had been with Goldwyn, that he'd been just terrible to her. She had eloped with Willy Wyler's brother the night before! This was after Wyler had left Goldwyn to be independent, with Capra and those people, and Goldwyn took this situation personally and said that Willy Wyler had put his brother up to marrying Cathy just to spite him! Can you believe that kind of ego? And he in*sisted* that Cathy annul the marriage im*me*diately, or she would never work again! I couldn't believe it! But it proved to be absolutely true. He just dumped her, got rid of her. And she really never did anything again."

To Goldwyn an actor was property. "Once I was told to go to Harry Cohn's office, at Columbia. When I got there, Harry Cohn told me that he had won me in a gin game the night before, from Goldwyn, and he wasn't sure whether he was gonna take Goldwyn up on it or not. Nothing ever came of it—but it was unbelievable!"

Much to Goldwyn's annoyance, Farley rebelled. "I wanted to work on the stage, in New York—but he wouldn't hear of it. I understand why, of course. I was beginning to get popular, and I was making money for him! I wanted to work

—but he wanted to loan me out for some things that I just thought were awful, and I wouldn't do them. So I would go on suspension. You were supposed to keep an actor on suspension only for as long as it took to make the film he turned down. But one time, he kept me on suspension for eight months, for turning down a film that took maybe two months. I could have taken him to court, but it wasn't worth it. So I began to be a bad boy.

"The suspension is like to *punish* you—you're supposed to sit home and cry and pout. I said To hell with that, I'm not going to sit here and do nothing. I can't work; I can't even park cars! They'll put an injunction on me! So that's when I started going to Europe. The first time was 1950."

Farley says Goldwyn's attitude was "igmatic." "Enigmatic?" I asked. "Yeah. Igmatic. After I started taking suspensions, he always referred to me either very politely as Mr. Granger or, if he was really pissed off at me, as That Boy. 'Get That Boy in here!' Then he began telling me what to do, and how to behave. I liked Chevy convertibles. He said that wasn't good for me, that I should buy a more expensive car now that I'd reached that bracket. *Dumb* things that began to dig away at my underpinning. He found out *everything*. During the McCarthy period, I had a lot of liberal friends. He said I was not allowed to be seen with certain people. I said I'm sorry, these are my friends. I'll be seen with anybody I please. He began to get very ritchety [sic] about *that* whole situation.

"I wanted to test my wings, and I felt I was being put into a mold—and I didn't know what the hell the mold was! I didn't know what I was supposed to be! I didn't have any *core!* 'Don't see these people. They may be Communists. They're bad.' I couldn't live that way. It was crazy!"

Personal appearance tours were more craziness. "Once I went to like twenty-four cities in twenty days. The publicity man with me had a nervous breakdown in Kansas City. The white coats just came and took him away! You're like a broken record. You say, 'Oh, I just *love* working with Dana Andrews! Yes, Sam Goldwyn is *such* a great producer, he's like a *daddy* to me.' All this bullshit that you had to say! I used to feel so *guilty* about it! I didn't think the films were that great! Why am

I telling these people to see it? I used to have great conflict about that. But it was what one had to do! You really were a property! As a piece of script was!"

Goldwyn loaned Farley to Hitchcock again, for *Strangers on a Train.* The part and the picture were outstanding, and Farley Granger suddenly became one of Goldwyn's most valuable assets—but only when he was working! Although Goldwyn used him in all but one of the pictures he made between 1948 and 1952, Sam only *made* six pictures in those four years—hardly enough to keep the actor busy. He tried to loan him out, but "All these other studios had young guys under contract my own age—the Rock Hudsons and the Tony Curtises, all those people—and they were paying them the regular stock contract money, three hundred dollars a week. Naturally, they wanted to promote their own people. Why should they build *me* up for *Goldwyn?* With him getting the dough *and* all the credit, *and* a more valuable actor? So as I became more popular, there was less work! Which I found harder and harder to take, 'cause I really wanted to work!"

When he did work at other studios, "That seemed like big time. Remember, I was young. There were other movies being made on the lot! I could go visit people I knew on the set! There was a big commissary, lots of showgirls—it was fun! Goldwyn's was a small operation—usually our film was the only one that was being made there. I didn't get any real feeling of show biz pizazz, or Hollywood. . . . But if a loanout came up for me that wasn't all that hotshot, he'd say Okay, he'll do it! I'd say, I'm *not* gonna do it, because I don't think it's any good! And then we'd have a fight, and I'd go on suspension again."

In 1948, Goldwyn costarred him with David Niven, Evelyn Keyes (who replaced Cathy O'Donnell) and Teresa Wright in *Enchantment,* a miserably mushy romantic epic. Next came *Roseanna McCoy,* a Hatfield-McCoy story. "Now it was during this period that Goldwyn began to lose his fabulous touch. It was a tight time, a rough time. Things were happening funny with the movies, because television was coming in. So Goldwyn decided to really cut down on the budget, to do a kind of cheap version of his classy movies. Then, too, there seemed to be great confusion when Bob McIntyre retired. A number of guys replaced him—somebody new on almost every film."

By 1951, after Goldwyn had used him in *Our Very Own* ("a sickie movie; the sugar content was too powerful for me"), *I Want You* ("unbelievable, old-fashioned") and *The Edge Of Doom* ("a real mistake from the very beginning"), Farley was doing everything he could to get out of his contract. "I felt claustrophobic. *Trapped!* He used to scream at me a lot—he'd shake and almost foam at the mouth. One thing he used to do to me—and this was typical, other people told me so—the day before filming would start on a picture, he'd call me into his office. He'd be sitting there behind his desk, with all the Academy Awards glistening and shining. He'd say, 'Do you like the part? You're gonna be marvelous in this! I know, because you're my boy. You're like a son to me!' He always said that he loved me more than Sammy, because I was more of an artist than Sammy, and I understood things. Then he'd say, 'You have to be good because you have to prove my faith in you. The director, he didn't want you in this picture at all. The writers, they saw your last film, you were very bad in that and *they* don't want you. But I have faith in you.' Of course, the first couple of times he did that to me, I was just destroyed! Then I began to realize it was his way of trying to get to me. He would pit people against each other so that he was always in control, the kingpin, pulling the strings. That was his way of working! But with me, after a while, it didn't work at all. He was treating me like a kid! I wanted him to be the boss, but not my father. I *had* a father!

"I was invited to the house for dinner a couple of times, which was all right. Frances was always very polite, very birdlike. You were given one drink, you were ushered in to have dinner and then you were made to practically *race* to the projection room. You always had a movie, no matter whose house you went to. But at Goldwyn's, you couldn't make jokes, which I always hated. You couldn't say, Oh, God, isn't it awful?! You had to be very *serious* about it.

"He had so few people under contract then. He split Dana's contract with Twentieth—and even *that* I wanted him to do with me! Various studios would have gone along with that. I *begged* him—but he wouldn't do it. So I just got more and more uptight. I was being so childish—I was doing everything I could to get him to kick me out. And he wouldn't, of course. He wanted me to have to buy my way out.

"It got to the point where we couldn't even talk to each other. But Goldwyn knew that TV was happening; he didn't know what he was gonna do then, and he didn't want me around his neck as an albatross. And I didn't want him around mine! So I finally did buy my contract out—it had two years to go. Which left me without a dime. Oh, he won! In the last years, I never got my full salary—I was always on suspension! And from then on, Goldwyn really did everything he could to keep me from working in Hollywood. As he did with Cathy, and as he did with David Niven. Fortunately, I was working in Europe and New York, in TV and theater. But out here, as far as movies are concerned, he really put the kibosh on me. They had a whole little rapport, the biggies. If someone was angry with some actor, they just picked up the phone. They'd say, 'Look, don't use him! He's on my shit list!' They were all-powerful, those people—and very vindictive! Mayer and Cohn, they were monsters! *Goldwyn* was a monster!

"Cohn was always the Boss, with the finger right in the face—*You do so-and-so!* Goldwyn, on the other hand, was more folksy—like Khrushchev. He had his homilies, his little mixed-up malaprops. He was more cutesy. He really liked to play Big Daddy. You were always breaking his heart if you didn't do what he wanted. He cried a lot—but I think it was all faking. I think he liked to cry. He could do it as well as Louis B. Mayer.

"They were monsters—but there's something missing now that they're gone. They were like bigger than life. I *liked* fighting with him, in a way. I would have *continued* working for him, if it weren't for the impossible situation—the loanouts, and his making so few movies.

"I think a big part of his trouble, as he got older, was that he would listen to whoever got to him last. He was getting unsure of himself. McCarthy and everything. He had gotten most of his best material, and his best writers, from the New York theater, which was quite liberal. Now, that was suspect. What kind of thing to do? Where to go?"

"I have joined the dropouts," Mary Wills told me over the phone in her Lillian Gish voice. "I wear levi's and jeans these days. I've become a rebel. I'm an Aquarian. What sign are you? Would you like to drop by tomorrow? You mustn't be shocked at my place—it's an absolute mess!"

Her house is in rustic (but nonetheless exclusive) Benedict Canyon, above the Beverly Hills Hotel. Inside, it is cluttered, comfortable, eclectic. Her Academy Award (costume design: *The Wonderful World of the Brothers Grimm*) is not in evidence.

Mary Wills is blonde ("I used to look a lot like Doris Day") and trim, and definitely does not look old enough to have gone to work for Goldwyn in 1945—which she did, as Irene Sharaff's assistant. When Sharaff left, Sam gave Mary a five-year contract, and she was his designer until 1952. "By the time I left," she says, "it was almost over. But I remember when it was the nicest studio in town to work at. You knew they cared about you, because they treated you so nicely. We had nice offices. I had my very own parking space on the lot. The man at the gate was polite. The janitor was polite. *Everybody* said Good morning. It was like a family, with Mr. Goldwyn being a very strict disciplinarian. The women on the lot—Julie Heron, Lelia Alexander, myself, my assistants—were expected to wear high-heeled shoes, and hats, and gloves. The seams of your stockings had to be straight.

"Mrs. Goldwyn set the example. She's a beautiful Irish lady. She worked around the clock for Mr. Goldwyn! He was *so* lucky to have her. And she thought she was lucky to have him, because her father had died when she was young, and he was a man that she could look up to. Frances grew up in Omaha, in a very proper big Victorian house. She had to kind of make do, making her own clothes and everything when she was a young actress. Frances left her home and her religion when she married Sam.

"Their family life was not homey. It was a very formal home. Frances *loved* entertaining. They always had somebody interesting like Tyrone Power, Joan Crawford, over for dinner. She also loved the intellectual contacts. Writers. She really enjoyed life. Such a *busy* life! As Mr. Goldwyn's social hostess. There were always dozens of people there to play croquet on the lawn, or to play tennis. It was a big producer's life.

"When they traveled, business came first. But they were wined and dined by the most interesting people. The Nixons became friends of theirs, and Eisenhower stayed with them. He gave a lot of money to Nixon's campaign; he backed him and believed in him, because he was Eisenhower's Vice President. They went to Palm Springs a lot, in two cars, with their complete staff—they did a lot of entertaining there.

"Mrs. Goldwyn was instrumental in the charity work they did, how they spent their money. She would try to find out in a very honest way if they were giving their money to the right things. She would call me sometimes to ask about a donation, what did I know about such-and-such.

"Their life was *very* disciplined! He got up early *every* morning and listened to the stock market reports around the world. She had to be up, she had to be dressed, she had to be ready to perform! She could never lie around, she could never be sick, she could never be tired. She happened to have this kind of nature. Gemini. Vitality and stamina. She'd bring her lunch in a bag, and she'd bring a sandwich for me. Oh, it was so good! She'd go to the Farmer's Market herself and buy the bread. She would do a lot of the marketing herself. She was really quite wonderful. She would have liked to have been much more human, I think. She was like an officer in the field, second in command. And *every day was an emergency with Mr. Goldwyn.* Any little thing that went wrong, he would start to freak out and go screaming, shouting through the house for her. '*Frances!*' And she'd have to go running. 'Now, Sam. Now, Sam. Now, wait a minute, Sam.' "

One of Frances' assignments was to serve as interpreter between her husband and Irene Sharaff, whom Goldwyn had fired and barred from the lot after a blowup during *Best Years.* Sharaff returned to do *Walter Mitty,* but only on the condition that Frances serve as liaison. "The problem," says Mary Wills, "was that Goldwyn couldn't read a sketch at all. And Sharaff, who has a very strong personality, couldn't explain it to him. So the costume would be made, and then he wouldn't be satisfied."

Goldwyn considered some of the costumes Sharaff designed for Virginia Mayo improper. He liked very, very ultra-feminine things—or else tailored. He was *fearful* of feathers and satin and jewels. He thought only a harlot would dress in things like that.

"He liked pastels. Their home had no red in it, and Mrs. Goldwyn would never wear red. He liked the virginal look. He thought all women should be virgins—or else they're bad women. That old Victorian thing. Once they gave a big party. All the gorgeous people were there, and Frances Goldwyn came downstairs in a lovely dress made by Travis Banton. It had a gold belt and embroidery or something—very elegant. His things were very theatrical. Goldwyn made her go back upstairs and change. He said she looked like a trollop.

"The wardrobe department had great stores of great materials left over from when Omar Kiam did *Marco Polo*. Beautiful, slinky things. One day I showed her a piece of slinky velvet and said, 'Oh, you should have a hostess gown of this!' She said, 'When would I wear it?' I said, 'Well, to put on for dinner.' She said, 'What do you think we *do* at night? Sam puts on his outing flannel pajamas and his old robe and comes down to dinner. And I put on something *very* respectable, covered up to here.' She said, 'You know, I don't live at all like you think I do.'

"I always got this lecture from Mr. Goldwyn about what people wore to bed, and how no decent woman would wear a nightgown. To him, a decent girl was like a girl living at the Barbizon Plaza. Tailored! And only wore *pajamas!* They could be *very* expensive—we used to go to the Maison de Blanc, or somewhere else in Beverly Hills and pay two or three hundred dollars for silk, handrolled with little embroidered initials and everything. But they were proper!

"When June Havoc played the alcoholic streetwalker in *Our Very Own*, we had to dress her as though, basically, she was a good woman. Because she was a *mother*. And when they remade *Ball Of Fire*, Virginia Mayo had to be clean-cut. It could not be implied that she was in any way a loose woman. Which, of course, the character was supposed to be! Mr. Goldwyn's morals had to do with such things as that. Outward appearances. It showed in all of his pictures."

Sam was never a womanizer, but he was not above making perfunctory passes at actresses "if he thought they were Bad Girls, Party Girls, Call Girls. That made them fair game. The Goldwyn Girls were pretty and young and, in a way, wild girls—but Goldwyn didn't like to think they were wild. Most of them married very well. One of them married Al Newman. Gregg Toland married one. We used to pile them all into two cars and go shopping at Magnin's or Bullocks. The Goldwyn Girls were the last of the fun times at Goldwyn's. After that, he got into wanting to make very serious pictures."

Although Mary Wills worked at the studio for five years as head designer, "Goldwyn never really knew my name. By the time I came there, he was quite an old man—like, sixty. Mrs. Goldwyn always said nobody knew his real age, or even his birthday. But he was very in-the-groove. He had a very impersonal, aloof manner, like the Supreme Commander who knows the face, he knows it's one of his men, but he doesn't know the *names*. When he came to my office, he knew that I was Miss Wills, the designer. But if he saw me out of context, or on the set, he'd look at me questioningly. I'm a warm person, outgoing. I'd say, Good morning! And he'd say, sort of hesitantly, 'Good morning, dear . . . Mary?' I'd say, Yes. 'Good morning!' he'd say. "Come on the set! We're doing a nice picture! I'd like you to see what we're doing!' I thought, My God, he thinks I'm Mary Pickford!

"Otherwise, I was Mrs. Goldwyn's little friend, Miss Wills. He always thought of me as a child, and he thought I really didn't know anything! He insisted that I have Edith Head to do some of the heavier costumes on *Enchantment*. He always took this *patronizing* tone with me—'Darling, now I know best, you know you shouldn't have it all fancy like you learn in art school.' I was a theatrical designer. And he held me down so terribly. They'd make me cut a collar down, to be even littler. And I couldn't have six buttons down the front, it had to be four. And he had no respect for a *period*, which insulted my integrity."

Enchantment was her first big picture for Goldwyn. "I designed a pretty pink little ball gown for Teresa Wright. Just a *darling* little piece of fluff. A *perfect* period piece. Teresa was like a little thistledown in it. Mrs. Goldwyn saw it, and she approved it. But when Goldwyn saw the test, he just went wild, because the dress had ruffles and a little bustle. He couldn't *stand* bustles! He wouldn't even talk to me! First he called in Edith Head, and she came out of his office crying. Mrs. Goldwyn went into his office, and *she* came out crying! She said, 'How could you *do* this to me? Mr. Goldwyn has just crucified us!' I said, 'What do you mean?' She said, 'You have let me down.' Tears were streaming down. I told her I was sorry, and she said, 'You should be! You really don't know, you don't know anything!' But she did say that Edith Head had said they were wonderful costumes.

"I wasn't afraid of him—but they wouldn't let me talk to him! I guess they were afraid he'd kick me off the lot, I would have fought him! I respected him and I admired him, but I didn't have that terrible fear of him."

Veterans of every department in the studio told me that the most dreaded hour of the day was nine A.M., when everyone who was employed in any creative capacity was expected to view the rushes with Sam and his executive staff. Mary Wills, who often worked nights, felt the strain of showing up bright and alert at that hour. "You'd drive on the lot and *run* up the stairs and *rush* in, breathless, to that pitch-dark projection room. It was like going up to meet your maker. Goldwyn was always early, and so were his henchmen, like Mr. Fromkess. His production men were always *very* serious in front of him; they had to back him right up.

"If you were five seconds late, the film had started. But you had to go in *anyway*. As you opened the door, the streak of sunlight went with you. You staggered in, absolutely blind, but you knew there were people sitting there from the fragrance of after-shave, and Mrs. Goldwyn's perfume. Your heart would be pounding. You'd fumble, and you'd *sit* on somebody; then someone would take your hand, and you'd try to slump down and be unnoticeable. Mr. Goldwyn always sat in the back row.

"Now, *I* was there to look at the costumes. The set decorator went to look at the set. The actress maybe was up there, and she was looking at her performance. The dialog coach was there, listening to the dialog, and if it was *really* a bad day, Frances Goldwyn was there to save anybody from getting killed.

"Mr. Goldwyn would *scream* at you the dark. He was beginning to be deaf by then, and would scream *loudly*. 'Why *can't they straighten the collar*?!?' What he didn't know was that the day before, Willy Wyler had said, 'Everybody off the set!' And you'd say, 'But Teresa's collar . . .' This was the collar Irene Sharaff designed for Teresa Wright. It cost five hundred dollars to make that blouse, because they kept redoing it. Teresa just played a normal little girl next door, but Sharaff was designing costumes for people like Lunt and Fontanne in her mind—these incredibly overworked costumes that required ten fittings! Then Wyler wouldn't allow Irene Sharaff on the set, so she told me, 'Go on the set and watch that collar, and if that collar gets out of line, you go up and straighten it!' But Teresa was trying to do a heavy scene, and Wyler said, 'Don't *anybody* come on this set, and don't *touch* her!' So I would then have to go to the projection room and hear Goldwyn say, 'Look at her collar! I'm paying a designer one thousand dollars a week, she has an assistant and two wardrobe men, and you can't straighten the collar!' Wyler would probably not even be there. Or if he was, he'd say, 'Sam! Mr. Goldwyn! Sam! It doesn't *matter* about the collar!' But Goldwyn would just keep on screaming. And everybody there *heard* you get it, and you'd just *hope* that he'd notice that the roses on the table were wilted or something, so he'd get after the set decorator and forget about the damn collar. This was what we called Getting The Projection Room. People would just want to jump off the balcony and *kill* themselves. I never, for the rest of my career, could go into a dark projection room without getting sick to my stomach.

I asked Mary Wills, as I had asked many other people, whether she happened to have any candid pictures of Goldwyn that I might borrow. Like everyone else, she said no—but she was the first to offer an explanation. "*Nothing* was candid on the Goldwyn lot," she said. "Neither behind the scenes nor on the stage were there any candid performances. That's why his daughter and his son don't want a book published about him. They will not let him be a dimensional person! Not even a human being!"

23. *The Worst Years*

As the forties ended, the industry as Sam had known it was going down for the last time. In 1948, the Supreme Court ruled that the major studios must divest themselves of their affiliated theater chains. Pictures would henceforth have to be sold on their individual merits, rather than being automatically booked into theaters controlled by the studios. Sam called the decision "essential to the health of our industry in order to break the stranglehold held by a few companies on the exhibitor market." On the surface, it seemed to strengthen his bargaining position. But the decision, though fair, was disastrous to the already precarious economy of the industry—and Sam, independent as he had always proclaimed himself to be, could not dissociate his fortunes from those of the industry as a whole.

In 1948, the number of studio personnel dropped by 25 percent. Those who didn't get laid off took salary cuts. Goldwyn halved every executive's salary, including his own. "The movie business is tottering on its last legs," he told a group of producers, and predicted that if they didn't start making better pictures for half the cost (he did not explain how this could be done), they should get ready to fold up. But the industry could not break its profligate habits overnight—and with stars beginning to demand percentage deals, and with television creeping into thousands of new living rooms every night, it was already too late.

As Goldwyn's output shrank to two and then (after 1950) one production a year, a new project took up the slack and provided a welcome distraction. Sam was becoming a Legend.

He had always had a mania for publicity; if a week went by without the publication of a feature article about him, he would fire a press agent. What he loved most of all were ghosted articles under his byline; these were planted in *Collier's, Liberty, Reader's Digest,* even *The New York Times Magazine.* He saw that his pictures were publicized long before they even went into production; actors were astonished to read in the trades that they had been cast in pictures they'd never heard of, and which never did get beyond the talking stage.

Over the years, the publicists with the longest staying power were, successively, Jock Lawrence, Lynn Farnol and Bill Hebert. Farnol, who handled the campaign for *Best Years,* was an Ivy League type who knew how to get "class" publicity into national magazines. Farnol's successor, Bill Hebert, was a more typical Hollywood press agent—Jack Carson in *A Star Is Born.* One of Hebert's brainchildren was a radio show called "Stars in Your Eyes." Scripts were distributed to radio stations "through the courtesy of Samuel Goldwyn Productions, Inc." One typical show began:

> FROM HOLLYWOOD, THE GLAMOUR CAPITAL OF THE WORLD, WE PRESENT THE LATEST INSIDE NEWS, CHATTER AND HUMAN INTEREST STORIES OF THE STARS AND THE MOTION PICTURE STUDIOS, GATHERED BY OUR ON-THE-SPOT REPORTER, WHOSE HOME BASE IS THE SAMUEL GOLDWYN STUDIO, GATHERING PLACE OF THE WORLD'S MOST BEAUTIFUL WOMEN—THE GOLDWYN GIRLS. LEARN WHAT GOES ON BEHIND THE STUDIO GATES, IN FILMDOM'S SOCIAL CIRCLES, IN THE SMART CLUBS AND STARS' HOMES—ALL UP AND DOWN HOLLYWOOD BOULEVARD.

Bill Hebert had ingenuity, but Sam wanted class. He knew that prior to *The Best Years,* he had been a figure of fun (thanks to that *schnorrer,* Goldfish) to Hollywood's elite. After *Best Years,* he began to be taken more seriously—thanks largely to the efforts of Ben Sonnenberg.

Sonnenberg was so classy that he didn't even call himself a press agent; he was a "public relations counsellor." His clients included Anaconda Copper, Standard Oil, Lever Brothers. He had emigrated from Russia at the age of nine, and had acquired the qualities Sam most admired: education, assimilation, an incalculable fortune, a royal life-style (his butler had worked for the Duke and Duchess of Windsor), and Respect. He described himself as "a Byzantine with Talmudic overtones." He was paid exorbitant retainers for unorthodox advice such as, in the case of Texaco, "Sell the cleanliness of your restrooms and introduce opera to the American people over the radio."

"When a man buys me," Sonnenberg told a *Town & Country* writer, "he buys cachet." When Goldwyn bought him, Sonnenberg appraised his new client's reputation as "powerful but, like a shillelagh, it had carbuncles on it. . . . I proceeded to assess his reputation on the basis of performance, and on the real contribution that he made as a fighting and stormy petrel independent in a business that was growing more and more monopolistic. I proceeded to add a measure of statesmanship, maturity and seasoning to what he did, so that he later appeared at Oxford University and received accolades by the dozen, and today he is taken seriously." *

Goldwyn was pleased with the job Sonnenberg did, but not with his blabbing about it to reporters. A few months after the above quote appeared in print, an article in the *Motion Picture Herald* indignantly admonished Sonnenberg for "taking the credit for the creative redemption of Mr. Goldwyn" and, in effect, called him a liar. But Sonnenberg had no reason to lie, and Niven Busch corroborates his story. "Sonnenberg told me that Goldwyn hired him to release a flood of stories saying that Goldwyn really spoke English like a member of the Academy, and that the stories about his malapropisms had been invented by Ben Hecht and Charles MacArthur. Sonnenberg asked me to write a piece for *The New York Times*, a profile or something, and help spread this canard. I said, No way! I wasn't going to make myself ridiculous doing this! But Ben began to circulate this shit!"

The Sonnenberg Touch bestowed, as promised, the sweet smell of cachet. A respectful profile in *Life* described Sam "sitting in a large wicker chair on a terrace outside his home surrounded

* *The New Yorker* (April 8, 1950).

by roses, oleanders and pepper trees. In one hand he held a cup of tea. Beside him on a plate was a twisted English biscuit and a small round pool of honey." The Los Angeles Chapter of the United Jewish Appeal named him Humanitarian of the Year, at a dinner given in his honor. The Mexican government, acknowledging his contribution of the proceeds from the Mexican premier of *Best Years* to a fund for undernourished children, awarded him a medal for his "outstanding depiction of democracy at work in the western hemisphere." His "statesmanlike" pronouncements appeared in hundreds of newspapers—attacking monopolistic theater chains; denouncing subsidies ("It only encourages bad pictures"); announcing that good pictures had nothing to fear from television; demanding a revised code of ethics so that "grown-up" films could be produced ("I don't believe in immoral pictures, but neither do I believe in just being able to produce pictures for children.").

Whatever the source, or sources, the Legend grew, feeding on a blend of fact and fancy which nobody had reason to challenge. In 1951, Sam the statesman introduced Israeli Prime Minister Ben-Gurion at a fund-raising rally at the Hollywood Bowl. In December, 1952, the Beverly Hills City Council declared "Samuel Goldwyn Day" and presented Sam with a medal "for his forty years of industry and civic leadership." If he occasionally contradicted or reversed himself (in 1953 he said 3-D would be "a bigger shot in the arm to the industry than either color or sound"; in 1954, he declared he had "never gone overboard for the novelty of 3-D"), nobody noticed or cared.

As the industry found itself in increasingly desperate straits, Sam took advantage of every opportunity to hang the blame on his long-time enemies, the exhibitors. In September of 1953, he went too far. Commenting on governmental attempts to impose a 20 percent "admissions tax" on theater box offices, Goldwyn said there were too many theaters anyway, and it would be no loss if many of them were forced to close—prompting this outraged response from the president of an association of small theater operators:

> With full recognition that Goldwyn has on occasion and only on occasion produced a boxoffice success, I would hardly

> relegate him to oblivion as readily as he has so glibly condemned thousands of theaters that have made it possible for him to shoot his mouth off. . . . I resent and protest these constant declarations that do the industry harm and benefit no one and nothing except Goldwyn's ego.

> A statement such as his must be taken seriously and not passed off as another inane Goldwynism. There's little doubt the loss of these theatres would be more harmful to the industry than the loss of Goldwyn.

The spokesman went on to announce that his organization's Iowa-Nebraska unit was forming a "Society for Muzzling Sammy." The spokesman for *that* unit issued a statement of his own, phrased in strangely familiar rhetoric: "It seems that savant of sagacious syllogisms, that peripatetic promoter of percentage pictures, that remonstrative repeater of the redundant remark, 40 percent Sammy Goldwyn is back in the news again. . . . Anybody agree with him? Or does he, as usual, stand alone?"

A representative of still another theater owners' group stated that "as far as exhibitors are concerned, Goldwyn should be permanently put on ice," and urged that "exhibs" pass up Goldwyn's pictures "from here on." *

It was unfortunate that Goldwyn continued to antagonize exhibitors at a time when his pictures needed all the help they could get. For example: *Enchantment.*

Nobody who worked on *Enchantment* has anything good to say about it, except that Gregg Toland's photography was, as always, outstanding. Sadly, it was Toland's last picture. Only weeks after its completion, in the summer of 1948, a heart attack killed him. He was forty-four years old.

Toland was a warm but introverted individual. To director Henry Koster, he was "Little Grief." "That's what he called him*self*," says Koster. "He used to come in my office and say, 'Henry, Little Grief is going to make trouble again.' I'd say, 'What's the matter?' He'd say, 'I don't like the close-up of Loretta. I'd like to do it over,' Never had a smile on his face, he

* *Variety* (September 16, 1953).

was so obsessed with his mission. He was the greatest cameraman alive."

A few months before he died, Toland gave a rare interview to Lester Koenig, printed in *Films in Review*. He expressed harsh criticism of cameramen less dedicated than himself, saying, "Cameramen often have ideas which would entail more work on their part, and they don't suggest them to the director for that reason. I stick out my neck."

He spoke candidly of the problem of the preponderance of "unstimulating" stories. "That's not an inducement to do your best work. When it's been my misfortune to have to photograph one of those pictures, I've said to my wife, 'I feel just like a whore, doing it for the money. If I had any guts, I'd quit this picture and we would go down to Rio or someplace.' But you never do. You just keep hoping the next opportunity will be better."

Toland deeply resented the star system. "It means we are making pictures with 'personality' rather than story . . . many cameramen are forced to sacrifice everything in order to keep some old bag playing young women. And when I say old bag, that's what I mean. A girl is often so old by the time she proves her ability that out comes the burlap in front of the lens.

"The average producer will answer, 'Pictures are a business for profit.' So they are, but it would be fine once-in-a-time, though, to see an honest motion picture. Aren't you tired of seeing some glamour star playing a shopgirl in New York, living in an apartment that would cost ten times her monthly salary, wearing dresses she couldn't possibly afford, and with a hairdo you could only get by coming to the movie studio and having a staff of specialists create for two hours before you come on the set?

"Some people might have the mistaken notion that I am referring to Goldwyn. This is definitely not the case. I sincerely believe that Goldwyn will allow me more freedom, more experiments and more ideas than anyone at the moment. I do not say this to protect my contented feeling, because Goldwyn may have my contract back any morning he chooses, and without a settlement, and he knows it. I believe he tries harder than any other person in this industry. He isn't always right, but he *tries*."

Leon Fromkess had to give Goldwyn the news of Toland's sudden death. "He cried like a baby. He loved Toland like a son." On the day of the funeral (attended by four hundred members of the industry), a five-minute silence was observed at the studio, and the flag flew at half-mast. But no gesture could begin to convey the enormity of the vacuum created by Gregg Toland's death. It was more than his artistic and engineering brilliance that made him irreplaceable. At Goldwyn's, as at every studio, an ongoing battle was waged between the money men in the front office and the creative people who made the pictures. During his eighteen-year association with Toland, Goldwyn had come to rely heavily on the cameraman's advice and judgment, not just in matters of photography but in all the creative aspects of picturemaking. Now, with his profit margin steadily shrinking and without the balancing weight of Toland's influence, the money men began winning most of the arguments. For the first time in Goldwyn's career, cost became the major consideration. The result was a series of pictures that were embarrassing to everyone connected with them. The first one was *Roseanna McCoy.*

Goldwyn told George Jenkins, art director on the picture, that he had bought the property—a novel based on the Hatfield-McCoy feud—because the jacket on the book said it was the greatest American love story, the Romeo and Juliet of the New World. He hired John Collier to do the screenplay.

Although Collier received sole credit, a recent viewing of *Roseanna McCoy* convinced me that that whimsical, urbane Englishman, who has done some fine writing, could not possibly have been the guilty party. Dialogue such as "When Randall McCoy shot my Pappy down, the earth was drinkin' up his blood like a hog drinks slops" could pass for vintage Ben Hecht, but not John Collier. I wrote to Collier in London, where he now makes his home, asking for clarification. He replied:

> I can't deny having written most of the screenplay of *Roseanna McCoy,* though I know that many changes were made in the course of the shooting. The lines you quote can't possibly be mine, though I must have done a very poor job.
>
> My relations with Sam Goldwyn were always distant and

formal. I have the feeling that I was thinking of something else all the time I was at the studio. Everyone else seems to have vivid and amusing stories about dealings with Sam. Unfortunately, I have absolutely none.

Farley Granger, who saw the original Collier script, thought it was "fantastic! A *beautiful* script! It really captured all the thing of the mountain people, with witches and weird folklore, like they really are. Some of those people speak almost with Elizabethan dialects, to this day!

"Then just before we were to start shooting, they threw the whole thing out! We were sent up to the Sierra Madre mountains where they had built sets, and we were up there for two weeks shooting with absolutely no script! Irving Reis, the director, shot 'Farley Granger riding horse from left to right, riding horse from right to left . . .' We just shot *things!* Then we were laid off for a couple of weeks. Then we started shooting the picture. It was just like television. We got the pages piecemeal, every day. We didn't know where we were, what was happening. We had no continuity or anything!"

Mary Wills provided the final piece of the puzzle. "There were some agents, you see, who had no brains whatsoever, but they were funny and amusing, and they would try to sell you a bill of goods. If you didn't want to buy what they were selling, they had some yard goods in the car you could get cheap, too. They were peddlers. And *one of them sold him Ben Hecht,* to rewrite *Roseanna McCoy.* He turned it into a terrible shoot-'em-up thing!"

The Hatfield-McCoy feud, never resolved in reality, was resolved in the movie with Joan Evans riding off with Farley on his horse, across the river and into the sunset.

The picture broke even.

In 1948, Goldwyn made a three-picture deal with director Mark Robson, best known for *Champion, Home of the Brave* and, most recently, *Earthquake.* Robson calls his three years with Goldwyn "one of the worst periods of my career. The pictures I made for him were just terrible: *My Foolish Heart, I Want You, Edge of Doom.* I never worked with a producer like Goldwyn. He'd say, 'I've got the greatest writer, the greatest designer, the greatest this, the greatest that.' I'd ask him, 'Then what do you need *me* for? Let everybody else do the work!' "

Goldwyn's production of *My Foolish Heart,* based on a short story ("Uncle Wiggily in Connecticut") by J. D. Salinger, may have had something to do with that author's self-imposed seclusion since that time. Salinger's story was an understated character study. The movie became a soapy morality play about the tragic consequences of illicit sex. (Ironically, Victor Young's theme song, which shot to the top of the hit parade, served as background music for a good deal of the illicit sex going on at the time.)

I Want You was described in a *Los Angeles Times* article (under Goldwyn's byline) as "a picture that tells the story of the effect of America's rearming on the lives of an American family today . . . in terms of the loves, the aspirations, the disappointments, the tears and the joys of real people—not cardboard characters—in times of stress. . . . It is not a 'message' picture or a propaganda picture, for I believe the function of the screen is to entertain."

Only Sam could have claimed (with a straight face) that *I Want You* was anything other than a propagandistic defense of our involvement in Korea. By the time it was finished, so was the war, and the audience for it was comparable to what it would be today for a picture about Vietnam.

Goldwyn even got Dick Day back to design sets for *My Foolish Heart, Our Very Own, The Edge of Doom* and *I Want You.* If anything, the beautiful frames merely emphasized the deficiencies of the pictures they contained. For the industry in general, and for Sam in particular, it was the worst of times. The nadir, in 1950, was *The Edge of Doom.*

The novel called *The Edge of Doom* was still in galleys when Goldwyn heard that Darryl Zanuck was interested in the property. That was enough to pique Sam's interest, and he obtained a set of galleys, which Frances read. Leon Fromkess, who was in on the debacle from the beginning, recalls that "Frances brought the galleys to my office, all excited. It would make a great picture, she said—I must drop everything and read it.

"The next day, we had a meeting in Goldwyn's office. Frances was all aglow and aglitter about it. She was one of the most ambitious women you would ever meet; she asserted herself more and more, but never in front of her husband. I told Goldwyn I'd never make it as a picture, that I thought it was sacrilegious even *trying* to make it! He jumped up from his chair—typical—and said, 'Goldwyn makes the pictures!' "

The Edge of Doom was a morbid, dreadfully written story about a young man who kills a priest—with a crucifix. How the novel got published in the first place is a mystery—unless the publisher was, like Frances Goldwyn, a guilt-ridden Catholic doing penance by reading it. For in the eyes of the Church, Frances, married to a divorced man, had been living in sin for the past twenty-seven years.

On Goldwyn's instructions, Fromkess went after "every top writer in town. When they read the book, they turned it down. Then Phil Yordan came to me. He'd written *Dillinger*—which was certainly not a Goldwyn-type picture. We offered him twenty-five hundred dollars a week and a twenty-week guarantee. He told me, 'I'll write anything for money. I've bought a lot of real estate, and I've got to keep pushing to make my payments.' "

Farley Granger, who played the murderer, was "very worried" about the picture. "If they'd really told the story of the religious torment of this man, why he hated the priest for what he had done to him and his mother, and about the corruption of the Church—but it was a whole false premise! It didn't *mean* anything! Mark Robson did everything he could, but it was such a dreary project, nobody could do anything to save it. There was nowhere to go with this stupid story!"

During production, Goldwyn underwent prostate surgery in New York. When he got back to the studio and saw the rough cut, he knew something was terribly wrong—but what? With no Toland or Wyler to tell him, he asked cameraman Harry Stradling what he should do. But Stradling, while a competent cameraman, had no desire to be consulted about scripts or direction. He simply wanted to do his job and go home at the end of the day, instead of looking at rushes long into the night. Mark Robson didn't mind; he had been a cutter (had edited *Citizen Kane,* in fact) and, like Wyler (and Goldwyn) could look at film until it was practically worn out. But Robson couldn't communicate with Goldwyn!

As often happened, Sam listened to the most insistent voice at hand—in this case, that of publicist Jock Lawrence. Lawrence persuaded him that what the picture needed was a love interest, which could be provided by adding a prologue and an epilogue. Goldwyn asked Danny Mandell what he thought of the idea. "I told him I didn't like it. He said, 'Do you have a better idea?' I said, 'Yeah, leave the picture as it is.' But he was convinced that Jock Lawrence was right. So we had to go ahead and do it. It was about three days' shooting. I thought it made the picture even worse."

The days when Sam could indulge in the extravagance of throwing everything out and starting over were gone forever. The salvage attempt on *Doom* cost $200,000, and an expensive ad campaign cost still more—but Farley Granger was right. Nothing could have saved the picture. Years later, Goldwyn admitted publicly that it lost more money than it cost to make —"which," said Sam, "isn't easy to do!"

24. *The Last Years*

Goldwyn's last three pictures were *Hans Christian Andersen* (1952), *Guys and Dolls* (1955), and *Porgy and Bess* (1959). *Hans Christian Andersen* was a moderate success; *Porgy and Bess,* an unmitigated disaster; and *Guys and Dolls,* a mitigated one.

Goldwyn's original choice to play *Hans Christian Andersen* was Gary Cooper, with Moira Shearer to costar as the ballerina. But Shearer got pregnant and Cooper became unavailable. The picture starred Danny Kaye, Farley Granger (in his last picture for Goldwyn) and Jeanmaire, with Roland Petit directing the dances.

In 1951, after spending a fortune on at least twenty-one different screenplays (all of which he rejected), Goldwyn finally settled on a version by Moss Hart. Hart's choice to write the music and lyrics was Frank Loesser, who had just had tremendous success with *Guys and Dolls* on Broadway. With all this talent signed, Goldwyn hired Charles Vidor, a competent but uninspired director.

William Dozier, then Goldwyn's executive assistant, recalls that "Sam poured a lot into *Hans Christian Andersen,* but he was visibly beginning to lose interest at that time. He didn't seem to care any more about hearing about things that somebody else might want to buy. I had known him for many years, and I had the feeling that the competitive instinct had gone out of him."

Dozier's job was supposedly to find stories and hire writers—"but that was not very preoccupying, because he didn't do many pictures then. Much of my time was spent *talking* about stories that never got bought. *Frances* used to come in and talk to me about stories a great deal, and I could never quite tell whether she was talking with me as a representative of Goldwyn, or whether it was on her own initiative. I didn't know whether the discussion was going to go back to Sam, or whether it was just for her own interest. It always used to puzzle me, just what she was doing. Everybody thought she had a tremendous influence on all his business decisions, but you never saw it happening. It was *in camera*, believe me."

Hans Christian Andersen, while hardly the picture "for children of all ages" that Goldwyn represented it to be, *was* an entertaining picture for children. Frank Loesser's songs—"Inchworm," "Thumbelina," "No Two People," "Wonderful Copenhagen"—all became popular hits. The only real problem came from an unexpected quarter: Denmark. The Danes, who consider Andersen a national hero, took exception to the fact that the character Danny Kaye played bore no resemblance whatever to the real man—nor did the plot resemble his life! A prominent Danish newspaper asked, "Is Hollywood really permitted to distort the life of a great man in such a reckless manner? It's a gigantic joke!"

Threatened with the loss of the substantial Scandinavian market, Goldwyn added a prologue to the film. "Once upon a time," says a narrator, "there lived in Denmark a great storyteller named Hans Christian Andersen. This is *not* the story of his life, but a fairy tale about this great spinner of fairy tales." To further placate the Danes, Sam sent Danny Kaye on a public appearance tour that included laying a wreath on Andersen's grave; and, in a masterful application of the Goldwyn touch, donated the proceeds of the Copenhagen premiere to charities for the benefit of Danish children.

Having thus protected his investment, he turned his attention to his next production: *Guys and Dolls*. By this time, Frances had taken over the function of what had been the story department. "I read all the scripts that come in," she told a reporter, "and if I think one will interest my husband, he gets it. He doesn't make a major decision without talking with me. He wouldn't have spent one million dollars for the story of *Guys and Dolls,* for example, if I hadn't said, 'Now listen, Sam, you go ahead and do it!' "

The fact that Sam had never produced a successful musical (the Cantor and Kaye pictures were, essentially, comedies with music) caused him no concern. He might have compensated by hiring a director experienced in the genre. Instead, he got Joseph Mankiewicz, whose credits included some fine (but no musical) films: *All About Eve, Letter to Three Wives, Julius Caesar.* Goldwyn cast Marlon Brando and Jean Simmons, neither of whom had ever sung or danced professionally, as Sky Masterson and Sarah Brown. To play Nathan Detroit, the quintessential Runyon character (portrayed to perfection on the stage by Sam Levene), he signed Frank Sinatra!

Goldwyn spent five-and-a-half million of his own dollars transforming the wondrously brash, vital "musical fable of Broadway" into a bloodless, boring picture—pastrami on Wonder Bread. Sam even included a new group of Goldwyn Girls; they came across as quaint and anachronistic. Reviews were mediocre, but thanks to elaborate promotion (BRANDO SINGS! the ads promised—or warned), the picture made money. By Sam's lights, that (and the fact that he liked it. He *liked* it!) made it successful.

In the case of *Porgy and Bess,* the property itself was an anachronism. If it was true, as Goldwyn claimed, that it had taken him ten years of negotiating with the Gershwin and DuBose Heyward estates to get the screen rights, that sealed the picture's fate. In 1947, *Porgy and Bess* might have been accepted as folk art. But in 1957, when Sam announced that Sidney Poitier would play Porgy, outraged civil rights leaders attacked the actor for agreeing to appear in a "condescending, insulting relic from a different age." Poitier's response was to withdraw from the cast. At that point, a boycott by all black actors seemed imminent.

Sam had paid $750,000 cash for *Porgy and Bess,* and he was not about to allow the production to go down the drain. Poitier, the first black actor to reach what appeared to be the brink of solid stardom, was exceptionally vulnerable to what he later described as "pressures brought to bear from a number of quarters and . . . a threat of my career stopping dead still." In December, 1957, Goldwyn announced that Poitier had "reconsidered" and would play Porgy after all. "I am confident," said Poitier (in a prepared statement) "that Mr. Goldwyn, with his characteristic good taste and integrity, will present the property in a sensitive manner." Years later, he admitted, "I have not yet completely forgiven myself." *

Without Poitier's support, the boycott had no backbone. Sammy Davis, Jr., Dorothy Dandridge, Brock Peters, Diahann Carroll and Pearl Bailey joined the cast, and preproduction work proceeded.

Rehearsals were set to begin on July 3. On July 2, Sam and Frances conducted a final inspection of the studio's mammoth Stage 8, which contained all of Irene Sharaff's costumes for the picture, Irving Sindler's props (eighteen full boxes of them), ten newly built dressing rooms and the Catfish Row set, designed by Oliver Smith, six months in construction. The Goldwyns declared everything okay, and went home.

Inside Porgy's little house on Catfish Row was a mattress on which someone, perhaps sneaking a quick nap late that afternoon, had left a lighted cigarette. That night, the stage and everything in it blazed up; after one nightmarish hour, only ashes and rubble remained.

Early on in his own motion picture career, coincidence had placed Sam with Adolph Zukor one evening at the scene of a potentially disastrous fire at Zukor's Manhattan studio. Zukor's reaction had so impressed Sam that he related the incident in *Behind the Screen*. Faced with financial ruin, all Zukor kept saying, over and over, was, "Is anybody hurt?"

Forty years later, in a similar crisis, Sam reacted with the same concern. Assured that there were no casualties, he appraised the situation with relative calm (aided, undoubtedly, by the knowledge that he was heavily insured). After several days of pondering the alternatives, he announced that the production would continue as planned, after an eight-week postponement.

Two stages were moved in from Eagle Lion, an inde-

* William Hoffman, *Sidney* (New York, Lyle Stuart, 1971).

pendent studio across the street from Goldwyn's. (Eventually, Sam would build three smaller, more practical stages to replace Stage 8.) Sets, props and costumes were rebuilt. Oliver Smith remained Production Designer, but Goldwyn replaced art director Joe Wright with Serge Krizman. Krizman, who had not worked for Goldwyn before, recalls their first meeting, in Sam's office. "He told me, 'Art directors are the backbone of a picture.' I suggested that the sets be designed cinematically, rather than theatrically, so that it wouldn't just look like a photographed play. He said. 'Fine, but I want it to be beautiful!' "

Three weeks after the fire, Goldwyn fired director Rouben Mamoulian.

Mamoulian had spent eight months working with Goldwyn and with N. Richard Nash, who wrote the screenplay. Nash was stunned when he heard that Mamoulian had been fired, but not really surprised. "What surprised me was that those two could have *ever* gotten along! Rouben is a man of *enormous* talent, *meticulous* in his ideas. He speaks with such specificity, you know *exactly* where his mind is. Their conflict was basic: Rouben, the articulate, and Sam, the inarticulate."

Nash preferred to work in New York, making periodic trips to California to meet with the producer and director. "I could see that while I was away, things kept getting worse between them. Rouben got into the habit of scoffing at everything Sam had to say. He didn't seem to be listening. One day Sam pointed his finger at Rouben and he said, 'You dunt listen to me!'

"Rouben said, 'Here is what you said,' and he repeated Sam's exact words. And Sam said, 'You listen to de voids, and Richard listens to vot I *mean!*' which was absolutely true.

"They finally got to the point where neither of them heard what the other was saying. Their battles slowed everything up. We weren't getting anywhere. Rouben, the intellectual, demanded the precise phrase for what you meant; Sam hoped you would understand what he meant, instead of what he was saying.

"Then there were other problems. Sam had assumed that his doing of *Porgy and Bess* would be greeted with huzzahs from the black community. But it was just the beginning of the black revolution, and everybody was very touchy. Sam was getting more and more nervous. He was putting a lot of money into the picture. Now he pulled his horns in a little, and pulled his budget down considerably. The biggest cut was in the matter of sets. The original screenplay was written for many locales, not at all like a stage play, and Rouben loved that script! At Sam's behest, we did pull it in some. But then he wanted us to pull it in further and further and still further, and finally Rouben and he had a big battle about it."

Mamoulian was no William Seiter, willing to take his money and quietly bow out of the picture. The director called a press conference at which he stated flatly that there had been "not one iota of dissension" between himself and Goldwyn concerning the picture. The basis for his "precipitous and irresponsible" dismissal, he charged, was Goldwyn's fear that Mamoulian might get some of the credit for the picture. Goldwyn, he said, had ordered him to fire his personal press agent. He had refused. Goldwyn had forbidden him to give interviews to the press. He had done so and, moreover, in discussing the production, never once had mentioned the producer's name! Finally, he said, Goldwyn had threatened to ruin him for having disobeyed.

Mamoulian filed a protest with the Screen Directors Guild, and *they* got into the act, alleging that Goldwyn's action was based on "frivolous, spiteful or dictatorial reasons not pertinent to the director's skill" and instructed its members to boycott Samuel Goldwyn productions—thus making it impossible for Sam to secure the services of *any* qualified director. Guild officers pointed out that Sam's contract with the Guild had expired.

When the dust settled, Goldwyn renewed his contract with the Guild, hired director Otto Preminger and rescheduled his starting date for August 27. Meanwhile, he offered Richard Nash, who had already fulfilled his commitment by delivering a shooting script, a substantial chunk of additional money if he would revise the script still again. "He wanted me to bring it down, down, down in terms of its camera mobility, and also cost. I refused to do it. I told him that if he brought in another writer, I'd understand. He said, 'But you'll have to share a credit!' I said

Okay, and I remember saying—kind of meanly, I later thought—'I'll also be sharing the blame.' He said, 'Dere will be no blame in dis picture. It's going to be a great big hit!' I told him I hoped so, and I left.

"Then *Frances* called me and tried to convince me to do it. She said, 'Don't walk out on him now. He really loves you. Do what he says. Do what he wants!' She put me through a slightly bad time. I knew I was right, but I had a terrible sense of responsibility to that project. I really worked like a dog on it! I did so much research on my own, on Dorothy and DuBose Heyward, on the prototypes of Catfish Row. I went down to the Carolinas. I was *terribly* proud of my first draft. It was going to be an active, moving kind of picture. I located music that Gershwin had discarded—music that I don't think has been heard! It was just . . . too bad.

"He never did give it to another writer. Preminger just changed the whole thing. And it turned out to be a film that could very easily have been the play. A relatively static film."

The next blow fell two weeks before rehearsals were to start. An organization called The Council for Improvement of Negro Theatre Arts ran a double-page ad in the Hollywood trade newspapers, reprinting an editorial that had appeared in a leading newspaper of Los Angeles' black community. The tone, although vicious and hysterical, indicated just how far out of touch Goldwyn was with the mood of the times. The writer, Almena Lomax, had attended a press conference held to hype the upcoming production. She had sensed "the tension, the battle for status, the people disprizement," she wrote, from the moment she drove onto the "lily-white lot. . . . The only Negroes we saw were a couple of guys trundling large containers of trash." She described Sam as "an ordinary mortal with a face like a plumber's wrench," and observed that the air was "heavy with sycophancy, although even it has to battle for a place in the sun with Goldwyn's own worship of himself.

"We watched Sidney Poitier put on his beamish black boy act. He did everything except scratch his 'haid.' Then we received Mr. Goldwyn's personal assurances that the Negro could just put his trust in Samuel Goldwyn, the Alpha and Omega of film making, the know-it-all-on-all-subjects. . . . Mr. Goldwyn smiled in gentle reproof that we should feel we knew more about being colored than he does, or that we would feel that a colored writer, like John O. Killens or Langston Hughes, could come anywhere near preparing a workable script for a Samuel Goldwyn picture."

In conclusion, readers were reminded that "directly after the earlier blasts at Goldwyn for his plans to make this piece of ante-bellum gingerbread, he gave a thousand dollars to the local NAACP drive . . . rather like blood-money, wouldn't you think?"

Sam was surprised, angered and hurt by the attack. "The only thing left to go wrong on this picture," he told a reporter, "is for me to go to jail." Wrong. The next crisis occurred on the first day of rehearsal, when the cast mutinied.

The new controversy centered on the dialogue. From the very beginning of his involvement in the project, Poitier had argued with his friend, Richard Nash, about the exaggerated dialect written into the dialogue of the residents of Catfish Row. Poitier felt that the ungrammatical speech was an affront to the civil rights movement. Nash says, "It seemed impossible to me to write a black in Catfish Row, South Carolina, in that era [1912], as Sidney said, *dicty*. Sidney said some of the characters seemed dumb. I argued that poverty stultifies whites *and* blacks. Anyway, by the time it got on the screen, the blacks were pretty *dicty*. Worst of all, it lacked poetry!"

Pursued to its logical ludicrous extreme, Poitier's argument would have had Porgy singing "Bess, You Are My Woman Now," and Sportin' Life, "It Isn't Necessarily So." What Sidney sought was a compromise. So during rehearsal, without consulting Preminger, Poitier's accent gradually shifted from Catfish Row to that of an English gentleman—and the rest of the cast followed his lead.

A compromise eventually *was* reached; the dialect was modified and the score—already recorded, with Poitier's songs dubbed by opera singer Robert McFerrin—*re*recorded, at considerable expense. In the end, the characters' relatively elegant diction and the lavish costumes they wore (Irene Sharaff again) gave the picture a basic dishonesty that not even Gershwin's magnificent music could overcome. "Make it beautiful," Sam had said. Beautiful was what he got.

Goldwyn and Preminger got along little better than had Goldwyn and Mamoulian. Except for occasional shouting matches, heard all over the lot, they barely spoke. At one point, Sam actually fired Preminger—but Preminger refused to leave!

Serge Krizman frequently found himself called upon to deliver messages between the two men. "I would have to tell Otto, 'Mr. Goldwyn wanted the scene played differently.' He would say, 'He's not directing this picture, *I* am!' Goldwyn was very actively involved in the production. He was into everything. He and Mrs. Goldwyn checked all the costumes, inspected all the props. As soon as we had a set part way up, they wanted to see it.

"When the picture was over, there was a big party and *every*body was invited. Goldwyn made a speech thanking everyone. I've never seen a man stand so straight—like an arrow, head straight up. And, like always when there have been explosions during a production, everything was patched up—arms around shoulders, pats on the back, Otto is a great director, et cetera."

Preminger, however, had nothing good to say about Goldwyn. Not then, not now. Preminger considered Goldwyn to be coldblooded, egotistical and so ignorant about the process of picturemaking that he didn't know that the film shot in "Todd A-O" seventy mm could be reduced to thirty-five mm in the laboratory. "He thought we would have to shoot two separate versions! When I tried to explain it to him, he didn't believe me!

"He had a good brain for business," Preminger admits, "but he contributed not one suggestion, not one helpful word of advice to *Porgy and Bess.* I couldn't possibly have any respect for a man like that."

For the first time in his life, Sam began using sleeping pills. His nervousness was understandable; it was said that the picture would have to gross $15,000,000 before he broke even. He poured additional millions into a promotional orgy—page after page of publicity in every newspaper, Sunday supplement, mass circulation and fan magazine, and countless plugs on radio and TV. All in vain. *Porgy and Bess* opened in New York in June, 1959, to unanimously bad reviews, even from Goldwyn's staunchest supporters. It was, said the reviewers, badly written, overdressed, badly photographed, poorly acted and sung. Dwight MacDonald, writing in *Esquire,* called it "Folkery-fakery—a patronizing caricature of Negro life."

(I TOLD YOU SO, said Sam Goldfish.)

25. *Fadeout*

Goldwyn was seventy-seven years old when *Porgy and Bess* was released, but he continued to deny any thought of retiring. "I've never had more hope and enthusiasm than I have today," he said, and referred somewhat coyly to pictures he was thinking of making but refused to name. One, he admitted, had a Middle East setting. "I have always been interested in the Middle East," he said.

With no more productions to hype, the press releases shifted their emphasis to Sam the Statesman, the Philanthropist, the Oracle, the Legend. In 1947 he had established a foundation, through which scholarships were awarded (Sam drove UCLA officials mad with his incessant complaints that the Samuel Goldwyn Playwriting Award was not sufficiently publicized) and charitable contributions made.*

In June, 1958, the National Fathers Day Committee named Sam Goldwyn and Sam Goldwyn, Jr., Father and Son of the Year. The story of Sam Goldwyn, Jr., is no less valid for being a cliché. Military school (with the sons of other moguls) at an early age. Indulgence alternated with discipline. His mother, determined not to spoil the boy, made him earn his spending money. Sam, mercurial with his son as with everyone else, was as likely to administer a verbal (or physical) beating

* Between 1942 and 1961, Goldwyn donated $550,000 to the Motion Picture Permanent Charities (which he had helped organize). In January, 1975, the Samuel Goldwyn Foundation's assets were estimated at $6,000,000.

for a minor offense as he was to shower the boy with ostentatious kisses. Frances, though she could gush when social occasion demanded, was undemonstrative. Loving his mother (though not uncritically; "She reads the preface and first three pages of a book," he confided to friends, "and passes herself off as an intellectual."), fearing his father, starved for affection and bearing that albatross of a name, how could he be himself? "I've gotta be another Sam Goldwyn" he told the showgirls he dated during his brief playboy period. Years of psychotherapy resolved the conflict somewhat, but Sammy could never completely escape his father's long shadow—particularly since, like the sons of many of the moguls,* he followed his father into the business.

Since 1952, Sam Goldwyn, Jr., has produced eight low-budget pictures—no smashes, a few flops. The most successful was the blaxploitation flick, *Cotton Comes to Harlem. Young Lovers,* the production he cared most about (and directed himself), was about a group of college students searching for values. It had a love story which its producer described as "an honest reflection of modern collegiate thinking on marriage, premarital sex and abortion." His parents considered it immoral, and refused to see it.

Now on his second marriage, Sammy has four children by his first wife. Neither of his sons is named Sam Goldwyn.

In Sam's last years, laurels threatened to inundate Laurel Lane. Accepting the 1959 Milestone Award from the Producers Guild (to which he did not belong), he said, "Conditions in the industry are worse than I have ever known them in the forty-seven years I have been connected with motion pictures." † Asked whether he thought things had come to such a pass because Hollywood lacked responsible leadership, he shrugged, "There never has been any leadership in this business. . . . Everybody wants to get into the act today. The writer, director, actor seems to believe he is a better producer than the fella who got the idea for the picture, raised the money, sweated out the development of the screenplay, hired the director and actors and technicians, and did everything necessary to get the picture

* Only David Selznick surpassed his father's achievements.
† Attendance had now shrunk to less than half what it had been in 1946.

before the camera." And because the producer has the final responsibility, Sam pointed out, "he must have the final authority."

In 1960, the Japanese government awarded Sam the Third Order of the Rising Sun Medal. In 1961, the Israeli government officially commended his "two decades of service to world Jewry through the United Jewish Welfare Fund," to which he was a generous contributor. In August, 1962, 1,200 members of the Hollywood Establishment—augmented by straight Establishment members including Leonard Firestone, Mayor Yorty and Richard Nixon—gathered at the Beverly Hilton Hotel to observe Sam's eightieth birthday and fiftieth year in the industry. The next morning, Sam held a press conference at the studio. He announced that he was preparing a new picture, but declined to name it. He called for the industry to adopt a "code of ethics" which he claimed to have been thinking about for more than fifteen years. He was *not,* he emphasized, calling for censorship. Just what he *was* talking about was not made clear, but it got Sam's name into banner headlines in the next day's trades.

Goldwyn negated his years of poormouthing by holding out longer than any other studio against television's bid for his films. In 1953, he had predicted that the novelty of TV would soon wear off. Two years later, it was disclosed that his old films were being edited for TV. In 1962, he called TV "the greatest medium yet." But not until June, 1964, when the price had escalated substantially, did he sell fifty of his pictures (not including his last three, for which ABC later paid $1,000,000 apiece) to CBS-TV, for a reported $4,250,000. ("I'm the only one who knows the real figure," he said, "and I'm not going to talk about it. Why should I? It won't make them pay me any more!")

He hit the headlines again that year by selling the same films to Great Britain's commercial television outlet, thereby breaking a boycott against United States films and ultimately benefiting the American film industry by hundreds of millions of dollars.

Sam continued to talk of vague plans for future productions. In 1964, he summoned N. Richard Nash to his New York hotel suite and tried to interest the writer in "at *least* a dozen projects that he wanted to do. There was only one that interested me at all, but I didn't want to work on it. It didn't seem to me that Goldwyn would go through with it. I hadn't seen him since the *Porgy and Bess* days, and the difference in him was dramatic. He was ailing. In the *Porgy and Bess* days, he was vigorous. He once told me that the secret of his staying so young was that every day after lunch he got into his pajamas and slept. I said, 'But Sam, it's no secret that you have a nap every afternoon!' He said, 'But it's a secret that I get into my pajamas!' "

During the sixties he still did some traveling (spending two months a year at a German spa), still issued pronouncements to the press, still hosted small dinner parties followed by screenings of movies (during which he frequently dozed off). King Vidor, who had not seen him in many years, encountered him at a cocktail party. "I shook hands with him and I said, 'Hello, Sam. You look wonderful!' He looked at me kind of with a frown and he said, 'Why not! Why not!' Instead of saying Thank you. He still had to challenge you."

During the last decade of his life, Sam, who had always been lawsuit-happy, had his biggest courtroom victory—and also his biggest courtroom defeat. The good news was an award of $7,000,000 in damages,* the culmination of ten years of litigation, thousands of pages of transcripts, and hundreds of exhibits. The original judge had died before he reached a decision. The defendants (theater owners who asserted that the suit was motivated by Sam's "personal pique") were found guilty of eliminating free competition (in violation of the Sherman Act)—sometimes having gone so far as to meet clandestinely in parked cars, where they illegally arranged bookings that clearly discriminated against Goldwyn productions.

The bad news, the case Sam lost, stemmed from his practice of rewarding his most loyal and valued employees with a small interest in the corporation—with the provision that when the employment was terminated, for whatever reason, Sam could buy back the interest for an amount to be determined by the accounting firm of Price-Waterhouse. This exclusive group included Gregg Toland, Leon Fromkess, Sam's brother Ben Fish,

* The decision was appealed, and finally settled out of court for $2,000,000.

and James Mulvey, for thirty-eight years Sam's most trusted associate.

James Mulvey was a dapper little Irishman who went to work for Sam in 1922 as a bookkeeper. When he retired in 1960, he was vice-president in charge of Sam's New York office and had grown rich and rotund in Goldwyn's employ. Mulvey disputed Price-Waterhouse's estimate of the value of his 5 percent interest, and he filed suit against Sam for the difference. In addition, the suit charged Goldwyn with violating the Sherman Act by offering his film library to television on an all-or-nothing basis —thus affecting Mulvey's share of the profits.

Goldwyn was terribly bitter. He felt he had been more than fair with Mulvey. Years before, he had sold Mulvey the reissue rights to *The Pride of the Yankees* for a token $10,000— Mulvey's profit allegedly exceeded, eventually, a half-million dollars.

In November, 1972, a jury awarded Mulvey $1,044,000 in damages. Both men were too ill to appear in court. Mulvey would be dead within a year. Goldwyn, already rendered helpless and senile after a series of strokes, may never have been aware of what would have been his most galling defeat.

There would be no quick, neat Hollywood ending for Sam. The first stroke disabled him in March, 1969; he would live on for nearly five years in that "smiling sleep." Frances, appointed conservator of his estate, discouraged company; only his children, his barber, his manicurist, his nurse and his servants were allowed to see him. One exception was the day in March, 1971, when he was wheeled out to his garden, where President Nixon awarded him the Medal of Freedom "for producing good, entertaining, exciting movies that were not dirty."

"You have a lot to do these days," said Sam, tears streaming down his cheeks. It was his last public utterance. In 1972, on his ninetieth birthday, Frances Goldwyn told a reporter that for the first time, Sam would have no birthday party. "Last year's was a fiasco," she said. "It was simply too upsetting and exhausting for Sam, and he was days getting over it. This year I have told the family not to mention the birthday and I'm praying that he doesn't know about it." Asked about her husband's health, she said, "I don't lie any more. He has the heart and the blood pressure of a young man, but nothing else seems to work." The manicurist, instructed to check with Mrs. Goldwyn by phone before reporting at Laurel Lane, was sometimes told, "Don't come today. He's off on a long ocean voyage."

At two o'clock in the morning of January 31, 1974, Samuel Goldfish, aka Goldwyn, died in his sleep, in his mansion, at the age of, approximately, ninety-one.

Epilogue

The obits paid predictable homage to the Legend and gave short shrift to the man. Eulogizers who had known Sam for decades spoke of him as a force, rather than as a friend. The inevitable Goldwynisms were disinterred and quoted (in a pseudosentimental tone), statistics recounted,* simplistic judgments made. Only Richard Schickel, who wrote, "Sam Goldwyn was his own greatest production," got the point.

The search for Sam yielded a dizzying diversity of images, reflected by the people who knew him (or thought they did), worked with him, fought with him, worshiped him, despised him, feared him, respected him, ridiculed him and, in most cases, survived him. My own feelings toward him changed continually; in the end, they are mixed. I can relate to his stubbornness, his impulsiveness, his lifelong battle with logic, his anxiety and his chronic, incurable insecurity. I can admire him for his independence, for he *was* the *only* independent producer in Hollywood to make it—and sustain it—on his own terms. The admiration is diluted by his insensitivity (his refusal to take the trouble even to get your name right), his pretensions and his inadequacies as a father. Certainly I preferred Goldfish the *schnorrer* to Goldwyn the snob.

The search ended in the Beverly Hills apartment of Frances Inglis, a lady of taste, education, sophistication and

* The most impressive: between 1939 and 1959, his pictures entertained over 200,000,000 people.

style. In the early forties, Miss Inglis was amanuensis to David Selznick; in the fifties, Executive Director of the Writers Guild; and in the sixties, Concert Manager for the Fine Arts Productions Department at UCLA. Only once in her career did she take a secretarial job: when she went to work for Sam Goldwyn, just after his *Best Years*.

She was a young woman then, and an extremely proper one. Knowing Goldwyn's reputation, she took the job on the condition that if he ever "blew up" at her, she would leave on the spot. Sam, who was quite capable of controlling himself when it served his interests, accepted her terms—and kept his word.

Observing Sam over a five-year period in his natural habitat—the studio—as well as on business trips, Miss Inglis' perspective was unique. So were her perceptions. She was young enough to be Sam's granddaughter, but she describes her feeling for him as "oddly maternal. I felt something really soft, tender, in need of protection. I fell under a spell while I was with him. That was his great talent—to make people believe that what he was doing was just the most vital thing in the world."

When she gave notice, believing that the Writers Guild needed her more than Sam did, "He paid me the compliment of spending the whole day trying to persuade me to stay. He said, 'Look, we've established a marvelous relationship. I've rarely worked with anybody as long as you. Don't you like me?' I felt very guilty for many years after I left him."

We talked for an hour or more about Sam and his scene. Miss Inglis apologized for the gaps in her memory, but promised to let me know if anything else occurred to her that might be of use to me. The next day, she wrote me this letter:

> Dear Carol Easton:
>
> One aspect I forgot to mention which, though trivial, may have some meaning for you. By the time I arrived, Goldwyn was in better command of the English language than his reputation for malapropisms would imply. But I was fascinated to discover that this man had an intense interest in language. Any time I used a word he did not know (and I tend to polysyllabic mutterings) he would ask me its meaning, note it

carefully (from his concentrated expression) and use it over the next few weeks until I was ready to climb the walls. When he had it firmly fixed in his vocabulary, he would stop torturing it—and me. I thought it was so remarkable that a man his age would still be so avid for knowledge. What he might have done with education—or, conversely, what education might have done *to* him—is an intriguing subject for speculation.

As to Mrs. Goldwyn and my statement that she carried him around on a satin cushion, I think my feeling could be more accurately expressed by the thought that she ran him like a business, not professionally of course but personally. . . . Hence concentrating her immense energy and enormous intelligence on seeing that Sam was freed of everything but the opportunity to be creative (in the widest possible sense of that word) assumed the proportions of an Omar Bradley Service of Supply.

A great many good wishes to you in your endeavor. This man deserves the sensitive treatment I sense you will give him, rather than the usual spectacular spectacle. He was blustering and brassy, remote and stoney, insidious and seductive in mercurial changes of mood, but never less than dignified (even in those outrageous rages because never really out of control), never vulgar even at his most vivid, and somewhere deep inside, vulnerable. I never learned just where that vulnerability lay, but I felt it—despite the barricade his pride built around any revelation of or intrusion into his real feelings. In a funny kind of way, this self-educated, steerage-class immigrant was a grand seigneur. As I said, I loved him dearly, so you must assume some prejudice somewhere along the line.

Most cordially,
Frances

Bibliography

Astor, Mary, *A Life on Film*. New York, Dell Publishing Co., Inc., 1969.

Atherton, Gertrude, *Adventures of a Novelist*. New York, Liveright Publishing Corp., 1932.

Barker, Felix, *The Oliviers*. London, Hamish Hamilton Ltd., 1953.

Beach, Rex, *Personal Exposures*. New York, Harper & Bros., 1940.

Behlmer. Rudy, ed.,, *Memo From David O. Selznick*. Viking, 1972.

Behrman, S. N., *People in a Diary*. Boston, Little, Brown & Co., 1972.

Brownlow, Kevin, *The Parade's Gone By*. New York, Ballantine Books, Inc., 1969.

Burke, Billie (with Cam Shipp), *With a Feather on My Nose*. New York, Appleton-Century-Crofts, Inc., 1948.

Cantor, Eddie, *Take My Life*. Doubleday & Co., Inc., 1957.

Capra, Frank, *The Name Above the Title*. New York, The Macmillan Company, 1971.

Carpozi, George, Jr., *The Gary Cooper Story*. New Rochelle, Arlington House, 1970.

Crowther, Bosley, *The Lion's Share*. New York, E. P. Dutton & Co., 1957.

Davis, Bette, *The Lonely Life*. New York, G. P. Putnam's Sons, 1962.

De Mille, C. B., *Autobiography.* Englewood Cliffs, Prentice-Hall, 1959.

De Mille, William, *Hollywood Saga.* New York, E. P. Dutton & Co., Inc., 1939.

Dietz, Howard, *Dancing in the Dark.* New York, Quadrangle Books, Inc., 1974.

Fadiman, William, *Hollywood Now.* New York, Liveright Publishing Corp., 1972.

Farrar, Geraldine, *The Autobiography of Geraldine Farrar.* New York, The Greystone Press, 1938.

French, Philip, *The Movie Moguls.* London, Weidenfeld Ltd., 1969.

Frischauer, Willi, *Behind the Scenes of Otto Preminger.* New York, William Morrow and Co., Inc., 1974.

Garden, Mary, and Louis Biancolli, *Mary Garden's Story.* New York, Simon & Schuster, 1951.

Goldwyn, Samuel. *Behind the Screen.* New York, George H. Doran Co., 1923.

Gourlay, Logan, *Olivier.* New York, Stein & Day, 1974.

Gow, Gordon, *Hollywood in the Fifties.* New York, A. S. Barnes & Co., 1971.

Griffith, Richard, and Arthur Mayer, *The Movies.* New York, Simon & Schuster, 1957.

Griffth, Richard, *Samuel Goldwyn, The Producer and His Films.* New York, The Museum of Modern Art, 1956.

Gussow, Mel, *Don't Say Yes Until I Finish Talking.* New York, Doubleday & Co., Inc., 1971.

Hampton, Benjamin B., *A History of the Movies.* New York, Covici-Friede, 1931.

Hecht, Ben, *A Child of the Century.* New York, Simon & Schuster, 1954.

———, *Charlie.* New York, Harper & Row, 1957.

Hellman, Lillian, *An Unfinished Woman.* Boston, Little, Brown & Co., 1969.

———, *The North Star. A Motion Picture About Some Russian People.* New York, The Viking Press, 1943.

Higham, Charles, *Ziegfeld.* Henry Regnery Co., 1974.

Higham, Charles, and Joel Greenberg, *Hollywood in the Forties.* London, A. Zwemmer Ltd., 1968.

———, *The Celluloid Muse.* London, Angus & Robertson, Ltd., 1969.

Hoffman, William, *Sidney.* New York, Lyle Stuart, 1971.

Jacobs, Lewis, *The Rise of the American Film.* New York, Harcourt, Brace & Co., 1939.

Johnston, Alva, *The Great Goldwyn.* New York, Random House, 1937.

Knight, Arthur, *The Liveliest Art.* New York, The Macmillan Company, 1957.

Lasky, Jesse, *I Blow My Own Horn.* New York, Doubleday & Co., Inc., 1957.

Lasky, Jesse, Jr., *What Ever Happened to Hollywood?* New York, Funk & Wagnalls, 1975.

Loos, Anita, *Kiss Hollywood Good-by.* New York, The Viking Press, 1974.

MacCann, Richard Dyer, *Hollywood in Transition.* Boston, Houghton Mifflin Company, 1962.

MacDonald, Dwight, *Dwight MacDonald on Movies.* Englewood Cliffs, Prentice-Hall, 1969.

Macgowan, Kenneth, *Behind the Screen.* New York, The Dial Press, Inc., 1965.

Madsen, Axel, *William Wyler.* New York, Thomas Y. Crowell Co., 1973.

Mahony, Patrick, *The Magic of Maeterlinck.* Millwood, N. Y., Kraus Reprint Co., 1970.

Marion, Frances, *Off With Their Heads.* New York, The Macmillan Company, 1972.

Mayer, Arthur, *Merely Colossal.* New York, Simon & Schuster, 1953.

Mayersberg, Paul, *Hollywood the Haunted House.* New York, Stein & Day, 1968.

Meredith, Scott, *George S. Kaufman & His Friends.* New York, Doubleday & Co., Inc., 1974.

Michael, Paul, *The American Movies Reference Book. The Sound Era.* Englewood Cliffs, Prentice-Hall, 1969.

Milne, Tom, *Mamoulian.* Bloomington, Indiana University Press, 1969.

Niven, David, *The Moon's a Balloon.* New York, G. P. Putnam's Sons, 1972.

Oppenheimer, George, *The View From the Sixties.* David McKay Co., Inc., 1966.

Ramsaye, Terry, *A Million and One Nights.* New York, Simon & Schuster, 1926 (2 volumes).

Rice, Elmer, *Minority Report: An Autobiography.* New York, Simon & Schuster, 1963.

Rinehart, Mary Roberts, *My Story.* New York, Farrar & Rinehart, 1931.

Rivkin, Allen, and Laura Kerr, *Hello, Hollywood!* New York, Doubleday & Co., Inc., 1962.

Robinson, Edward G., with Leonard Spigelgass, *All My Yesterdays.* New York, Hawthorn Books, Inc., 1973.

Rogers, Betty, *Will Rogers.* Garden City, N. Y., Garden City Publishing Co., 1943.

Rogers, Will, *The Autobiography of Will Rogers.* Boston, Houghton Mifflin, 1926.

Rosenberg, Bernard, and Harry Silverstein, *The Real Tinsel.* New York, Macmillan Company, 1970.

Rosten, Leo, *Hollywood, the Movie Colony.* New York, Harcourt, Brace & Co., 1941.

Rotha, Paul, and Richard Griffith, *The Film Till Now.* London, Vision-Mayflower, 1960.

Schickel, Richard, *His Picture in the Papers.* New York, Charterhouse Books, Inc., 1973.

Scott, Evelyn F., *Hollywood When Silents Were Golden.* McGraw-Hill Book Company, 1972.

Shipman, David, *Great Movie Stars; The Golden Years.* New York, Crown Publishers, Inc., 1970.

Singer, Kurt, *The Danny Kaye Story.* New York, Thomas Nelson & Sons, 1958.

Smith, Ella, *Starring Miss Barbara Stanwyck.* New York, Crown Publishers, Inc., 1974.

Talbot, Daniel, *Film: An Anthology.* New York, Simon & Schuster, 1959.

Talmey, Alice, *Doug, Mary and Others.* New York, Macy-Masius, 1927.

Taper, Bernard, *Balanchine.* New York, Harper & Row, 1960.

Thomas, Bob, *Selznick.* New York, Doubleday & Co., Inc., 1970.

———, *Thalberg.* New York, Doubleday & Co., Inc., 1969.

Thomas, Tony, *Music for the Movies.* New York, A. S. Barnes & Co., 1973.

Vidor, King, *A Tree Is a Tree.* London, Longmans Green & Co., 1954.

Wagenknecht, Edward, *The Movies in the Age of Innocence.* Norman, University of Oklahoma Press, 1962.

Walker, Alexander, *Stardom.* New York, Stein & Day, 1970.

West, Jessamyn, *To See the Dream.* New York, Harcourt, Brace & Co., 1956.

Wilk, Max, *The Wit and Wisdom of Hollywood.* New York, Atheneum, 1971.

Zierold, Norman, *The Moguls.* New York, Coward-McCann, 1969.

Zukor, Adolph, *The Public Is Never Wrong.* New York, G. P. Putnam's Sons, 1953.

Index